D0678465

SHOWING
HOW

Gabriel Moran

SHOWING HOW

THE
ACT OF
TEACHING

TRINITY PRESS INTERNATIONAL
Valley Forge, Pennsylvania

Copyright © 1997 by Gabriel Moran

All rights reserved. No part of this book may be reproduced, stored in a retrieval system, or transmitted, in any form or by any means, electronic, mechanical, photocopying, recording, or otherwise, without the written permission of the publisher.

Trinity Press International, P.O. Box 851, Valley Forge, PA 19482–0851
Trinity Press International is a division of the Morehouse Publishing Group

Library of Congress Cataloging-in-Publication Data

Moran, Gabriel.
    Showing how : the act of teaching / Gabriel Moran.
      p. cm.
    Includes bibliographical references (p.) and index.
    ISBN 1-56338-187-7 (alk. paper)
    1. Teaching. 2. Teaching – Moral and ethical aspects.
    3. Education – Philosophy. 4. Moral education. I. Title.
    LB1025.3.M664 1997
    371.102 – dc21   96-50492
                         CIP

Printed in the United States of America

97   98   99   00   01   02   10 9 8 7 6 5 4 3 2 1

Contents

Introduction

THIS BOOK is about the activity of teaching; more precisely it is about the meaning of the verb "to teach." Despite a steady flow of books that have "Teaching" in the title, I do not know of a book that covers the same ground as this one. At first glance, answering the question, "What does it mean to teach?" seems simple. A small dictionary will supply an uncomplicated definition, such as "to instruct" (Random House). A larger dictionary (Oxford English Dictionary) will reveal a range of meanings that can vary according to time and place.

Acknowledging the diversity in meaning, we have two options for an answer: either "Let's agree on one definition," or "There are so many kinds of teaching that no single answer is possible." The first choice, agreeing on one definition, allows you to converse with anyone who accepts the same definition. However, that tactic does not take into account how living languages work, nor does it get at troubling inconsistencies in the use of the word. The alternative — no single answer is possible — avoids the question of what is the common bond that holds the diversity together. If the term is not simply equivocal, there has to be a core, root, or foundation from which diversity issues.

Nearly all books on teaching leave out the main story. Most often, they do not even raise the question of the meaning of "to teach." If they do examine the activity, they concentrate on only one form of teaching. This book asks why people avoid the topic of teaching, or if they do not entirely avoid it, why they study only one unusual form of teaching. My thesis is that people are uneasy with the very idea of teaching. By "people" I mean a good part of the general population, including people who write books on education. At some level of consciousness and conscience, people have an ethical problem with the activity of teaching. Put more simply and most starkly, many people have a deep suspicion that teaching is an immoral activity.

Because this suspicion exists as a vague anxiety about an action that is supposedly praiseworthy, not many people readily acknowledge the suspicion. The uneasiness with the morality of teaching is seldom articulated and therefore not resolved. Most of the population can go its way to other problems in life that do have to be resolved, such as preparing dinner or paying the mortgage. The ambivalence about teaching only occasionally surfaces, perhaps when a child has a conflict with the first-grade teacher or a school bond issue is up for approval. The question raised in this book may seem peripheral to most people's pressing problems, but I think that our whole culture suffers from an unresolved moral ambivalence about teaching.

I recently participated in a seminar on the nature of teaching. All the participants were professors in a school of education (that is, a school of a university concerned with the preparation of professional school-teachers). Three hours into the discussion, one professor said, "I try to avoid the words 'teacher' and 'teaching' because of their bad connotations. Instead I try to talk only about 'learning.'" To most people outside this discussion, the remark must surely sound absurd. A professor whose job description is "teacher training" but who tries to avoid the words "teacher" and "teaching" would seem to be in the wrong line of work.

The professor of education who made this remark was dipping into a standard cliché of educational literature, namely, that we have concentrated too much on teaching and not enough on learning. This oft-repeated statement strikes me as preposterous. I am not about to argue that we need fewer studies of learning. I do argue that we need more attention to the inherent relation between teaching and learning. That topic is not studied because of an assumption during the last half-century that there is *no* inherent relation between teaching and learning. Teaching and learning are taken to be separate processes. Teaching is at best an optional extra; at worst it is seen as an oppressive interference.

What I offer in this book is an alternative assumption and the resulting description of the relation teach-learn. In much of human history, especially in religious history, there is nothing peculiar about my assumption. Human beings learn because they are taught: by other human beings, by the religious tradition, by the marvels of creation, and ultimately by the divine teacher. In nearly all religions the highest title given to the religion's founder is "teacher." In many languages, "religion" and "teaching" are derived from the same root.

I have been teaching in a classroom every year since 1958, and have constantly puzzled over what it means to teach someone something. During most of this time I have been engaged in the teaching of religion, an area that offers special problems for the meaning of teaching. But it was while teaching courses in the history of education and the philosophy of education that I discovered the piece of the intellectual puzzle I had been missing: modern theories of education denigrate teaching because of an antireligious bias. When modern European writers rebelled against Christianity, they also fled from teaching. Eighteenth-and nineteenth-century writers did not eliminate the term, but they narrowed its meaning to a rationalistic core devoid of religious meaning. Teaching remained a part of the necessary burden that a child carried until the child could overthrow the oppressive power of adults. In educational literature of the twentieth century it is assumed that teaching is an explanation from the front of a classroom. As a result, discussions of teaching cannot draw upon a comparison of what teachers do in classrooms and what teachers do in other settings for teaching. For example, the ubiquitous phrase "parents and teachers" is the denial of a central activity of the parent, namely, to teach.

For teachers in religious education, the effect of a rationalistic meaning of teaching is to limit the possibilities of their work. Any effective teaching of a religious way of life requires a range of settings for teaching: in the family, in the religious congregation, in struggles for justice, in contemplative silence, as well as in the classroom. However, modern educational writing, which is indispensable to the Christian or Jewish educator, has the side effect of undermining the significance of teaching.

There is another possibility to consider in this relation of modern education and religious teachers. The flight from religion may be nearing its historical limit. The term "modern" is no longer a certificate of superiority. The eighteenth-century project to replace the church with the schoolroom has not turned out as well as expected; there is constant complaint about the failures of the school system. Any successful revolution in education will have to include a reappropriation of the many forms of teaching. The religious traditions are the chief repositories of a richer meaning of teaching. However, the modern world is not going to discover this fact unless religious people retrieve the best of their own traditions and bring that wisdom into conversation with modern writing on education.

Part 1 of this book establishes a fundamental meaning for "to teach."

The first chapter explores teaching as a moral dilemma, tracing some of the historical journey that has brought us to our present plight. The deep-seated fear that teaching is an immoral act must have some realistic basis. The dilemma cannot be resolved by a quick change of attitude or by simply avoiding everything that suggests threat and coercion. The dilemma continues to exist because discussions of teaching nearly always begin several steps removed from its basic meaning. The second chapter attempts to ground the meaning of "to teach" in its most basic forms, moving from examples in the nonhuman world to communal and nonverbal forms of teaching among humans. The third chapter describes the physical design of teaching, exemplified by the writings of modern reformers of education and in situations where speech functions as a choreographing of bodily movement.

Part 2 of this book explores the languages of teaching. With the basic meaning of "to teach" established, it is possible to discuss the diverse forms of speech that are appropriate to teaching. The fourth chapter explores rhetorical forms of speech that are familiar to any religious person; these include storytelling and preaching. The fifth chapter discusses languages that are called "therapeutic"; they had nearly disappeared in modern philosophy but recently have returned with a vengeance. Religion preserved these languages and still offers a proper ritualized setting for their exercise. The sixth chapter is on languages that call language itself into question; it is here that the conversation of a classroom should be situated.

Part 3 draws out implications for education. In chapter 7, I reflect on the meaning of education in the light of what teaching is. A correlation is drawn between forms of speech in teaching and forms of education. In chapter 8 I focus on the school and the several forms of teaching it contains. Chapter 9 tests the moral solution that has been offered, extending the argument to the teaching of morality. The conclusion recapitulates the book's thesis by contrasting two meanings of "to teach."

Perhaps an initial warning is in order about what this book is not. The first seven chapters are not preparation of a theory that is finally tested out in chapter 8's "teaching in school." Readers who are sure they know what teaching is may be impatient to know what I have to offer as solutions to the "real problems of real teachers." But each chapter of this book is about real teachers and real teaching. I do hope that classroom instructors and other teachers in school read this book.

But it will not be a productive venture unless they are willing to let go temporarily of the terms "teach" and "teacher" so as to consider the possibility that teaching is a mysterious activity in human life that needs to be investigated at length.

I have great respect for classroom instructors and other school staff, but my task is not to offer them solutions to their very real problems. My hope is to open a conversation about teaching that, among other things, will lead schoolteachers to have better conversations both among themselves and, just as important, with other teachers about teaching. To some people this approach may seem unrealistic and impractical. I can only respond by inviting the reader to a discussion that will not go over the well-worn ground of "tips for teachers." Instead, I invite the reader to reflect on the practice of teaching in human life and our peculiar way of speaking that prevents us from having lively, practical discussions about improving teaching, including teaching in schools.

On Hiding "To Teach"

Contemporary literature that claims to deal with teaching usually treats teaching only within the classroom. This form lacks the context needed to describe an effective — and moral — approach to teaching, even in this particular setting. That is, when teaching is equated with classroom instruction in a school, what disappears are not only most kinds of teaching but also the language, imagery, and techniques for improving classroom instruction itself. The one kind of teaching that is thought to be defensible is left morally indefensible.

The jump from "to teach" to one peculiar form of teaching is sometimes made unconsciously. But since everyone does have some awareness of the difference, writers usually acknowledge they are making the jump. Seldom is any argument provided for the move, other than one about the efficient use of the space at hand. Most often the jump is made with a single statement of fact that suggests no need for explanation. The similar case would be someone writing a book on fishing, and who, after a sentence on the first page acknowledging other things that might have been written about, concentrates on the goldfish bowl in the living room. There is nothing wrong with writing a book on goldfish so long as one does not confuse the task with writing a treatise on fish and fishing.

Take, for examples, two minor classics of twentieth-century writing on teaching: Gilbert Highet's *The Art of Teaching* and Jacques Barzun's *Teacher in America*.[1] These books are among the best in their genre, written with style and learning. They have been helpful to generations of readers. But even these expert treatises on teaching are strangely narrowed down to a small area that counts (at least seriously counts) as teaching at all. An obligatory nod is given to all the other teaching in the world. The typical example of another form of teaching that they cite is what parents do.

In *Teacher in America*, the allusion is in the first chapter: "The odd thing is that almost everybody is a teacher at some time or other during his life. Besides Socrates and Jesus, the great teachers of mankind are mankind itself — your parents and mine." The author does not explain why he considers this an "odd" fact instead of one of the most important facts to be explored about teaching. In any case, after this one paragraph praising parents, the book does not return to them.[2]

In *The Art of Teaching*, there is also one paragraph on parents found in the chapter entitled "Teaching in Ordinary Life." Curiously, this chapter is the last one in the book, whereas it would seem most logical to put that chapter first. Either way, however, the 240 pages on the school remain untouched by "teaching in ordinary life." The major forms that teaching takes in *The Art of Teaching* are the lecture and the tutorial. Jesus was the first great lecturer, Socrates founded the tutorial.[3]

The process, as I have described it so far, is to collapse the meaning of teaching into what is done in the classroom. From that beginning, discussions of teaching can proceed to elaborate descriptions of the work of schoolteachers. Notice, however, that there is not just one collapsed distinction here but three. Before we can get to the meaning of "to teach," we have to peel back three layers of covering.

First, the verb "to teach" slides into the noun or gerund "teaching." In the English language, we can indeed use "teaching" to convey the active verb, and I will occasionally do so. I do indeed wish to keep "to teach" and "teaching" in close relation, that is, to distinguish the two terms without separating them. But I will most often use the infinitive form "to teach" so as to pinpoint the question as the activity or event of teaching.

The second collapse is from teaching to teacher. Books about teaching tend to become descriptions of teachers. The question of good teaching, for example, becomes the desired personal qualities of the teacher. Of course, there are excellent reasons here for keeping a close relation between "teaching" and "teachers." Eventually, "to teach" and "teaching" need to be situated as the activities of "teachers." But one should not presume without question that the "teacher" is necessarily an individual human being.

The third blurring is between teacher and professional schoolteacher. This move is a typical case of a modern professional group taking over an important human activity. Educational literature then turns back on its own professionalized meanings; references to "teacher" — unless otherwise qualified — mean a member of the profession. As a result, the meaning of "to teach" is further obscured by all the professional issues surrounding the staffing of schools.

There are numerous examples throughout this book to illustrate this triple folding over of the meaning of "to teach." Examples are not difficult to find; in fact, what is difficult to find are counter examples. Any writer in an educational journal who wishes to maintain seriously (as opposed to paying lip service) that teaching is performed, for example, by parents, is forced to resist nearly all the trappings and jargon of the journal. This book is an exercise in such resistance. I will regularly remind the reader that I am asking a question that is almost too simple for words: What is the meaning of "to teach"?

On the Meaning of Words

The remainder of this introduction will be an extended comment on the approach of concentrating upon language. The quotation marks that I have several times placed around "to teach" are intended to call attention to the term. This distinction between to teach and "to teach" could be interpreted as a fourth level that has to be peeled back. However, I think it is more helpful to consider this issue to be one that cuts across the previous three (teaching, teacher, professional schoolteacher). I refer to the difference between discussing an *idea* about something and getting at the meaning of the *term* that appears in the discussion. A focus on the meaning of "to teach" or "teaching" is a more pointed discussion than talking about ideas or concepts or models of teaching. And

I wish to claim that attention to the term is more effective in changing not only the understanding but also the practice of teaching.

I will not attempt to justify this approach in the introduction. If there is any proof of its value, the evidence lies in the execution of the approach. Here I simply note that my attention to the meaning of the term "to teach" is not based on an idiosyncrasy but is a theme of numerous twentieth-century thinkers. Various schools of philosophy that have little else in common agree that our words are not transparencies for thought but the place where thought is born. Language thereby becomes the source of our difficulties in thinking, speaking, communicating, and agreeing. As Ludwig Wittgenstein, perhaps the best-known philosopher of language in this century, puts it, "It is what human beings *say* that is true and false; and they agree in the *language* they use."[4]

Why has this century been so concerned with language? Is it a sign of progress or despair? One can view the concentration on words as a possible gain in understanding. But it is also a sign of the modern distrust in just about every claim that is made in words.

First, the distrust of words is manifest. What has slowly but surely spread throughout this century is a doubt that words can convey truth. Regarding the collapse of "all the regnant world systems," Irving Howe says of the effect, "This leads to a mood of skepticism, an agnosticism of judgment, sometimes a world-weary nihilism in which even the most conventional minds begin to question both distinctions of value and the value of distinctions."[5]

This result is not likely what any philosopher, linguist, or literary theorist had in mind when calling attention to the fragility of our words. Alexander Bickel, the political theorist, used to say, "No one wants everyone not to believe in anything."[6] But the corrosive effect of questioning every word is not under anyone's control and it could lead us into a nihilism, the likes of which have never been imagined.

Friedrich Nietzsche, who died in 1900, is at least symbolically at the head of this parade. Nietzsche is blamed for too much; Nazism — the most horrific result sometimes attributed to him — is not a necessary or direct effect of his philosophy.[7] Nonetheless, after Nietzsche, Nazism and other frightening things become possible because so many defenses and subterfuges have been unmasked. For the moment my interest is that Nietzsche's withering criticism went at the connection between the words and the things. A contemporary commentator calls attention to the method on a page of Nietzsche's studded with quotation marks ("revelation," "sin," "sacred book"): "As opposed to conceptual analysis, it refuses to grant that its objects are part of an impersonal world of ideas to be assessed on their own merits. Instead, they are texts which issue from and are signs of power."[8]

The effect of reading Nietzsche is not so much that one agrees with him, but henceforth every term becomes questionable and suspect: it becomes a sign of power. Once one sees this, one can never not see it again. The questioning of language does not necessarily lead to philosophical skepticism or outright nihilism. But any philosophical outlook has to have a chance of standing against the kind of criticism that Nietzsche helped to unleash and others have spread far and wide throughout the twentieth century.

I suggested above that there might be a more positive way to look at the attentiveness to language. It may represent, if not progress, at least a regrounding in rich strands of the past that had become obscured in recent centuries. And in returning to a method of asking the meaning of our ordinary words we may have more to bring to the question than could Aristotle, Aquinas, or Spinoza, who employed a similar approach. Our capacity for tracing the ambiguities of speech should provide us with insights into how language limits us while sustaining us. Perhaps a limited kind of progress could then be hoped for.

In tracing the history of language, Aristotle did not have the benefit of the Oxford English Dictionary. What Aristotle did have was an extraordinary genius for examining the "phenomena" at hand. This starting point was not a collection of facts but the common beliefs people hold: "These are the things we say." Aristotle's quest was for the meaning of "the things we say." If definitions arise, they come only at the end, not the beginning, of Aristotle's process of inquiry.[9]

For example, in investigating nature, Aristotle assembles seven different meanings that the term "nature" had already acquired.[10] Aristotle's own use of the term tried to respect the variety of meanings that the term brought with it. One does not eliminate meaning or meanings by announcing a definition. At most one can bring one meaning to center stage, while trying to relegate other meanings to the wings. Aristotle was brilliantly successful in handling the term "nature"; that is, he stamped his own reshaping of "nature," which still lives on in every use of the term. Our contemporary use of "nature" still embodies the multiple meanings that Aristotle discovered, his reconfiguration of those

meanings, and all that has happened in the two millennia since then.[11]
This example is not a trivial one. Much of modern history revolves
around the uses and abuses of "nature," whether we are discussing
science, politics, ethics, religion, or economics.

Whether people are consciously aware of the etymology and the history of a term, they are always working with and against the limits set
by the term itself. This history is often a history of forgetting, the narrowing of meaning in the hands of those who use language for their
own purposes of ordering the world. This process is not necessarily devious or ominous; human life can only bear so much disorder. It is left
to poets and philosophers to resist such "practicality" and to retrieve
the latent meaning of our most important words.

Like "nature," the story of "to teach" goes back to well before Aristotle. Its story is even more complicated than nature's because it is a
simple, more universal term. In the course of this work I will refer to
Plato, Aristotle, and other philosophers in my inquiry into the meaning
of teaching. I do so not because any one philosopher supplies the right
definition of teaching, but to resist a narrowing of the term and to retrieve forgotten elements. With a term such as "to teach," the meaning
is found in ordinary people's usage both past and present. Perhaps at the
end of a long reflection, a "technical definition" of teaching may serve
some purpose, but at the beginning it would almost certainly obstruct a
search for meaning. Since the landscape is strewn with such definitions
of teaching, the first part of this book is antidefinitional, an attempt to
get behind the *definition* of teaching to the *meaning(s)* of "to teach."

Some people assume that attention to the issue of language and the
search for the meaning embodied in the use of language take us into a
realm of "abstractions." Ironically, the reverse is the case. A discussion
of teaching (that is, an idea about the reality) is an abstraction. The
attention to "teaching," to the use of the term, roots us more deeply in
ordinary life and its concerns. The metaphorical direction for Aristotle
and Wittgenstein is *down*, not up, down into the meanings embodied in
the words rather than up to ideas abstracted from words.

The Middle Ages distorted Aristotle's method by choosing the term
"abstraction" for what Aristotle describes as incomplete enumeration.[12]
That is, when it is impossible to study all instances of a set (induction
for Aristotle), we must penetrate deeply whatever cases are at hand.
And the beginning point for these cases are the words we use and the
beliefs we hold.

Despite the distortion introduced by "abstraction," Aristotle's approach to language was not lost to much of the Middle Ages. It generated great intellectual inquiry until, when atrophied by lesser minds, it became the butt of ridicule in the seventeenth and eighteenth centuries. Thomas Aquinas, while differing from Aristotle on fundamental points of philosophy, was a true disciple on the question of meaning and definition. For Aquinas, a definition is never decisive; one has to look to "use." Agreeing explicitly with Aristotle, Aquinas held that in the naming of things "one must go with the crowd."[13]

Aquinas's position may seem to be a shocking capitulation for a philosopher to make. The "crowd" does not supply the answer to philosophical questions. But the answer will not be entirely outside the human crowd's conversation. The philosopher has to argue that some ways of speaking are better than others, though one must reckon with the possibility that the "better" speaking — more honest, truthful, just, effective, inclusive — will be found at the edge of the crowd or among muffled voices throughout the crowd.

Every human being finds him- or herself in one crowd that is a minuscule part of the complete crowd. Our choice of whom we listen to is within a selection that our time, place, and circumstances have already chosen for us. We can only start with the voices available to us. From there we can try to widen the circle of acquaintances through traveling in space and time, through listening, reading, and conversing on those issues that strike us as worth our effort.

If I were to choose one book from which my dialogue begins, it would be Ludwig Wittgenstein's *Philosophical Investigations*. I make no attempt to exegete this complex and intriguing book, but it provides the inspiration and much of the guidance for what follows. Wittgenstein's book does not announce itself to be on teaching; it is most centrally about the nature of language and how we learn language. But in reflecting on primitive languages, Wittgenstein describes how a child learns a language, that is, how the whole environment and individuals within a human community teach the child to speak. Teaching as explaining or giving reasons plays almost no part at the beginning of teaching. The teacher teaches by showing someone how to do something. The teacher goes through moves and encourages the child to do the same. Then, at some point, "we can go on in the same way as those who are teaching us."[14]

What Wittgenstein gives us is a description of teaching that appeals to a universal experience: Someone shows me how to do something; at a certain point I can go on in the same way. This bedrock description cries out for detail, analysis, and distinctions. But each step of trying to articulate a scientific-sounding definition of teaching threatens to create a set of abstract ideas that prevent us seeing what is everywhere before our eyes, namely, examples of someone showing someone how to do something. That does not mean we should forsake detail, analysis, and distinctions, but they have to serve rather than replace the force of Wittgenstein's seemingly naive beginning. Wittgenstein considered using as a motto for *Philosophical Investigations* the line from *King Lear:* "I'll teach you differences."[15] Indeed, he does teach differences and he is able to do so because he starts at the simplest and deepest meaning of teaching.

This book is an attempt, however modestly, to join the conversation of great thinkers on the meaning of "to teach." Even though one's best thoughts have in all likelihood been thought before, there is still the impulse to express thoughts for whatever crowd of listeners might be interested. The many writers referred to in what follows and many of my teachers who are not named here have shown me how to do it. What I am trying to do is "go on in the same way as those who are teaching us."

Part One

Chapter 1

Teaching as a Moral Dilemma

A BOOK that attracted more publicity for its contract than for its content is *To Renew America* by Newt Gingrich. Although the book did not sell well, it contains some remarkable contrasts revelatory of contemporary controversies. One of the book's revealing contrasts is between "education" and "learning." "Education," according to the author, "describes a system of teachers and students that has grown inefficient and expensive," while "learning" "describes a dynamic community of people using whatever means they have to improve their performances and better their lives."[1]

That contrast leads immediately to five others, including "the learner versus the student," and "learner focused versus teacher focused." According to Gingrich's model, "in the Industrial Age the education model has been a passive student dominated by an active teacher." But in the "Third Wave model... responsibility is placed on the learner rather than the teacher."[2]

Gingrich is enthusiastic about the learner while he disparages the teacher. That contrast is especially strange when one considers that *To Renew America* is largely adapted from Professor Gingrich's televised academic lectures. A tension between teaching and learning has existed throughout the history of Western culture. But a total contrast of the terms "teach" and "learn" is especially to be found in the 1960s, a decade Gingrich is fond of attacking.

At the end of the 1960s, one of the most popular speakers in the country was Ivan Illich. After analyzing many modern institutions, Illich hit upon the school as the linchpin of oppression. His prescription for liberation was contained in the small tract, *De-Schooling Society*, published in 1970.[3] There probably would have been an audience for such a book in every decade of U.S. history, but the end of the 1960s — with its relentless rebellion on college campuses — was primed for Illich's message.

15

The message Illich stated most succinctly was "to teach is to corrupt." During the short time in which he was hailed as prophet and liberator, large audiences of schoolteachers listened to his attacks on teaching, and then dutifully filed back into their classrooms and continued to teach. Those who agreed with his thesis presumably felt more guilty than before for morally subverting the young.

Illich soon progressed to criticizing other institutions; the schools continued through cycles of public apathy and passionate proposals for reform. That Illich had identified a political and cultural system worth criticizing can hardly be denied, but his failure to make any relevant distinctions regarding "teach," "teaching," "teacher," and "schoolteacher" undermined the possibility of his saying anything helpful about education in general and about the meaning of "to teach" in particular. Illich's typical opposition was between teaching and learning; more teaching meant less learning, hence the passionate attack upon teaching.[4]

In some education books the opposition is not between teaching and learning, but there is nonetheless a moral problem with being a teacher. Jacques Barzun's *Teacher in America* is ostensibly in praise of teaching. But the moral dilemma is created at the beginning of the book in this description:

> To be sure there is an age-old prejudice against teaching. Teachers must share with doctors the world's most celebrated sneers, and with them also the world's unbounded hero-worship. Always and everywhere, "He is a schoolteacher" has meant "He is an underpaid pitiable drudge." Even a politician stands higher, because power in the streets seems less of a mockery than power in the classroom. But when we speak of Socrates, Jesus, Buddha and "other great teachers of humanity," the atmosphere somehow changes and the politician's power begins to look shrunken and mean. August examples show that no limit can be set to the power of a teacher, but this is equally true in the other direction: no career can so nearly approach zero in its effect.[5]

In this passage the plight of a person called "teacher" might have been the springboard for a helpful analysis of the meaning of "to teach." But the author has already narrowed his focus to the career problems of the schoolteacher; these issues are what occupies the rest of Barzun's book. That track is the standard one to follow, but it leaves unresolved the "age-old prejudice against teaching."

The claim that "he is a schoolteacher" has always and everywhere meant "he is an underpaid pitiable drudge" seems to be an over-generalization. In most times and places, "schoolteacher" has sparked ambiguous thoughts of dedication, idealism, limited possibilities, and an underappreciated public worker. If always and everywhere "school-teacher" has meant that he (or very often she) is an underpaid pitiable drudge, what hope could be offered to change the situation? Pre-sumably, Professor Barzun is not including college teachers in this characterization; in fact, most books giving advice to schoolteachers are written by university professors from above the fray.

There is in the passage a positive portrait of "the teacher." The great teachers of humanity are set on a pedestal that no schoolteacher can hope to approach. The contrast between those people who have power without limit and those people who have a career that approaches zero places the great teachers on one side and schoolteachers on the other; Jesus, Socrates, and Buddha are not the ones with a career problem. Great teaching is exemplified by three men who tried to teach the human race how to be good. Would it not be better for all of us if we were to follow Socrates, Jesus, and Buddha? Alas! We seldom do follow their advice. And, indeed, *Teacher in America* does not have much to say of their teaching beyond this brief rhetorical flourish.

Socrates, Buddha, and Jesus are indeed interesting figures in the his-tory of teaching, though they certainly do not teach the same lesson. Each rebelled in his own way against the established teachings of his time. To each of the three we easily attach the term "teacher," but the relation that each of them had to the term was and is problematic.

In the case of Gautama, the Buddha, one of his titles is "the silent one." The experience that transformed him seemed at first to be be-yond communication to others. He was therefore skeptical of trying to teach disciples his newfound truth. He did come to influence others by his example and his enigmatic stories. Eventually there grew up a reli-gion that is called Buddhism, and books summarize this religion under headings such as "The Four Noble Truths" and "The Eightfold Path." The word "teachings" is used to refer to Buddhism just as it is used of the religion he was rebelling against. The Buddha comes to be called a teacher.

Somewhat similarly, Jesus of Nazareth began as a reformer of Jew-ish teachings. Like Gautama, his own teaching or counter-teaching is a combination of example and enigmatic statements. As befits the

Semitic thread of religious history, there is more verbal jousting in Jesus' teaching and longer debates about individual teachings. Jesus seems to be comfortable in having disciples who address him as "teacher." After his death, his sayings and stories were gathered in a book that Christians hold to be as sacred as the teachings that nourished Jesus' life.

In Jaroslav Pelikan's study of the images of Jesus, the author places "Jesus the teacher" first.[6] Pelikan says that "teacher" was the "least controversial title" attributed to Jesus in the first century. However, by the second century, the title was embarrassing and by the third century obscure. What had happened was that a radical split between Judaism and Christianity left the title of teacher (rabbi) in Judaism. Although "Jesus the teacher" is regularly brought back in Christian reform movements, Christianity has not especially exalted the title of teacher. In Judaism, Islam, and most religions, nothing greater can be said of a religious leader than "teacher." The fact that "teacher" was applied to Jesus in the first century suggests that he was not as much of a rebel as later Christianity portrayed him. The fact that the title is almost lost in later Christianity undercuts the historical relation of Christianity and Judaism.

In considering religious leaders such as Moses and Buddha, Jesus and Muhammad, one can see the close relation between religion and teaching. In some languages, the terms almost blend together. Two dangers to this close identification are evident. First, the act of "to teach" is nearly rendered invisible by the prominence of the religion's teachings. When that happens, a lot of things that were not necessarily taught by Moses or Muhammad get associated with the teaching. The great teachings acquire cultural accretions that later generations may find foreign and unacceptable.

That situation leads to the second danger, a wholesale rejection of teaching by the individual critic or a critical-minded era. If the teachings of a prophet are rejected because of preference for teachings from another source, society may suffer no loss. But if the identification of the people's religion and teaching is complete, an era might react against the idea and term "teaching." Here is where the moral dilemma of teaching in modern times emerged. The choice was seen to be between subservience to the teachers of the established religion and — in Immanuel Kant's description of enlightenment — daring to be wise and having the courage to use your own reason.[7]

Socrates: The Ambiguity of Teaching

Before going ahead with the modern plight of the activity of teaching, I take note of the third great teacher that Barzun listed: Socrates. His relation to teaching is perhaps the most interesting of the three people named. To this day, Socrates is held out as the great precursor of modern man, the founder of our modern educational ideal. But he remains a complex and mysterious character. We piece together his thinking from the early dialogues of Plato (the later dialogues probably represent a more fictionalized Socrates) and a few other references in Xenophon and Aristophanes.

What is evident in almost every reference to teaching in the Socratic dialogues is the moral issue at stake. I do not mean only that the question of teaching is often posed in the context of asking, Can anyone teach *virtue?* Rather, the claim to possess knowledge and to be able to impart such knowledge to other people is understood to be a claim to moral superiority. If the claim cannot be sustained, then the "teachers" are not technical failures but moral frauds.

The argument between Socrates and the Sophists is told to us in a one-sided way with Socrates as the hero. Some twentieth-century scholars raise the question of whether Socrates' opponents might not have something to teach us about teaching. For example, the Sophist Protagoras speaks eloquently of the whole community teaching people through the laws it has and of punishment as intelligible only as a form of teaching. Socrates may be a great teacher but might it be that his form of teaching presupposes a form of teaching that is communal and nonverbal?[8]

On a textual level, the case could be made that Socrates rejects teaching and teachers. For example, in the *Apology*, Socrates says, "I counted Evenus fortunate indeed if he really does possess that art and teaches for such a modest fee. For my own part, at any rate, I would be puffed up with vanity and pride if I had such knowledge. But fellow Athenians, I just don't have it."[9]

Such statements need to be read in the context of the irony that abounds in Socrates' speech. One could say that Socrates founded our modern meaning of irony: saying one thing while giving a signal that the opposite is true. In this instance, the first sentence is laced with irony: the huge fee that Evenus charges for his teaching would be a modest fee — if he really could teach what he claimed to teach. But he is no teacher. For true teaching one has to look to someone (Socrates) who is directly contrasted with Evenus: one who sponsors a free inquiry that produces a "service to the god."

The moral dilemma that Socrates was wrestling with and could not resolve by a straightforward answer was, Who anoints anyone as "teacher" and gives that person the right to teach? Who gave that person or persons the right to have their word assumed as true and beyond challenge? Socrates and the Sophists come down to us in history as irreconcilable opposites. And yet Aristophanes could picture them doing the same thing, and from his view it was not a very good thing.[10] Both were engaged in what other people call "teaching." But whose knowledge and what authority supports the teaching? Socrates regularly denied that he possessed knowledge, but he attacked one knowledge on the basis of another. Clearly, he thought he had discovered the most important kind of knowing. He called it a "human wisdom" in contrast to the claim of a "wisdom that is more than human."[11]

This formula does not resolve the question of who or what legitimates Socrates' vocation. There is an unmistakable religious element in Socrates, a "demon" that moved him to do what he did.[12] This power remains somewhat mysterious, as perhaps it had to, but the appeal to some force greater than human reason is what keeps the Socratic search for the good from turning into an egocentric instrumentalism. That is, Socrates' criticism of the Sophists was that they reduced knowledge to an instrument of human good. Socrates was not in the vocation of selling knowledge of the good life.[13]

Anything that claimed to be divinely guaranteed knowledge was subjected to Socrates' critical questioning. The knowledge we think we have may not be knowledge at all, while the knowledge that is most important may be in some sense present to us beyond our immediate awareness. If that is the case, then the one who is "teacher" will be forced to use strange methods, always trying to turn the question back on a deeper question.

The issue of whether Socrates "teaches" is well summed up by Gregory Vlastos:

> In the conventional sense, where to "teach" is simply to transfer knowledge from the teacher's to the learner's mind, Socrates means what he says: that sort of teaching he does not do. But in the sense which *he* would give to "teaching" — engaging would-be

learners in elencthic argument to make them aware of their own ignorance and enable them to discover for themselves the truth the teacher has held back — in that sense of "teaching" Socrates would want to say he is a teacher, the only true teacher.[14]

Vlastos's use of quotation marks in the above passage is to indicate that the question is, "What is the meaning of the term 'to teach'?" In our day, as in Socrates' time, there is perhaps a "conventional" sense of teaching (to transfer knowledge). Given any sustained reflection on the matter, it quickly becomes apparent that such a transfer is impossible. Probably in every decade of every century someone "discovers" that there is no such thing as teaching. He or she announces to the world a new finding: No one can teach anyone anything.[15]

The verb "to teach," however, does not disappear. In fact, the word is everywhere. If no one can teach anyone anything, why is it that everyone has the sense that at least on some occasions they were taught? Over the years, I have asked thousands of people to engage in an exercise concerning teaching. I ask them to write out in detail a description of when someone taught them something; that is all the instruction I provide for the exercise. I have never had a person who could not come up with a description. Most people set about the task immediately and usually come up with a precisely detailed description.

The search in this book is for meaning *in use*. How does the "crowd" use the word? Regarding "teaching," the crowd obviously has mixed feelings. The activity seems to be all but universal and yet it also seems to be impossible to realize. Giving up on the word, if that were possible, would not resolve our problems. But we still have to test out possible directions for use of the term so as to clarify what the moral dilemma is and how best to work with it.

The Modern Dilemma

Socrates may still exemplify the essential dilemma of teaching, but I think the actual embodied problem has become worse in recent centuries. The early founders of modernity would probably be astounded at our plight. The scientific revolution, it was assumed, would solve the problem of teaching. Surely teaching was a minor problem compared to the problems of astronomy and physics. One of the earliest of these scientists of the new education, Johann Comenius, wrote, "As soon as we have succeeded in finding the proper method, it will be no harder to teach schoolboys in any number desired, than with the help of the printing press to cover a thousand sheets daily with the neatest writing."[16] Thus arose one of the favorite metaphors for teaching in modern times: writing on a slate or, better still, printing on paper.

This kind of passage, dear to humanistic critics of education, can be unfair to Comenius. He is commenting here on teaching large groups instead of small groups, not on what teaching is. For the most part, his writing on teaching is not posed in mechanical terms. In fact, the term that dominates almost every page of his educational writings is "natural." Comenius and others after him believed that teaching will be easy once the laws of nature have been discovered; education is simply a following of nature.[17] As the plant when supplied with water and sunlight grows of itself, so the child needs only the nurturing of its environment and it too will grow to maturity. Jean-Jacques Rousseau's statement at the beginning of *Emile* — "Plants are shaped by cultivation, and men by education" — is the most common source for this image, but it is an image found in numerous other educational treatises.[18]

It is ironic that Rousseau is the one who is assumed to represent this position, because Rousseau opposed "man and nature." In his educational writing, Rousseau's sympathies seem to lie on the side of "nature." But the contemporary reader can misread this choice to mean that the nonhuman world (nature) provides the path for man to follow. Rousseau was writing at one of the moments in Western history when "nature" was in transition. Rousseau's meaning of "nature" is actually close to what later centuries have meant by "man." That is, the great conflict is not between the human race and the nonhuman world; rather, it is between "man" (meaning society) and "nature" (meaning the individual).[19]

For Rousseau's educational purposes, "nature" is the boy's inherent structure of growth. For teaching "according to nature," Rousseau set out a very rational program for the tutor to follow. It seems to work well at the early stages and Rousseau's work was a great inspiration to bettering the education of young children. Rousseau, like his British counterpart John Locke, did not have children in his care. Whatever the source of the wisdom they tapped into, they helped to improve the care of children according to "nature's" wisest ways.

What they could not do was cure the split between the individual and society. At the beginning of *Emile*, Rousseau says it is impossible to educate both a man and a citizen; he opts for trying to produce an individual man according to nature; that means one who would forever be in conflict with society. The tutor doggedly follows a plan that allows his young student to discover knowledge — so long as it is knowledge that is innocent of society's economic, political, sexual, and religious forces. Eventually the tutor must fall back as society's sex, religion, and politics come to bear. The desperate hope is that Emile's individuality will then be strong enough to withstand the assault of these social forces when teaching has come to an end.

Religion, for example, is a key element in the whole plot. Rousseau would have his young student shielded from religion until the age of 15. Then everything about religion would be put into a straightforward, persuasive explanation. About fifty pages of *Emile* consist of a long, boring sermon on what Rousseau takes to be Christianity, but is in fact a summary of the eighteenth-century's newly minted religion, Deism.[20] In other times and other places one might be able to root knowledge of religion more closely in "nature." But even "nature religions" go beyond nature; that is, humans ask questions and search for meaning in a way that sets them adrift from other beings "in nature" or other natures.

It is at that juncture — when the child begins to reason and to socialize — that teaching becomes a moral crisis. The child, it would seem, has to know certain things to function in even the most primitive society. Those things begin to be conveyed before the child has a reflective consciousness. Some revolutionary reformers suggest that children should discover everything by and for themselves. It is doubtful that the program has ever been seriously entertained because its execution is unimaginable. Each culture and each generation have very particular things for the children to learn.

Rousseau was realistic on this point, despite what may seem to be a curriculum guided only by the child's interests. The tutor knows what is best; it is he alone who knows where the process is leading. The system is authoritarian, although as all authoritarians know, the trick is to hide the coercive power in what appears to be complete liberty. When a conflict does arise, Rousseau's advice to the tutor is brutally realistic: "Let him know only that he is weak and you are strong; that from your respective situation he necessarily lies at your mercy.... Let the bridle which constrains him be compulsion and not authority."[21] As in John Locke's educational writing, there is sweet reasonableness on the part of the teacher, because, if necessary, the child can be intimidated ("shamed") by sheer power.[22]

Locke and Rousseau did not resolve the moral dilemma of teaching and, in some ways, they worsened it. Both focus on what they take to be the ideal teaching situation: one male tutor confronting one young, male student. In this context, teaching gets confused with the power that adults have over children. The male tutor knows that some day the boy will be grown up and able to reject the teaching. While the boy is young, he can and must be taught; when he gets to be an adult he is free of this oppression. Educational reformers who wish to liberate children usually find no other recourse than to attack teaching.

Donald Schön identifies the problem of educational reform as having two parts: how we name what we attend to and how we frame its context.[23] The premise of *Emile*, that one male tutor confronts one young, male student, is unduly limited in its "framing" in many ways. One of the assumptions in this framing is that the ideal situation has one pupil.

When school reformers try to bring Rousseau into the classroom, they are frustrated by having twelve, twenty-two, or fifty-two students in front of them. How can one follow "nature" (the *individual* child's bent) when one is dealing with a large group? The schoolteacher is led to feel that Rousseau-like theories do not work only because the schoolteacher's situation is deficient. But is it possible that the original framing is deficient?

One of Kurt Lewin's famous studies that helped to found our knowledge of group process was a study of a hospital. The staff of the hospital instructed each new mother on how to take care of the newborn infant. The hospital staff gave twenty minutes to each mother; eventually, however, the staff found that instructing six mothers for almost the same length of time was *more* effective; and obviously it was more time-efficient for the hospital. The fact that most people most of the time learn better in groups than individually is now commonplace knowledge.[24] But the picture of Rousseau's tutor and pupil still haunts the subconscious of educational reformers. If only each pupil had his or her own teacher, then would not educational reform work? The answer, I suspect, is no; in fact, we would have a more obvious problem with the meaning of "to teach."

Another problem with Rousseau's framing of teaching is that the teacher is male and so is the student; or at least the main part of *Emile* is about the education of the boy; the girl Sophie appears only in the last of the five books. To his credit, Rousseau was aware of an important question here: the possible differences between boys and girls in education. The same awareness cannot be attributed to most of the reformers in his wake.[25]

Emile is educated to become an "autonomous man." Sophie's education is to prepare her to be the mother of Emile's children and the manager of his home. While Emile is supposedly independent, he is in fact dependent on his partner for all of life's earthy necessities. In public the man is powerful, in private the woman is; but this relation of public man and private woman does not produce two whole human beings. In a novel written after *Emile*, Rousseau acknowledged that the project would fail. In that novel, Sophie rebels against her role, becoming sexually promiscuous; Emile goes through various hardships and ends up a loner.[26] The lack of an integral *relation* between Emile and Sophie reveals that Emile's education is at least as deficient as Sophie's.

It is interesting to note that Sophie is more easily taught than Emile and will never have to rebel against teaching. Women were thought to be closer to "nature." Mothers were to teach their daughters sewing, cleaning, cooking, caring for infants. The powers that are exercised pertain to nurturing bodily functions. In religion, Sophie does not have to be shielded as Emile is, nor is she ever given the deistic system to digest. Religion is the comfortable set of attitudes and practices that the mother will maintain and pass on to her daughter.

Rousseau's program for the education of girls finds few takers today. But what is the alternative? One route is to demand that Sophie be given the same education as Emile so that she, too, can become an autonomous individual. Writing thirty years after Rousseau's *Emile*, Mary Wollstonecraft sounded this theme in her *Vindication of the Rights of Woman*. The term that dominates her book is "reason," and the contention is that women can be every bit as reasonable as men. "Children cannot be taught too early to submit to reason...for to submit to reason is to submit to the nature of things."[27]

Mary Wollstonecraft gives short shrift to all the "womanly" things that occupy Sophie's upbringing. If forced to choose between these two models, most educational writers today would presumably go with Wollstonecraft. But is it certain that she has framed the context with sufficient breadth? Jane Martin points out that much of what Sophie is taught are necessities of human life. They are not things that can be or should be transcended in the name of reason.[28]

Sophie might be a good reminder of where all human teaching starts. Although teaching should go beyond where Sophie goes, human teaching can never entirely leave behind being born, fed, clothed, nurtured, visited, and the like. Jane Martin, in examining books in the philosophy of education, found that these necessities of life are excluded from teaching. What mothers do is not counted as deficient teaching; it is not counted as teaching at all. Teaching, it is still assumed, consists of a man giving reasons to a boy. And, if some girls are allowed into the room, that fact does not of itself change what it means "to teach."

What the eighteenth century has given us is a meaning of "teaching" in which an adult exercises power over a child. It is assumed (not without reason) that children need to be controlled. In addition to the parents, a special group is allowed to exercise this power; they are the "teachers." In other circumstances, the teacher's power would be immoral. When the child has the power to direct his or her own life, then the power of the teacher will be overthrown. Philip Jackson, in *The Practice of Teaching*, says there are two things that liberals and conservatives in education agree on: remove unnecessary pain in learning and increase the independence of the learner. Commenting on the second, Jackson writes, "Nor would anyone in his or her right mind recommend keeping students dutifully servile to their teachers a day longer than is necessary."[29] The shocking thing explicitly said to be agreed upon by all spokespersons is that students should be *dutifully servile* at all.

Suppose that children decide that being servile for even one day is a state no one should have to put up with. That may be the situation we are now experiencing. In the eighteenth century, it was possible and acceptable to intimidate the child, to "shame" the child into submission. The power of shame played a key role. As late as 1930, Willard Waller, a humane sociologist of education, describes how to control a child by the sheer power of shaming.[30] Schoolteachers might still be able to do that, but most find Waller's description repellent; they are, so to speak, ashamed of the idea. Even those adults who are not ready to subscribe to a children's bill of rights recognize that children should be respected and treated with human dignity. This development has not made life easier for schoolteachers; in fact, it is central to the crisis that has gripped schools for several decades. The children have discovered that the school cannot or will not exercise the power to make them servile. At that point, "to teach" becomes unclear if adults cannot tell children what to think.

If this analysis is correct — that teaching has been equated with an ethically questionable exercise of power by adults over children — then there would be two places in modern educational literature where teaching is attacked or avoided. That turns out to be the case with "moral education" and "adult education."

In the twentieth century, the phrase "moral education" came to mean a specialized area — not the opposite of "immoral education" but of "neutral education." While most of education was left to its assumed neutrality, a special set of techniques was developed for moral education through moral development. The literature on "moral education" is suspicious of "teaching." At the most extreme (for example, "values clarification") teaching comes under direct attack. The teacher should never say that something is right or wrong.

In most of "moral education," the attack on teaching is more subtle. What is affirmed is "moral development," a process that simply makes teaching moot. Jean Piaget's work on moral judgment (later extended by Lawrence Kohlberg) has been influential in setting the direction of "moral education."[31] Piaget was critical of adult interference in the development of the child's moral judgment. He was most critical of schoolteachers because their attempts to teach morality are detrimental.

Piaget was reacting to a book by Emile Durkheim entitled *Moral Education*. Durkheim thought that the school was a "locus, par excellence of moral development."[32] Piaget rejected that idea. Durkheim, writes Piaget, was still relying on the "authority" that comes from society, and society's priests, the schoolmasters. In Piaget's framework, to teach morality to a child is almost a contradiction in terms. Beyond "facilitating" discussions among children, the task of the parent and the schoolteacher is to get out of the way.[33]

In twentieth-century "adult education," it is even more obvious that teaching does not fit. If to teach is to exercise power over a child, then (to try) to teach an adult is an insult. Adult-education literature tried to invent a new vocabulary (the centerpiece was "andragogy") which was to gain its clarity by a contrast to the teaching of children.[34] Children study a subject, adults solve problems; children's learning is directed by others, adults are self-directed learners. Most important, children need teachers, adults need anything but teachers.

There was no agreement on the name of the people directing adult education, so long as it was not the oppressive "teacher." The index of *Handbook of Adult and Continuing Education* does not contain an entry for "teaching."[35] An international conference on adult education stated, "In adult education practice it was now widely accepted that the concepts of 'student' and 'teacher' were inadequate. Instead of 'teacher,' the word 'guide' or 'counselor' or 'animateur' were increasingly being used."[36]

As it turns out, however, it is not that easy to get rid of teachers and teaching in education. For example, in the book reporting the above objection to "teacher," the author twenty pages later bewails the failure of "teacher-training programs" to study adults and their learning abilities.[37] But this exclusion of adults would seem to be consistent with the author's advocacy: teacher training would study children; animateur training would study adults.

In actual practice, the thousands of adult-education programs do not seem to get free of what most people call teaching and teachers; the words have not disappeared. There is a lot of group discussion, although these days "group work" can be found in almost any school. The total contrast between the education of children and the education of adults is — fortunately — not borne out in practice.

I say it is fortunate because the method of totally contrasting children and adults put what is supposedly all the good and liberating activity (for example, self-directed learning) on the adult's side. The child was to be left to the oppression of external forces. There was no inclination here to reform children's education; that would only cause a blurring again as to the specific nature of "adult education."

I would applaud the fact that the adult-education movement recognized a problem with the meaning of "to teach." There is an urgent need to examine the power relations between child and adult. One can acquiesce in a reduced and ethically questionable use of teaching by separating adult education from teaching. Or, by starting our thinking with adults, we could get a much richer picture of *all* teaching. Teaching is the way to major social, economic, and political transformation. This is where the great hopes of the founders of the adult-education movement in the nineteenth century remain unfulfilled.

Consider the provocative thesis of Peter Elbow: "When the sexuality of teaching is more generally felt and admitted, we may finally draw the obvious moral: it is a practice that should only be performed upon the persons of consenting adults."[38] I doubt that Elbow really wishes to *exclude* children from teaching; he does wish to wrench our thinking away from typical assumptions in both educational writing and "adult education." If we begin by thinking of teaching in its most complete form as something that happens between adults, we would have a rich relation to explore. Among other things we would get a better picture of where children fit in the relation of teach-learn. We would be more sensitive to the child's gradual entrance into the exchanges of adult power.

Children are, so to speak, an exception in teaching. They are an important exception; the very youngest children, I will argue in the next chapter, are a test of all theories of teaching. If we were to proceed on this path, the existence of "adult education" would be cast in doubt. We would not need a theory of adult education; instead, more than ever, we would need a theory of education that excludes neither children nor grownups.

Liberating the Verb "To Teach"

In this final section, I will document the claim that schoolteaching is only one form of teaching but, even as writers admit other forms, teaching is cast as obvious in the one case and discernible only by shadowy extension in the other cases. Educational literature usually assumes the image of an adult standing in front of a group of children. The image was set in the eighteenth century before the advent of universal schooling. Neither John Locke nor Jean-Jacques Rousseau was describing classroom instruction. But the modern school was able to embrace the image of the individual (male) tutor and (boy) child pupil. Even when women generally replaced men (at the "lower levels" of teaching) and the pupils multiplied in numbers, the idea of what a teacher is and does did not substantially change.

Philip Jackson, in *The Practice of Teaching*, says of teachers, "Among the first things to note is how many kinds of teachers there are. Leaving aside the large number of non-professional teachers (most parents, for example), we are still left with an impressive variety of types, the major ones well known."[39] With one parenthetical sweep, most teachers are dismissed from the topic of teaching.

More important, when Jackson brings up the meaning of "to teach," he introduces a reference to home, street, synagogue, church, and doctor's office, with the premise, "although formal schooling is obviously the chief source." For many writers on education, "formal schooling" is apparently the chief source, but it is not at all obvious that that is how most human beings have experienced and understood the primary meaning of "to teach." Writers on education need to consider the possibility that they are looking at teaching through the wrong end of a telescope. What teaching means in the setting of "formal schooling" cannot be enriched if all the other instances of teaching are assumed to be lesser imitations of what schoolteachers do.

Consider the astounding assumption by Brenda Cohen in this fairly typical paragraph in the philosophy of education: "Teaching can, of course, take place outside schools, but it is arguable that the term is then used by analogy with what does go on in these special institutions."[40] There is the liberal granting that "of course, teaching takes place outside schools" but it is "arguable" that any usage outside schools is only by analogy to schoolteaching. Saying it is "arguable" might suggest that the author at least thinks this premise is debatable. But she immediately points out that if parents wish to teach their children at home they have to set up a time schedule, place, and materials on the analogy of the school. The logic is consistent: If teacher means schoolteacher, then when a parent teaches, he or she has to set up a school. The author does not consider the possibility that parents teach by the fact of being parents; that parental teaching is more basic than classroom teaching; that parental teaching and the school's teaching have to be seen as complementary forms. Her assumed meaning of teaching excludes this line of inquiry.

The assumption that "to teach" is approximately equivalent to what schoolteachers do in classrooms has the advantage of providing a simple, brief answer to the meaning of "to teach." Socrates, lacking that clear-cut reference, can only leave us somewhat confused as to what does or does not count as teaching. Rousseau sets out to describe all the actions that might possibly fall under the category of teaching. He goes on for 500 pages without it being clear that he has covered all the ground. If one meditates on the meaning of "to teach," it becomes distressingly obvious that the activity is not one clear-cut gesture or set of words. How exactly do we circumscribe an area so that all the gestures and ways of speaking within this area constitute the activity "to teach"? Are we indeed sure that *any activity* corresponds to this verb?

Consider contrasting cases. If one asks the meaning of "to eat," we may occasionally be mistaken or there may be questionable cases. But we are confident there is an activity that most people most of the time have no doubt about. Each day they move digestible material by hand or utensil to an open mouth; chewing and swallowing are followed by the body's reception and treatment of the material. Similarly, hundreds of other verbs have clear-cut correlatives in human life. Nearly always we can recognize cases of seeing, walking, swimming, talking, sweating, jumping, excreting, or reading.

Some activities, indicated by a single verb, are a combination of activities but are still easy to identify: driving a car, mowing the lawn, fixing a broken pipe, acting in a play. In contrast, there are other complex activities that may seem to correspond to an important verb, but we are hard put to say, "These are all the cases and only these are the cases." What does it mean, for example, "to love," "to govern," or "to achieve success?" What are the gestures and forms of speaking that constitute each of these activities? Teaching seems to fall into this last category. Any attempt to define it is likely to leave us bewildered.

Hence arises the temptation to answer, "What does it mean to teach," by saying, "I don't know how to tell you but if you look in that classroom you will see a person doing it; teaching is what schoolteachers do." The problem, however, is not entirely solved by that maneuver. Is everything that this person is doing part of the meaning of "to teach"? That is, if you are called a "teacher," does each of your activities fall within "to teach"? If not, we still have to sort out the teaching and the nonteaching activities of the teacher.

Thomas Green's *The Activities of Teaching* deserves extended comment because it sets out promisingly to ask and to answer just that question.[41] Green recognizes that teaching can be broken down into dozens of activities. Such activities as explaining, questioning, and comparing are part of a set that he calls *logical* acts connected with teaching. He also has *strategic* acts, such as planning and evaluating, that are part of the execution of teaching. Finally, he has *institutional* acts associated with teaching, things that schoolteachers are called upon to do. His intention is to distinguish the act of teaching itself from other activities that teachers perform: "The activity of teaching can go on without the institutional activities of teaching. Teaching, in short, does not require the institutional arrangement we associate with schools. It can and does go on between father and son, for example."[42] His intended distinction between teaching and schoolteaching is a crucial one, though his sole example (father and son) is not very encouraging, given the modern premise of teaching as adult male confronting boy child.

What obstructs Green's analysis of teaching is his choice of "institutional acts." He lists seven such acts: collecting money, chaperoning, patrolling the halls, attending meetings, taking attendance, consulting parents, keeping reports. Green has put in this list activities that are almost always easily disconnected from the central meaning of "to teach."[43] Hardly anyone thinks that these activities are inherent to the meaning of teaching. His intention of examining teaching in a context distinct from the school's institutional activities is a good one. But I would suggest an alternative list of school activities, ones that *do* get collapsed into the meaning of "to teach." These activities would include the following: being in a classroom, speaking to pupils, having pupils listen to instruction, referring to a book, writing on a chalkboard, talking about "subjects," starting a semester, passing out exams.

Because Green does not, in fact, distinguish teaching from the institutional trappings of the school, we do not hear again about father and son (or mother and daughter, rabbi and congregation, supervisor and intern, and dozens of other relations). A book that sets out to examine the activities of teaching is still about teaching as seen from behind the lectern at the front of a classroom. As I will repeatedly affirm, we do need a view of teaching from the front of the classroom, but not when this view is given within the illusion that it has been distinguished from institutional acts associated with schools.

The Activities of Teaching settles into a series of technical distinctions and elaborate arguments, but the book can never get outside the corner into which it has been painted. When he comes to make the first distinction within teaching, Green sets the direction for all that follows. He asserts, with little attempt to argue the case, that teaching breaks down into "teaching someone to do so and so" and "teaching someone that so and so is the case." The distinction is often shortened into "teaching to" and "teaching that."[44]

The first of the two cases, teaching someone to do something, is clear and requires little defense. What it needs is to be taken seriously with extended discussion and examples. The second case is an amazing assumption, that one of the two main meanings of "to teach" is telling someone that so and so is the case. Is this what the instructor in the classroom does? Green seems to think so and has to spend most of the book in elaborate explanations of why and how this can be justified. No matter how much one twists and turns within "teaching someone that so and so is the case," one can never get entirely free of the suspicion that indoctrination has just become more subtle and therefore more dangerous.

No doubt telling someone that so and so is the case is something that teachers frequently do; in fact, human beings do it every day. But to assume that "teaching that so and so is the case" is one of the two ways (seemingly the main way) to teach is an amazing assumption. It begins an analysis of teaching within the narrow power arrangements that are in question today. The world remains in need of occasions when someone who knows something stands up and says, "So and so is the case." But if there is to be any hope that such teachers will speak, and equally important that they will he heard, we need a richer context for the meaning of "to teach" than theories of how to explain things to children without indoctrination.

I do not mean to scapegoat *The Activities of Teaching*. It is a carefully constructed book, better than most in the philosophy of education. Its author has continued to raise a clear and humane voice in educational reform. But this particular book is tragically flawed. It asks precisely the right question, namely, the meaning of "to teach" when it is distinguished from schoolteaching. But the answer fails to free teaching from the school's institutional control of the meaning of the term.

Most textbooks on "teacher preparation" or "teacher training" give up the wider, deeper meaning of "to teach" on page 1. They plunge into explaining all the activities that a (school)teacher must confront. The ethical problem of teaching, which has been present with us since Socrates and exacerbated by modern theories of education, cannot be addressed. Instead, we have idyllic and idealistic things said of education in textbooks of (school)teacher preparation. In other literature, we have cycles of elaborate praise of and snide attacks on the work of schoolteachers. Perhaps most of what is in the textbooks on teacher preparation is true, but these books need a sound grounding for the basic meaning of "to teach" so that schoolteachers have a realistic and fighting chance.

Chapter 2

Regrounding the Verb "To Teach"

THE DILEMMA described in the previous chapter concerns the assumptions built into the discussion of teaching. In this assumed context, a person called "teacher" and a child called "student" confront one another in a way that only allows for subservience or rebellion. Adults do, in fact, have responsibility for children's lives, especially to protect small children from forces that could overwhelm them. When the child is two years old, the adult on occasion must exercise a complete controlling power (for example, against running into the street). But this power to enforce behavior — which ought to shift yearly or even daily — is at best a primitive form of teaching.

Most discussions of teaching move the power struggle out of the street and into the school. In that context, teaching becomes not the assertion of gross power but an appeal to reasonableness. Thus, in most theorizing on education, teaching is closely associated with reasonableness.[1] The child is gradually initiated into the world of grown-up discourse.

There is much that is admirable in this ideal; I certainly would not wish to reject a move toward reasonableness. But most of life does not consist of reasonable explanations. Children along with adults are often dissatisfied with explanation alone. Radical critics of school infer from this fact that the walls of the school should come down. My own inclination would be to strengthen the school walls. But at the same time, one must ask whether there are things about teaching in school that need changing, helped by a comparison with teaching outside school. That question cannot even be asked if teaching, for all effective purposes, is equated with the activity of the schoolmaster.

Emile's contemporary tutor finds himself (or herself) backed into a corner by students who do not necessarily trust in reasonable explanations. Rousseau's advice to "remember you are strong and he is weak" indicates that a child in the eighteenth century could also be suspicious of reasonable explanations.

While sheer power may still control the situation with two-year-olds, what happens when the student is six-foot-three and 200 pounds? Perhaps the insinuation that "this is going on your permanent record in the principal's office" is the exercise of power that can stabilize the situation. In any case, teaching always has been and always will be situated in a power relation. To reduce teaching to explaining is to be blind to the full context of human life in which teaching is embedded. There is nothing in itself wrong with explaining; it is just that explaining is nowhere near wide enough to be the ground for "to teach."

A meaning for teaching that has an adult explaining things to children is attractive because it seems so clear. It is familiar territory for people who read books, and especially for people who write books. We are comfortable with the assumption that the adult teaches by giving explanations; the child learns by grasping explanations. We know that a lot of gesturing and talking at the front of a classroom may not be productive. We call this situation a "learning problem." Nevertheless, we are sure that teaching is in process, whatever the result.

The act of teaching looked at externally takes the form of explanation. But what is the indispensable condition for the activity to be called "teaching" at all? Teaching is identified with the rational activity of an individual called "the teacher." Behind the gestures, procedures, pronouncements, and questions, that individual determines when teaching occurs by the conscious intention to teach. That is, if teaching is severed from learning, and if teaching cannot be identified with everything a teacher does, then the one sure note of teaching is an inner, psychological act.

In most educational literature, the indispensable note for teaching is intention. To teach is to intend to teach. Such a circular statement may not seem to get very far, but it does specify what is under the teacher's control. What teachers have to do is "make an effort" to have something happen with their pupils. The teacher can only teach — intend something; it is up to someone else to engage in another activity, that of learning.

There is an admirable modesty in this modern position. Philosophers from Aristotle to Wittgenstein, and religious thinkers, especially in the East, have counseled humility on the part of the individual human teacher. Unfortunately, however, the modern emphasis on intention takes place within an individualism that only recognizes the subjective world of the individual and the external facts of perception. Thus, the result of equating intention with teaching is not humility for teachers but a reduction of teaching to an inner, subjective world. Whether teaching has any connection to a "real world" of fact and accomplishment is beyond anyone's control.

Although intention is obviously central to human life, its importance can be overdone. Bringing intention to center stage without playwright, scenery, and actors does not produce good drama. With teaching, as with many other activities, intention ought to emerge at the center of physical interactions and social relations. Human intention may alter what is already occurring, but one must attend to all the elements of the situation rather than only to one's intention.

I think that the emphasis on intention is an extraordinary deficiency and naivete in literature on teaching. Everything that follows in this chapter and throughout the book is based on the refusal to accept the naive equation of teaching with the intention to teach. Literature on teaching goes its way as if Nietzsche, Freud, and most of twentieth-century thought had not occurred. But for better and worse, the twentieth century has happened. The conscious intention of anyone cannot be taken at face value; context has to be examined. Nietzsche's statement of a century ago unmasks the trust in intention:

> The suspicion has arisen that the decisive value of an action resides in precisely that which is *not intentional* in it, and that all that in it which is intentional, all of it that can be seen, known, "conscious," still belongs to its surface and skin — which like every skin, betrays something but *conceals* still more.[2]

In many areas of life we have learned the point that Nietzsche (as precursor of Freud) is making here. If someone is accused of making a bigoted statement, the first line of defense is often, "But I didn't intend to offend." Far from ending the matter, the fact that the bigoted statement was *not* intended makes it the more serious. The bigotry is embedded in the subconscious and unconscious, in history and culture, in symbols and institutions. If bigotry could be eliminated just by changing people's intentions, the task would be relatively easy. We also have to get at what is behind intention, around intention, underneath intention. Nietzsche and Freud were themselves getting behind the reasonable thinking and conscious intention of eighteenth- and nineteenth-century thinkers, making contact with an older wisdom that knew what the road to hell is paved with.

The story of the unintended is not always about the dark, duplicitous, and evil doings of human beings. In the case of teaching, most of the story is about the good and joyful teaching of human beings, teaching in which intention plays at most an indirect part. As I will describe later in this chapter, much of the daily teaching in small affairs as well as the historic teaching across the generations is not intended. Thus, the literature on education that equates teaching with intention simply eliminates most of what is taught.

An Alternative Path

If teaching is reduced to intention, then the verb "to teach" and the noun "teaching" are left without any intrinsic connection. That is, what one intends as teaching (the verb) is not necessarily what results as teaching (the noun). The teachings of Moses, Jesus, Newton, or Darwin are, we hope, what each intended to leave. The connection, however, is tenuous between what is taught and what is learned by others as teachings. Any connection between, say, Jesus's teaching and his disciples' learning is fortuitous.

I wish to lay out a genuine alternative to this use of language for the relation between teach and teaching, teaching and learning. But first it is necessary to establish a meaning of "to teach" which is neither reducible to the inner world of intention nor surreptitiously the work of schoolteaching. I brought in this meaning of "teaching" in the introduction via Wittgenstein. This meaning has been present in the term "to teach" for more than a thousand years back through Old English and Middle English. "To teach" has always meant and still means "to show," and by immediate extension, to show someone how to do something. An adult explaining a math problem to a child is engaging in such "show how," although there are hundreds of other examples that might first come to mind. "Showing how" starts with bodily gestures that invite a bodily response.

I think that "show how" is the best beginning phrase for describing teaching. I have to admit that it has two drawbacks, one that is inherent to the phrase and another that can easily be supposed. The first drawback is that "show" calls attention to visual elements; we show something that can be seen. This drawback is partly overcome by adding the word "how." Usually one cannot show someone how to do something simply by presenting a visual pattern. To show someone how usually requires a bodily demonstration and the learner's body in motion.

For example, if you are going to teach a child to swim, you do not show a picture of someone swimming and say, "Imitate that." A picture of accomplishment may or may not be an encouragement to learn. But for certain, to teach a child how to swim involves putting hands under stomach or on legs, and shouting words such as "kick" or "breathe." In ordinary English, "showing how" includes aural, oral, and tactile relations. The smallest child who is trying to tie a shoelace or drink through a straw knows exactly what he or she is asking by the words, "Show me how to do that."

The second drawback, which is not intrinsic to the phrase but is likely to be present, is that "show how" is understood to be superficial, pertaining only to technical details. In this assumption, "show how" is usually correlated with "know how." Although having "know how" would seem to be valuable for automobile makers, is that what philosophers, poets, or schoolteachers are about? Part of my argument is that schoolteachers, poets, and philosophers do indeed need their own form of know-how.

I would also point out that "show how" is most closely correlated with "learn how," rather than "know-how." In "learning how" to do something, the exclusive emphasis is not knowledge or know-how. One can learn to do some physical activities in which knowledge does not seem to play a prominent role. The child who learns to swim or ride a bicycle or tie a shoelace does not necessarily have much knowledge of the activity. There is a certain amount of "know how" in doing these things but "learning how" includes more than "know how."[3]

My attempt to reground the meaning of "to teach" would be prevented if "showing how" were understood as merely knowing how to get things done efficiently. "Show how" can be the basis for complicated theorizing about the human condition and the whole universe. Furthermore, the really challenging problem with teaching is not only about propositions of science but about how we live. As traditional religions knew, and the ancient meaning of philosophy connoted, the fundamental correlation with "show how" is "to live." And showing someone how to live must eventually include how to die. Thus, the meaning of teaching as "show how" that does not limit its comprehensiveness is, "To teach is to show someone how to live and how to die."

The question might still be raised whether I have broken free of the subjective captivity described earlier. Am I in fact just saying that "to teach" is "to intend to show someone how to live and die"? That is not the case because this alternative path has presupposed what I need to make explicit: the continuity of teaching and learning.

Teach-Learn

Do teaching and learning necessarily go together? Most educational writers in the last few decades give a negative answer to that question. They are countering what they see as the naive fallacy of an earlier era. Their point of reference is the attempt during the first half of the twentieth century to develop a "science" of teacher effectiveness.[4]

A movement to study the relation of teaching and learning began at the turn of the century. It surely is a worthwhile venture to examine this relation. Unfortunately, the whole movement was undermined by naive assumptions about measuring behavior and determining causality. Mountains of data were collected to discover which behaviors on the part of the (school)teacher would cause learning in the pupil.

As often happens with reactions, critics of this movement accepted the main terms of what was being criticized. In this case, the question was still posed as a causal relation between (school)teaching and learning. Because the science of education had failed to prove any causal relations between the behavior of the (school)teacher and the student's learning, teaching and learning were declared to be totally separable activities. A more radical criticism would have asked a different kind of question. For a start, it would not have equated teaching with the activities of schoolteachers.

H. S. Broudy, one of the critics of the previous orthodoxy, wrote, "Many educators rather glibly pronounce the dictum: 'If there is no learning, there is no teaching.' This is a way of speaking because no educator really believes it to be true, or if he did he would in all honesty refuse to take most of his salary."[5] Broudy is surely right on one thing: "No learning, therefore no teaching is a way of speaking." But so is the alternative he proposes: "As long as the effort was there, there was teaching." The educator who prefers the first way of speaking would

presumably say, "I should get paid today because I made every effort
to teach them — even though I failed. At least, I failed to teach them
what I set out to teach them. Perhaps my efforts were misplaced; perhaps I taught them something different from what I had intended to
teach."

What we have here are two plausible ways of speaking which may
seem to differ only slightly. "I taught them (that is, I made the effort);
they didn't learn" versus "I tried (that is, I made the effort) to teach
them; they didn't learn." The slight difference will turn out to have
profound consequences; the following chapters attempt to make this
point. Most books in the philosophy of education presume that people
who say that teaching and learning necessarily go together have made
a naive error of logic. It is said they are guilty of a "category mistake."

Gilbert Ryle is the philosopher who is regularly invoked to explain
this error. We have confused a "task verb" with an "achievement verb."
We think that teaching is a cause, the effect of which is learning (that
is, the students have been taught). We fail to observe that on many
occasions someone is teaching but no one is learning. One of Ryle's
examples is the difference between kicking (the task of the kicker) and
scoring (an achievement). If kicking always led to scoring, the scores of
soccer games would be much higher.[6]

Some writers are willing to tolerate a use of teaching as either task
or achievement. John Passmore seems to accept this double meaning by
saying, "I do not know of any important pedagogical confusion which *in
fact* has this ambiguity as its source." But he also says that "it is a very
important fact that there can be learning where no one teaches."[7] I wish
to deny Passmore's supposed fact that there can be learning where no
one teaches. Saying that teaching and learning are separate processes
is simply a debatable way of speaking. John Dewey, for example, writes,
"Teaching may be compared to selling commodities. No one can sell
unless someone else buys. There is the same exact equation between
teaching and learning that there is between selling and buying." Dewey
is not stating a fact; he is proposing a way to speak about the act of
teaching.[8]

The rejection of the assumption that teaching and learning are separate things will lead to new questions about what teaching means and
has meant for a thousand years. I begin with the premise that learning
always implies teaching. In fact, the only proof that teaching exists is
the existence of learning. The way to avoid the equation of teaching

and intention is to say that teaching is the showing how in the process of teaching-learning. Teaching is showing someone how to live and how to die. Someone learns these things because he or she has been taught. With that assumption, one is directed to interesting questions about the who, what, where, and how of teaching.

A more fruitful comparison to teaching is found in baseball rather than soccer. Baseball has an ambiguity with "hit" as education does with "teaching." The batter hits the ball; the hoped-for result is a hit. Baseball fans do not get confused by what seems to be a terrible "category" confusion. Whenever there is "a hit," it has followed from the batter hitting. The proof that someone has hit is the fact that there is a hit.

The guarantee does not seem to hold in the opposite direction. In most cases (seven or eight out of ten), hitting does not lead to a hit. However, there is still a connection and the batter can improve his approach to hitting and increase his number of hits. However, his intention to hit better may not do that; as every athlete knows, intention can get in the way. The cruel thing about baseball is that the batter may drive the ball 400 feet and not get credit for a hit; the next batter may hit the ball 30 feet while trying to get out of the way — and find he has a hit. The patient player, the only ones who last, know that with a smooth swing the hits will come in the course of 162 games. But on a particular occasion, the connection between "hitting" and "a hit" is controlled by providence, fate, luck, or the fallible judgment of the official scorer.

The analogy of teaching and hitting is not perfect; analogies never are. But ordinary speech about each of them recognizes both the continuity of a process and the human individual having only partial control of success within the process. Does the batter swinging a bat cause the hit? If that means that a repetition of the same action would produce the same result, the answer is no. And yet "hitting" is an indispensable element in the occurrence of "a hit."

Is teaching the cause of learning? Instead of applying what is presumed to be the obvious meaning of cause, we might reconsider causal relations in the light of teach-learn. Teaching-learning is one of life's mysteries that should make us wonder whether we understand causality. The eighteenth-century image of cause and effect — one billiard ball striking another — is obviously inadequate to describe teaching-learning. In Aristotle's sense of cause — one of the four be-causes — teaching can be spoken of as a cause. I am not advocating a return to Aristotle's categories, though his complex pattern of meaning for "cause" may be more relevant to the late twentieth century than is the eighteenth-century meaning.

Aristotle in fact speaks of teaching-learning as an example of his agent/patient relation. That is, there is a single "actualization" at issue which can be viewed from opposite ends: "the actualization of x in y and the actualization of y through the action of x." Unless the student is learning, the teacher is not teaching. There is only one activity (or motion) and it occurs in the student.[9] Aristotle may be overly optimistic about the ability of the individual teacher to bring about this actualizing of the learner's power. Presumably he recognized the common case where the teacher is trying to bring about this movement and fails. Nonetheless, Aristotle's linguistic premise — that teaching and learning are not two separate processes — is a helpful way to examine teaching.

If there is a single process, how can it be that the student does not learn what the teacher teaches? The answer to this question lies in the recognition that the student is always facing more than one teacher. The child learns what has been taught by one or more teachers, but it may not be the lesson that the schoolmaster is trying to teach. David Elkind comments on what is called the slow learner, "the one who does not acquire the curriculum at a 'normal' rate." Elkind notes, however, that "the slow learner is fast to learn that he is slow." Drawing his conclusion from Piaget's view of learning, Elkind writes, "Once we acknowledge that children are learning something, all of the time — even if it is not what we set out to teach them — then we have considerably broadened our options for reaching children and directing their mental growth."[10]

I would agree and add that it is every bit as important to recognize that in addition to always learning, the child is always being taught. In the case of the "slow learner," the child does not invent or imagine something that is not there. The child learns what he or she has been taught. Plenty of things in the child's environment teach the child that he or she is slow. Some of that teaching may come from the behavior of the adult at the front of the room. In some conscious ways, and probably more so in unconscious ways, the school instructor conveys an attitude that the slow learner quickly grasps. A system of tests, grades, rewards, and punishments confirms to the child where he or she fits. Keeping the term "to teach" here is important. The child is not just learning, but is systematically being *taught* that he or she is a slow learner. Only by recognizing that teaching is occurring are we led to examine the teaching, and perhaps change some of it.

Who and What Teaches

The next crucial step is to free the meaning of "to teach" not only from the conscious intent of the individual teacher but also from individual human teachers. We have to examine the unconscious behavior and indirect intention of the teacher; we also have to examine the nonpersonal world, including nonhuman nature and human institutions. A kind of obsession with the interpersonal relation of teacher and student can obscure the world of teaching that the individual human teacher is trying to work with and work in. The ultimate subject of "to show someone how to do something" is the universe of living and nonliving things.

In Michael Oakeshott's essay, "Learning and Teaching," he allows that we might learn from a book or the sea, and we might be self-directed in our learning. But then he asserts, "To say that the book, the sky or the sea has taught us anything, or that we have taught ourselves, is to speak in the language of unfortunate metaphor."[11] The author does not explain why the metaphor is "unfortunate." More basic and questionable is the dismissal of these cases as "metaphor" instead of the genuine and original sense of teaching. Each of the cases that he cites deserves comment on its own. They are not all one "metaphor." Sea and sky are perhaps of a piece and can be treated together. Books are different, and the self as teacher raises further complications.

Does it make any sense to say that the sea teaches us? Obviously if teaching requires either a human intention to teach or human explanations, then there is nothing to discuss. But if "to teach" means to show someone how to live and how to die, then the sea as teacher is not a vague figure of speech. It is just about the biggest and most powerful teacher on earth. When the sea speaks, humans had better listen. I have a friend who says that he only feels fully alive when he is in the ocean. The ocean conveys — as nothing else does — our most elemental relation to life's forces; it was not by chance that Freud called the sense of connection to all the "oceanic" feeling. At the same time, the sea's enveloping power undermines all of our feelings of strength and security. Few things are more soothing than the gentle roll of waves onto the shore; few things are more terrifying than a hurricane-driven sea.

There are no doubt people who would say that the sea has never taught them anything. Many people live (relatively) far from the sea and cannot engage it regularly. They cannot absorb a daily lesson, though the human race is subjected to its teaching every minute of the day. Some people are fortunate enough to listen to the sea daily. They learn from the moods of the ocean that change each day. A crowded summer beach is not to be disparaged, but to learn from the sea one has to contemplate it in winter bleakness and in all the transitions between summer and winter.

As for Oakeshott's second case — books as teachers — one does not have to reach far at all. The book is the closest we can get to most of our human teachers, living and dead. Surely, there is nothing vague or outlandish in saying, "Aristotle has taught me..." by which we mean Aristotle's books. I think Erasmus went too far when he claimed that reading the New Testament provides closer contact with Jesus than what the disciples of Jesus had who looked on him in the first century. Erasmus's point is that we get to know a person best through *listening* to his or her words. That is often, if not always, more enlightening than simply looking at them.[12]

It is significant that when referring, for example, to Plato's *Republic* we use the verb in the present tense: "Plato says in Book II..." Plato is dead and does not say anything, but the Plato embodied in the text is present and is still a great teacher. I would proudly say I have been taught by Aquinas and Wittgenstein, Karl Rahner and Hannah Arendt. They are real people, real teachers, though I have only their words on paper. I am surprised that Oakeshott rejects the book as teacher; even in a highly interpersonal image of teaching in which words are the medium, the book fits right into that image, just a step removed from the human teacher in the flesh.

The third case — the self as teacher of the self — does raise some problems. Here I would share a concern with Oakeshott that we maintain a consistent and logical description. The phrase "self-directed learning" is, as mentioned in chapter 1, a favorite of adult-education literature. The phrase is often used as an attack on teaching. The one who is self-directed supposedly needs no teaching.

At one end of its meaning, the term "self-directed" is practically redundant. The self is always giving direction for learning. If the self is never absent from human learning, then all learning is self-directed. At the other end of its meaning, the claim to self-directedness approaches absurdity. The claim that I and only I am the source of the learning is to be oblivious to all the people and books, not to mention the sea and sky, that give direction, resources, and substance to my learning.

To refer to teaching oneself could be a way of feeding this solipsism. However, I think it is more likely that by recognizing the value of self-teaching the most introverted image of learning is avoided. Without the use of the term "teaching," the phrase "self-directed learning" is not likely to include political debates, social reconstruction, or examination of institutional power. The language of myself as teacher is at least a first step out to where the learner has to be shown something that is not immediately evident in his or her experience.

It is thus "within" the individual's experience that he or she can act as teacher. I use "experience" here as a complex relational term: passive/active, rational/nonrational, and even in some sense subjective/objective. A person can experience her- or himself as a subject of the act of teaching (I as teaching) and the indirect object of the teaching (me as taught). An "outside" teacher (human or nonhuman) likely provides the beginning example, pattern, or way of doing things; the teacher within takes it from there.

It is often noted that the student cannot just passively accept teaching; the student has to respond with his or her own distinctive powers. What is less often noted is that the response includes becoming the teacher of ourselves so as to continue the pattern or fill out the design. After saying that "didactic influence" can be exerted by a person upon himself, Gilbert Ryle adds, "He can coach himself to say and do things which are not echoes of the words in which that coaching is given."[13] The "coaching" here seems to need an outside teacher to begin the process, but it is just as necessary to have the pupil then become the teacher.

The myth of the "self-taught man" does need some pointed criticism. When the phrase means that someone is an avid reader or has had the initiative to learn carpentry, TV repair, skiing, or making money in the bond market, admiration may be in order. If the phrase is used boastfully to mean he trusted no one, listened to no one, and had no need to learn from others, then the self-taught, self-made man is living an illusion that could collapse at any time. People who are truly governed from the center of the self know that the self as teacher can use all the help it can get.

Teaching by Living Beings

The language of a person teaching him- or herself is not a vague or confused image of speech; nor is there anything unclear about a book teaching; the voice of the author reaches us not through the air but on the page. The other example discussed — the sea — may still strike the reader as metaphor or analogy.

It may seem that what we have recognized in human activity we have projected on to a screen of inanimate objects. "The sea teaches," a poet might say, but literally and scientifically we know that the ocean lacks that power.

I wish to dispute this objection on the basis that it is up to human beings to decide how to use the term "to teach." In this case, the poet is worth listening to. There is no scientific evidence against the sea teaching. The question is simply whether in this way of speaking the human race is using a confused grammar or else is recognizing a continuity of life on earth. Wittgenstein notes that we cannot say "a machine has a toothache"; the grammar of "machine games" does not allow the sentence.[14] Similarly, in reference to sea games, the imposition of an entire range of human emotions can become confusing anthropomorphism. But "to teach" is a fairly controlled reference to an encounter between the ocean and a teachable being.

What I have said of the sea by way of example could be said, *mutatis mutandis*, of the other great forces of nature: mountains, forests, deserts, sunsets, snowstorms. Each can teach and has taught powerful lessons to those who encounter these forces. In Gary Snyder's book on wilderness, he writes, "For those who would seek directly by entering the primary temple, the wilderness can be a ferocious teaching, rapidly stripping down the inexperienced or the careless."[15] Even miniature forces can teach those who are willing to respond: the snowflake, the seashell, the pebble, the flower, the diamond. Jacob Needleman, in exploring religious traditions up through the Middle Ages, found it to be a constant principle that "the universe" teaches. I wish to assert nothing less.[16]

The reference to the Christian Middle Ages may suggest that the idea of everything in the universe teaching is dependent on a religious interpretation. Is the real meaning of "the sea teaches" the belief that "God teaches us through the sea"? I would grant that listening to the sea for wisdom and meaning does imply what is often called a "religious" outlook. I would add that it does not imply a Christian interpretation; in fact, being taught by the sea or the mountain or especially the forest was mostly frowned on by the Christian church and survived despite the suspicion. In any case, I am not interested in turning the sea into an instrument of teaching, a kind of audiovisual aid for divine instruction. I am interested in the human-nonhuman interplay and the most comprehensive context for teaching.

It is true that we would not use "to teach" of the sea or the mountain if we did not know what it meant in human exchanges. That is true of every term we apply to inanimate objects, with some terms being more of an anthropomorphic stretch than others. To say "the volcano is angry" is taken as a figure of speech by modern people. To say "the mountain taught a lesson to the mountain climber" is to describe a precise interaction. The mountain climber learned something in response to being shown something by the mountain.

The resistance to this form of speech comes from those who have closely identified teaching and conscious intention. Presumably the mountain did not have in mind setting out to teach a lesson. Further along in this book I wish to celebrate consciousness, intention, and the power to speak. I do not wish to reduce all teaching to the way it is done by sea or mountain. However magnificent the things of nature, they do sometimes need a human voice to speak on their behalf.

Nonetheless, the relation is not all one way, with nature's teaching a general context for the real teaching, human speech. It is instead a dialectical relation in which sea or mountain may provide an instructive element for understanding teach-learn in the world of living beings. Most of the teaching done by humans is — like that of sea and mountain — unintentional and nonverbal. Before getting to these human interactions, it will be helpful to consider the example of living beings other than humans, especially the humans' next of kin: the sentient animal.

One of the helpful developments of this century has been the renewed interest in studying (nonhuman) animals. The Middle Ages often argued from analogy with the animal world. The idea was not so crazy as the seventeenth, eighteenth, and early nineteenth centuries, with their radical split of "man and beast," assumed. Many terrible mistakes in the Middle Ages came not from the study of animals but from having facts that were entangled with myths. Conclusions about human life were often based on mistaken information. In the twentieth century it can sometimes seem almost the reverse. Our detailed knowledge of the animal or insect world can be used as an exhaustive measure of the human world. Whatever the excesses, however, the study of nonhuman animals can be very helpful in understanding such human phenomena as sexuality, aggression, and fear.

The fact of continuity between human and nonhuman animals has been widely recognized during the past century. Few people would now resist the application of the verb "to learn" to many, if not all, animals. There is endless debate about what the learning of the chimp, horse, or dolphin means, the similarity with and difference from human learning. But that animals take in a kind of knowledge and retain it for future use seems clear.

Animals learn, but are they taught? With the use of the language I have been advocating, the answer has to be yes. The case is clearest when the teacher of the animal is a human being. Some people distinguish sharply between teaching and training. They would agree that the animal trainer trains but not that he or she teaches. There will come a time to specify terms such as "to train," but for the present, teaching as showing how embraces elements of training, drilling, and coaching. The animal trainer's teaching methods are very restricted; nevertheless, it can be said that the animal learns a trick because it has been taught to do the trick.

A more problematic step is replacing the animal trainer with an animal. Do we still have teaching-learning when both parties are non-human animals? Does the mother bird teach the small bird to fly? Does one deer teach another how to get food? Does a dominant tiger teach a lesson to a would-be replacement? I think the grammar of animal games can easily bear this way of speaking.[17] The *how* of teaching is restricted by the given structure of teacher and student. So *what* can be taught is highly limited. The mother robin cannot teach her young to build a DC-10 or even a small Lear jet. The human world is tempted to look down snobbishly on the restrictions built into one animal teaching another animal.

Despite the restrictions, animals might be able to teach human beings some important lessons. For example, the place of ritual in intraspecies conflict is a lesson that humans have yet to learn from their next of kin. But beyond such individual lessons, the animal world's great importance to human learning is in the reminder to humans that they, too, are animals. Whatever humans try to teach, in a specifically human fashion, they can never get away from their animality. With very young children, the relation is most evident; the way to teach is to show the child how to do something—with whatever bodily gestures are needed. The principle becomes modified but it is not retracted when the pupil is 6, 16, or 46 years old.

The animal part of teaching is found in the physical continuity of teaching-learning. Animals perpetuate practices that are life-preserving without going into explanations. The mature animal performs the physical activity and at some point the young one can continue the same act. The first thing a cat does after eating is clean itself. Mother cats know that the best chance for cleaning a kitten is while it is eating. Throughout its life afterward, the cat will associate eating and cleaning. That is presumably not a lesson the mother cat intended but it is a lesson the kitten learned. Life, health, and safety tips are passed down from one generation to another.

Any theory of human teaching has to include infants. In fact, the youngest children are one of the main tests for our understanding of teaching. If someone supposes that to teach is to explain and to give reasons, he or she should test out that meaning with a two-year-old. Instead of doing that, most authors simply exclude infants from the meaning of teaching. What typically follows from this exclusion is that discussions of teaching take place without awareness of the whole physical organism and with little appreciation of the relation between speech and bodiliness.

The moral dilemma in the meaning of "to teach" arises when the words and the bodily movements separate. The moral dilemma becomes an impossible problem when teaching is equated with words alone. At the most physical level of teaching, there is usually neither moral confusion nor moral rebellion. The child's body is receptive to learning physical skills; the way to teach the child is to tune into the rhythms of the child's movements. Teaching a child to use eating utensils includes putting the food on a spoon and raising it to the child's mouth and developing a ritual for the practice. So long as no violence is done to a child, each little piece of physical learning is a plus.

As the child will eventually learn about all human life, there are moments when one has to overcome immediate feelings of fear or laziness to master a complex human skill. But no teacher can simply run roughshod over the immediate feeling, even when the teacher is oneself. As a medieval prayer voiced it, "Beyond a wholesome discipline, be gentle with yourself."

Teaching oneself or someone else requires discovering the rhythms of the learner's constitution. It is in the developing of physical abilities that teach-learn is most clearly seen as a single process. The teacher and the student succeed together or they fail together. The question does not arise whether there can be teaching without learning, whether the teacher is kicking but not scoring. The ability, say, of a child to use the toilet is a power in the child. The adult has no doubt whether the teaching has succeeded; teacher and learner rejoice together at success.

The usual evidence that the child wishes to learn a physical skill is the presentation of a receptive organism. The child says, "Teach me to ride the bicycle." The teacher complies not by explaining bicycles in the living room but by running up and down the street. The child's desire to learn is shown by getting up and trying again after falling off the bicycle. The teacher's teaching is mainly to provide a temporary balance by physically holding the bicycle and occasionally saying "push," "stop," or "tip to the right." No adult comes in from the street and announces, "I taught Jimmy to ride the bicycle but he didn't learn."

If Jimmy fails to learn, there are several possible reasons to be explored within the single process of teach-learn. The deficiency may lie on the teacher's side, the learner's side, or on both sides. If Jimmy does learn, the teacher and student know that they have succeeded together. One of the overused and underexamined phrases in contemporary educational literature is "hands-on learning." Human teaching does begin with "hands on," in this case on the back of the bicycle and the backside of the bicyclist. The human mouth will have its place but the hands come first.

Human Teaching: Example and Tradition

In the previous section, I emphasized that at least all animals with sensory abilities teach-learn. If they are attentive, human beings might learn from the way other animals teach. The human beings are able to transcend the limitations of other animals, but the humans cannot with impunity leave behind the physical basis of all teaching-learning.

Every mammal mother, including every human mother, knows how teaching begins: place the nipple before the newborn's mouth and the learner sucks.

In the next chapter, I will describe how humans try to improve on what nature gives them for teaching. Especially through speech used in a variety of ways, the human environment can be redesigned. Before getting to that step, there is an intermediate stage between a mother suckling her young and a professor explaining black holes in the universe. There is a kind of teaching that arises in the human community and has distinct human qualities. However, for the most part, the teaching is not verbal. Insofar as the actors are human, the patterns may have a degree of consciousness and intention connected to them. Nevertheless, this kind of teaching occurs without any one individual intending to teach. In the acknowledgment at the beginning of his book, *How We Die*, Sherwin Nuland writes, "Even when I had no idea I was learning from one or another of the vast number of men and women whose lives have entered mine, they were nevertheless teaching me, usually with equal unawareness of the gift they were bestowing."[18]

I would emphasize that this kind of teaching is not simply a deficient form of *real* teaching. On the contrary, all human teaching rests on two pillars: the bodily organism and silence. Speech arises in the middle of body and silence. Very often in human teaching, speech will clinch the case, but not without a silent bodily presence as precondition. Occasionally, speech is a distraction from the power of silent example. We teach by showing people how to live and how to die. At the beginning, words are unnecessary, at the end words are inadequate. Nonverbal teaching can be examined in two ways: a cross-section of the present gives us teaching by example; looking at the flow of the generations gives us teaching by tradition.

Teaching by example, like parental teaching, is simultaneously praised and dismissed in treatises on teaching. John Locke would seem more positive than most in asserting, "But of all the Ways whereby children are to be instructed, and their Manners formed, the plainest, easiest and most efficacious is, to set before their Eyes the *Examples* of those things you would have them do or avoid."[19] A close reading of this text, however, reveals that Locke is starting with the question, "How does an adult instruct a child?" His answer is that examples are the best instrument of instruction. Although I will later affirm the great value of using examples in several forms of verbal instruction,

Locke's language actually undermines a fuller meaning of "teaching by example."

The most effective teachers do not begin by setting out examples, but by being examples. They may or may not be instructors of anything. Their lives include examples of what to do, though the multiplicity is usually rooted in a single example: this is the way to live and to die. For such a person, "to set out examples" (even when the example is from one's own life or perhaps especially when it is from one's own life) is far too directive of other people. Here we have one of the great paradoxes of human life: not only is intention not the essence of teaching, but some of the most important teaching can only occur when it is not intended. The wise, talented, disciplined, accomplished person is aware that others will be inspired by his or her life. What any individual on any occasion may be inspired to do is not up to the teacher to determine.

Some interviewer is always asking a prominent athlete, "Do you think you are a role model?" The athlete is usually confused or embarrassed by the question. If he or she says yes, it sounds arrogant; if he or she says no, it sounds like a shirking of responsibility. The athlete's problem is not his or her fault. The question is not deserving of an answer. Charles Barkley caught the attention of the country with a statement in a Nike commercial, "I am not a role model. I am not paid to be a role model. I am paid to wreak havoc on the basketball court."[20] Not surprisingly, people lined up in support of or in denunciation of Barkley's statement. Unfortunately, not much gets clarified here about the power of teaching by example. The simple fact is that a Charles Barkley or a Michael Jordan is a powerful teacher. A person from any celebrated profession can provide an inspiring example of how to discipline personal talent and achieve brilliant results.

Barkley's real argument should have been with the stilted phrase "role model." Instead, he used the phrase in the punchline of the statement: "Parents should be role models." Of course, a parent can model the role of parent for his or her children, but that is hardly an encompassing statement of what children need. Children need good example from adults; some of that can come from celebrities in sports or in music; much more of it should come from parents, schoolteachers, politicians, police officers, and other adults that the child encounters.

The phrase "role model" is assumed to be clear because it is thrown around so frequently. If one wishes to appreciate teaching by example, then neither "role" nor "model" is particularly helpful. "Role" is too narrow for what is taught; "model" is too rigid for how to teach. If a social scientist wishes to talk about role models, it may make sense in some contexts. But role models is not the place to begin exploring how human beings teach one another every day.[21] A study of black youngsters in the Bronx of the 1950s found that the majority wished to have the same job: center fielder on the Giants. That was Willie Mays as role model. Unfortunately, having a "role model" does not just mean wishing to be a ballplayer, but to be center fielder on the Giants or small forward on the Bulls. That kind of teaching — including the social science jargon that becomes part of it — is mostly a cruel hoax. It is no help to youngsters and adults who need people to admire, to trust, and to emulate. Millions of young black men in the country could learn something from Charles Barkley; but what they should not aspire to learn from him — and he could not teach 99.9% of them — is how to be a forward on the Suns.

We all depend on human teaching every day, people doing things in our presence which inspire us to believe that there is goodness in the world, that one can say yes to living another day. And most of the time, the smile, the gesture of politeness or care, is all the more powerful as teaching because it is not intended as teaching. There is no moral dilemma here; the learner is free to take whatever he or she wishes to take and is able to take from the available teaching.

Consider this example of example as teacher from Malcolm X's auto-biography. He was in Jedda on the way to Mecca in 1964; in the crowded conditions of the city, a government official gave up his own room so Malcolm could sleep. Malcolm, reflecting on the incident, writes, "That white man ... related to Arabia's ruler, to whom he was a close adviser, truly an international man, with nothing in the world to gain, had given up his suite for me, for my transient comfort. ... That morning was when I first began to reappraise the white man."[22] Malcolm X's life was profoundly changed by the new situation he was in, by the physical, historical, and social influences all around him. But he nonetheless pinpoints the connection between a simple act of kindness and the beginning transformation of his thinking on race.

Writers in education get tangled up in their own language when they refer to this simple, but all important phenomenon, teaching by example. It does not fit their definition of teaching; unfortunately, however, that does not lead them to question if their definition is wrong. For example, Page Smith, in *Killing the Spirit*, writes that the "true person" must have love: "None of us is worthy of it, and yet all of us must have it to live. *It can't be taught.*" Two sentences later in the same paragraph, Smith writes, "Teachers who love their students are of course by that very fact teaching their students the nature of love, although the course may in fact be chemistry or computer science."[23]

If Smith decided by the end of the paragraph that "of course" love can be taught, I think he should have gone back two sentences and changed the flat assertion that "it can't be taught." The contradiction may seem minor, but it is in a chapter entitled "Teaching" in a book that caustically attacks the lack of critical-minded thinking in the university of today. If one writes a chapter on teaching, there ought to be some consistency in the meaning of "to teach."

The same confusion regularly shows up in essays with the title "Can Virtue Be Taught?" Nearly always the answer is no, with appeals made to thinkers from Socrates to Kohlberg. And yet if one begins by not unduly limiting the meaning of "to teach," the obvious answer is yes. People do learn to be virtuous; they do so having been taught to be virtuous. How does that happen? Aristotle supplies the simple, clear answer: the way to become virtuous is to grow up in a virtuous community. Virtue is what is taught all day long by virtuous members of the community.[24]

Aristotle's answer is one of those circular-sounding statements that could be ridiculed once it has been taken out of its matrix of related assumptions about community, teaching, virtue, and causality. What Aristotle is getting at is a wisdom that goes back millennia. His philosophical formulation draws upon principles that were practically self-evident for Jewish, Christian, Buddhist, Muslim, and other religious groups. The way to get good people is by providing good example. Good example does not guarantee good students, but the absence of good example will assuredly guarantee a deficiency of learning.

I caution, once more, that this principle does *not* mean "to set out good examples." That procedure comes later. Teaching by example means first and mainly living with people and showing, by the way one lives, a "way of life." I think it is amazing that, despite the vast differences among religions, they are in nearly perfect agreement on this point: the way people learn goodness or virtue is by the presence of good, virtuous people.

The principle of teaching by community example is perhaps clearest in the case of a small child learning to speak his or her native language. The child is able to pick out the sounds of human speech and respond with similar patterns of sound. Without any explanations of grammar or syntax (they should come later) the child grasps the structure of speech and joins the human conversation. Once the pattern is in place, the child becomes a voracious namer, with an explosion of "What's the name for that?" It is possible to say, "No one teaches the child to speak." That can mean there are no teachers. A more helpful statement of the situation is, "No one teaches the child to speak" because (nearly) everyone and everything teaches the child.

Steven Pinker, in *The Language Instinct*, overstates his case by saying, "First, let us do away with the folklore that parents teach their children language.... Many parents (and some child psychologists who should know better) think that mothers provide children with implicit lessons. These lessons take the form of a special speech variety called *Motherese*."[25] Pinker's object of scorn here is Motherese. While he may be right on that point, he fails to give credit to mothers (and fathers, sisters, brothers, uncles, television programs, and numerous other teachers) for teaching the child to speak. Parents teach their children not by "lessons" but by conversing with each other and speaking with the child.

What could be more obvious: the way to speak English is to grow up in an English-speaking community. The practice of English by its users and teachers is an invitation to speak English. The child for survival's sake accepts the invitation. We could improve the quality of English spoken and so improve the teaching. But even with good examples in the environment, an individual may for a myriad of reasons not learn well. These learning problems are issues to be explored. For the moment, however, it should be clear that the way *not* to teach language is by sitting a person in a chair with a list of words and rules of grammar to memorize. Language teachers in schools have a very important job in *improving* spoken and written language, but classrooms are poor places for starting to learn how to speak a language.

The very young child, I said above, is one of the best tests for the meaning of "to teach." The infant is thrust into the middle of human bodies, human institutions, and nonhuman nature. If there is no violent interference, the child can learn from all of these sources. The burden of teaching a child does not fall on one human individual; no one should have to bear that responsibility. The primary bearer is the "community," a much overused and abused word, but still indispensable. A community is a small group of people getting on with life; birth, feeding, thinking, talking, planning, aging, dying. The child learns to live by doing what the community does. Throughout life the individual continues to learn by doing what many overlapping communities do.

Groups of people and their work get taken up into human "institutions" that also become powerful teachers. Large institutions are very suspect in our day, as well they might be. Simple flight from them, however, does not make them go away or lessen their teaching influence. Institutions are in need of continual reform or else their teaching goes sour.

Our concentration on personal relations tends to reduce teach-learn to the question of individual teacher and (ideally) one student. An awareness of group process only gets us one small step beyond the tutorial image. But teaching goes on every day insofar as communities live and institutions function. And although communities can become introverted and institutions can become corrupt, the learning of the human race is nevertheless passed down over the centuries by being embodied in communal rituals and institutional arrangements. Most of this story is for the next chapter in which we consider teaching by *design*.

My focus in this chapter has been on foundational forms of teaching that occur with little or no conscious intent, with few, if any, human words. One last aspect of this mostly unintended and nonverbal teaching provides a bridge to teaching by design. I refer to tradition. It is a term that does not have good standing in educational writing. Indeed, since the late eighteenth century, education has often been posed as the opposite of tradition. "To teach" often means to free people from tradition, which is assumed to be a collection of myths, superstitions, and prejudices. Some kinder words have been said about tradition in recent decades. On the whole, however, tradition is taken to be the stone that rational explanation has to dislodge.

How schools interact with tradition is a major concern of chapter 8. Here I am interested in highlighting *that* tradition teaches and *how* tradition teaches. The fact that tradition does teach follows from the meaning of "to teach" as "show someone how to live and to die." Fortunately, for all of us, tradition has continued to supply us with wisdom about living and dying so that each generation does not have to rely solely on its own insights.

The *how* of tradition's teaching is the most interesting part. I said earlier that all teaching begins with "hands on" (one on the bicycle, one on the backside; one under the stomach, one moving the legs). Not by accident the etymological meaning of "tradition" is "to hand on." The term often connoted a conspiratorial whispering in the ear. What was handed on was secret teaching that the master could not entrust to writing. Tradition is aural, oral, and tactile, even in the era, or especially in the era, when writing dominates. At the beginning "oral tradition" was redundant, "written tradition" a near contradiction.

Eventually, the act of handing on secret wisdom does produce written statements that are codified. The name "tradition" slides over to refer to what is the *result* of tradition. What is often called "tradition" is the corpse that is left. But even when tradition appears to be moribund, when tradition(s) become the name of an oppressive code of conduct, the revolutionary power of tradition does not disappear. The oral/aural/tactile basis of tradition is still a threat to established power.

The most obvious example of tradition has for most of history resided in what mothers do with infants. (The father still remains an outsider to some of the secrets.) The mother *handles* the child, conveying through touch the experience of human care, love, and security. Speech to very young children is mostly in the form of repetitive melodies and ritual sayings. The infant does not grasp the meaning of individual words, but clearly it responds to the tactile and the oral. This basic trust, as Erik Erikson calls it, is the basis for all teaching to come.[26]

I noted earlier Jane Martin's discovery that what mothers do is routinely excluded from the meaning of teaching. Beyond saying that the problem involves bias against women, what can we say about the exclusion of tradition's teaching from the meaning of "to teach"? An immediate inclination is to think that educational writers simply do not think the mother's teaching is important enough or powerful enough to qualify as teaching. I would suggest that the real reason is just the opposite. The mother's way of teaching — handing on — is so powerful and frightening to anyone in charge of things that this revolutionary power has to be excluded from the meaning of "to teach."

All teaching is showing how. If you show a child with your hands how to do something, there is a tremendous satisfaction without any feeling of guilt. There is almost never a moral dilemma in silently doing something that the child is gradually able to continue doing. If the child is later *told* something that does not agree with this learning, the verbal teaching will almost certainly fail. The schoolmaster is awed and frightened by maternal teaching because in any showdown mother's way will win.

The human race, of course, does not remain two years old. Even in the generational act of handing on, there is design to the process. Spoken and written words have to protect the tradition from internal atrophy and external attack. We do not "hand on tradition"; rather, tradition is the handing on; we hand on whatever we can hand on of life. For the process to be humanly rich, we need to put our minds and mouths to giving shape and form to whatever it is we are trying to hand on.

Chapter 3

Teaching by Design

T HE FIRST appropriate thing for a chapter with this title is to indicate its design. I explore in this chapter the way that human beings teach by design. The phrase has a double meaning. To teach by design can refer to a conscious human intention in contrast to the unintentional, or at least indirect, way to teach described in the previous chapter. To teach by design can also refer to the design or designs that the teacher uses. The person who sets out to teach someone something inevitably attempts to impose some design. What the teacher discovers in this attempt is that every human design is a redesign. The best that a teacher can do is work with student and environment to improve the present design.

My design in this chapter is to present some relevant distinctions of language that will help to deal with such ethically questionable phrases as "impose some design." I will cite some authors and the metaphors they use for describing what a person does who wishes to help others by teaching them. I try to provide examples, some brief and others extended, of people who teach others by design and what some of the designs are.

The material I have to work with in this chapter, and throughout the book, is words. I design, or rather redesign, language in the hope of evoking within the reader images and understanding. Words are fragile material for the design of meaning. When Wittgenstein chose examples of the design of meaning, he often turned for help to architectural blueprints or Western movies.[1] This chapter does not have accompanying blueprints or videotape, but such referents are needed if my sentence designs are to convey the process of teaching by design.

In the previous chapter, I described teaching-learning as a single process. I did not prove that to be the case; I assumed the language of such a description in order to have a richer context in which to explore teaching. The value of such an assumption still has to be shown in this chapter and those that follow. Here I concentrate on instances of teaching in which human language is present, but is firmly embedded in physical contours. Or I could say that the main *language* in the teaching to be described is a physical design; *speech* in this case is a directive about the design.

I have said that teaching is not best understood as the *cause* of learning because that term still suggests two different things, teaching and learning. Instead, I have related teaching and learning more closely than cause and effect. They are descriptions of one process, seen from two different directions. Where there is teaching, there is learning, and where there is learning, there is teaching.

My premise conflicts with the modern educational assumption that there is a gap between "to teach" and "to learn." However, it is not my intention to disagree with several philosophers (Wittgenstein and Aquinas, in particular) who may seem to have an even wider gap between the efforts of the teacher and the results in the student. Aquinas and Wittgenstein insist that the teacher can only engage in "movements" that may or may not issue in the student's learning.[2]

The crucial question here is where to draw the line that acknowledges a gap between two related terms. Most of contemporary literature has the gap between "teach" and "learn," whereas I have asserted a continuity between the two. The place to draw the line and admit a gap is between the individual human teacher and the learning. There is a gap that can never be eliminated between the *intention* of the (human) teacher, translated into a set of gestures, and a result called learning on the part of another.

As an analysis of teaching shifts from mostly physical movement to mostly human speech, the gap between intention and effect becomes more evident. That is, the more specifically human the teaching is, the less assurance the teacher has that his or her movements deserve the name "teaching." Thus, at one end of the spectrum, the gestures of a mother with a newborn infant are most likely to be effective teaching; the mother does things similar to, but one step removed from, what other mammals do with their young. The case is similar for all teaching in which physical action predominates. The teacher of bicycle riding has a feeling of achievement when the child succeeds; surely, the teacher thinks, I had a part in that success. The case is different, however, when someone tries to teach by relying almost exclusively on words. In that situation, the connection between the movement of the teacher's mouth and the learning of a student is, at best, tenuous.

Even the best of teachers cannot fill this gap. Indeed, the best teachers do not try to fill the gap; they know when to stop. The insecure teacher wishes to be certain that his or her efforts produce results. "I will teach this; you will learn this; and we will leave no room for error, daydreaming, or surprise." Few things in life are sadder to watch than a well-intentioned, hard-working, totally dedicated "teacher" who does not have a glimmer of the paradox that the teacher's effort is not what brings about the student's learning.

This principle, which both Wittgenstein and Aquinas maintain, is part of a "mystical" strand in their thinking. And it is connected to a central strand in Eastern religion, which both exalts the place of "teacher" and simultaneously warns any would-be teacher to be humble in trying to play the part. That is what "mystical" means here: a recognition of mystery in the midst of the most common, everyday activities. The paradox of trying to be a teacher does not apply only to classroom instructors or religious gurus. Every human being is regularly in the position of trying to be a teacher, while a big obstacle to being a teacher is the "trying to be."

Modern treatises on teaching often pick up on part of this paradox but they usually collapse the tension. Carl Rogers writes, "When I try to teach, as I do sometimes, I am appalled by the results, which seem a little more than inconsequential, because sometimes the teaching appears to succeed. When this happens I find that the results are damaging." His solution, a typical one, is to abandon the term "teaching." He argues that since the "outcomes of teaching are either unimportant or hurtful," we should stop trying to teach; "I am only interested in being a learner."[3]

I have suggested an alternative understanding of "to teach." The position that I advocate is: Find out what *is* teaching in a particular situation and then direct one's attention to redesigning these forces. What is the difference between these two positions? The abandonment of the term "teaching" leaves us with "learning" alone, usually meaning the reduction of educational discussions to psychological categories. In contrast, insisting on the relation of teach-learn presses us to attend to the relation of organism and environment, and to the political, economic, and institutional forces that influence the structure of teach-learn.

In Eastern religious literature the paradox is sometimes pushed too much in the opposite direction; learning collapses into teaching. Psychological theories of learning would be a helpful restraint to placing all the attention on the teaching end. Similar to what was said of learning, if the issue is only looked at from the teaching side, the political, economic, and institutional contexts tend to fade.

In this traditional literature, the individual human teacher is both exalted and humbled without enough attention being paid to other forms of teaching. The guru's words may be self-deprecating, but the format of teaching is nonetheless a (male) guru giving out words. In the next chapter, I have some positive things to say about this kind of teaching, but it desperately needs a context in which women and men teach, and the design is both verbal and nonverbal.

The paradox in the guru/disciple relation is that the learner is encouraged to trust, to identify with, to practically become the teacher. For his part, the teacher is supposed to want nothing from the student — not even that he or she learn. When Trunga Rinpoche is asked how a person can have the ultimate experience of "no-self," he responds, "It could only come about through admiration for one's teacher. You have to become one with the teacher and mix your mind with the teacher's mind."[4] The outsider can see here a situation ripe for exploitation. What if the teacher is power-hungry or sexually disturbed? The answer to that query is: He is not a *real* teacher. True enough, which raises a further question of how the real teachers are discovered and "licensed" to teach.

In Western educational systems, we generally have a series of bureaucratic controls to weed out the bad prospects for (school)teacher. We do not expend as much effort in trying to find the best teachers, those who might find it difficult to work within the limits of our educational designs. Traditional religions of the East relied on an apprentice system and on the test of time to identify true teachers. No one has a statistical study concerning the success of such a system. From reading and personal experience, I would say that the most striking quality of these "real" teachers is an ironic sense of humor. The guru has disciples solemnly trying to mix their minds with the teacher, but the guru has a playful twinkle in his eye. Imitate me, if you must, but I am not really the teacher at all.

With this description, we come around again to Socrates, who surely believed in teaching but did not think he possessed the wisdom to be a teacher. That disclaimer may raise suspicions. When famous, successful, and powerful people say that they really don't have much power, we suspect fraud. If they do not manifest some sense of ironic humor, we have reason to suspect that the delicate paradox of teacher/teaching is not being maintained.

Take, for example, the writings of Krishnamurti, a well-known guru of this century. He was relentless in his attacks on teachers. Teachers are not to be trusted; they are power-hungry and egotistical, seeking only to control their disciples. What Krishnamurti may have conveyed in person I do not know, but his books are long, humorless sermons that can only call attention to his opinions, while attacking dependency on all (other?) teachers.[5]

The best of educational reformers through the centuries did not reject teaching, even though they have been severe critics of teachers and the systems around these teachers. The test of educational reform is to offer a redesign of the process of teach-learn, in which the potential teacher finds a better way to work within the process. Such a redesign takes patience, skill, and cooperation with others. The last of these qualities may be the most difficult for many reformers. If he or she is trying to radically reform education, he or she has to teach other teachers how this new process works.

Design and Good Teachers

Take four examples of modern reformers who have struggled with teaching by design. The examples are from Russia, Italy, New Zealand, and Brazil: Leo Tolstoy, Maria Montessori, Sylvia Ashton-Warner, and Paulo Freire. Each of them expresses great ambivalence about "teachers" while being fascinated with teaching.

Leo Tolstoy is probably the most impatient of this group. Tolstoy did many things in life; writing *War and Peace* was no doubt more important than any theory of teaching he devised. However, he did get intensely interested in school reform for a short period of his life.[6] He founded his own experimental school and tried his hand at teaching children. He is still regularly quoted by reformers inclined to remove restrictions on the child's learning.

In the small body of educational writing that he left, Tolstoy says extremely radical things. For example, he writes, "There is only one criteria of pedagogy — freedom." More important, however, he attends with a novelist's eye to the details of adult-child interaction.[7] He writes with a sophistication that includes knowledge of several European languages but also with an appreciation of Russian peasant simplicity. Tolstoy was not so naive as to think that there is no design to what teachers should do with students. But he was truly shocked when he discovered that the children are sometimes the teachers. A passage from "Should We Teach Children or They Teach Us?" describing work with one child, captures the theme of Tolstoy's discovery:

> As soon as I gave him complete freedom and stopped teaching him, he wrote a poetical work which had no equal in Russian literature. And therefore it is my conviction that we must not teach writing and composition in particular, to children in general and to peasant children especially. All that we can do is to teach them how to set about composition.[8]

The last sentence is surprising, a seeming reversal of what precedes. As soon as Tolstoy "stopped teaching him," the child produced a work unequaled in Russian literature (perhaps some poetic license in that judgment). He goes on to generalize that "we must not teach writing and composition," artistic composition being the worst subject and peasant children the worst group to be violated with teaching. And yet, in the end, Tolstoy says we must teach: "Teach them how to set about composition." His distinction between "teach composition" and "teach how to set about composition" invites further reflection, which Tolstoy does not offer. We will have to engage the distinction later in asking how a teacher might design, or rather redesign, a student's composition.

A second famous educational reformer came from a period just after Tolstoy and is cited by many of the same people who cite him. Maria Montessori stayed with the work of changing education. Her reforms continue to exist in a large network of schools and, less successfully, in her educational writing. Like Tolstoy, Montessori appeals to a kind of peasant simplicity, especially among women. At the same time, there is need for exquisite design of the environment.[9]

Montessori developed a method, the control of which, after Montessori's death, has led to some strong infighting. Is this a true Montessori school with a real Montessori teacher? But why cannot anyone, having read Montessori's books, set up his or her own school on the same principles? The method, it is argued by Montessorians, cannot be conveyed through the written word. The master of the method must show teachers how to design the environment and work with the design. The success of Montessori schools in the United States might have surprised Montessori. She was skeptical of "teachers," by which she usually meant professional schoolteachers. She often contrasted the Italian peasant women who were receptive to her method and the professionally trained teachers in the United States who knew too much of the wrong thing:

> In America experiments never succeeded because they looked for the best teachers, and a good teacher meant one who has studied all the things that do not help the child, and was full of ideas which were opposed to the child's freedom. The imposition of the teacher on the child can only hinder him.[10]

Montessori writes with irony here; that is obvious enough but it still raises troubling questions. "The good teacher" or "the best teachers" are obviously not people opposed to the child's freedom. But if a good teacher is one who has "studied all the things that do not help the child," should a teacher simply stop studying? Should she be a bad teacher? In other words, does one abandon the terms "teacher" and "teaching" or study all the ways we might better describe the relation of teaching-learning?

The third example is a woman who is associated with Maria Montessori in educational writing but who had a different approach to classroom design and who wrote in a different style. Sylvia Ashton-Warner was a New Zealander who taught Maori children. One of her best-known books is a novel; the central character describes her successes and failures teaching in "the infant room." There is more emphasis on speech than in Montessori, who concentrates on physical design until the "explosion of literacy." Ashton-Warner's teacher keeps probing for the most emotionally charged words (which she discovers in her situation to be "ghost" and "kiss") that will lead to the sound of "erupting creativity."[11]

The meaning of "teacher" remains puzzling for the woman called teacher. The word does not take on the negative connotations it often has in the hands of other reformers. Ashton-Warner's teacher treasures the vocation but is constantly puzzled as to how one is to carry out the vocation. She looks for a "light enough touch" so that "the teacher is at last with the stream and not against it; the stream of children's inexorable creativeness."[12]

She constantly goes back to the world "locked inside." Like Tolstoy and Montessori, she wishes to avoid "plastering on." The ultimate trust is in the children's creativity. Nevertheless, the term that is never far from her lips is "design." She looks at the volcanic eruptions of her infant room and sees: "What wonderful movement and mood. What lovely behavior of silksack clouds! An organic design. A growing, loving, changing design. The normal and healthful design. Unsentimental and merciless and shockingly beautiful."[13]

Paulo Freire, a contemporary educator who worked mainly in Brazil, provides a grown-up's version of the three previous pictures. Most of Freire's work was in adult literacy. The basis of the work is similar to the other three theorists: trust in the simple, peasant-like qualities of the learners and unleash their creative possibilities through careful design of the environment. Like Ashton-Warner, Freire sought out the most powerful (political as well as emotional) words for the particular group. Like Montessori, he found an explosion of literacy once that power center had been located.

As do the previous three writers, Freire had a certain ambivalence about "teachers." In the adult-education document referred to in chapter 1, the author says of Freire's work, "This identification is to be brought about by a free dialogue between a coordinator (obviously the designation 'teacher' is inappropriate) and a group designed to unravel the social significance of key words germane to the learners' everyday lives."[14] The parenthetical reference to the inappropriateness of "teacher" is not at all obvious in Freire's writing. Instead, Freire speaks of the need to create a teacher-student and student-teacher.[15] Like Socrates or Tolstoy, Freire attacked one idea of teacher, but he was intent on the precise design of a teaching-learning situation. A term such as "coordinator" may sometimes be useful but it is not a substitute for the teacher who designs.

Freire has been an inspiring genius of educational revolution. Probably his best-known distinction is between "banking" and "dialogue" forms of education.[16] The contrast expresses a stark choice in repressive situations. Unfortunately, the contrast is easily turned into a cliché in cultures where talk is "free" and dialogue about "problem solving" is comfortably acceptable. "Dialogue" is one of the ultimate terms for a fully human life and for the best education. But it needs plenty of support in physical forms of teaching (human and nonhuman) and several forms of discourse that the term "dialogue" does not capture.

Dialogue can suggest an equality that is usually lacking in the teaching situation. The teacher (who is also a student) is not the same as the student (who is also a teacher) and cannot pretend to be. Equality of power may be what teaching leads toward but it is not where teaching starts. The one who is playing teacher has the responsibility for designing the environment to make dialogue more possible. Freire knows the paradox: the learner identifying with the teacher's learning; the teacher acting to break the link of dependence on the teacher.

The four great reformers cited here had a sense of the gap between the teacher's intention and the student's learning. The recognition that the teacher can neither take credit for success nor be burdened with guilt by failure can have opposite effects. Either the teacher is liberated to do the best that he or she knows, without having to worry about the results. Or else the teacher becomes depressed, lazy, and in search of a new job. What is the point of working hard if there is no connection between my movements and the learning that results? There is no simple answer to this question, which has to be pondered by all teachers, not just schoolteachers.

A Governing Metaphor for Teaching

The teacher cannot fill the gap between his or her intent to teach and the learning that occurs in the student. In the most physical kinds of teaching, the gap may seem indiscernible. Teacher and learner succeed together or fail together in riding a bike, swimming, tying a knot, or catching a ball. The teacher "lays on hands" and the teaching seems to flow from body to body.

Although I have insisted that these cases of teach-learn are fruitful for understanding all teaching, I think that the wrong lesson is often drawn from them. The act of physically shaping the material can be taken too literally. True, words can be shaped just as bodies are shaped. But as the teacher's words take on more importance in teaching, one has to be careful of what one attempts to shape with the words. The mind of the student cannot be shaped in the way that the child's hand can be physically shaped in teaching him or her to catch a ball.

The term "to shape" can be helpful to discussions of teaching. From

Comenius and Locke down to B. F. Skinner, this metaphor of shaping has had a privileged position. The most common images embodying "to shape" have been the shaping of water, wax, or slate. When crudely used, the image implies that the mind of the child is completely pliable material on which knowledge can be stamped or written. Skinner often uses "shape up," which conveys the most direct behavioral control of the student. Pigeons and people are shaped up to behave.[17]

Most writers on education have allowed some give-and-take with the image of shape. For example, in George Dennison's Lives of Children, a book celebrating the freedom of the child, the author writes, "The work of the teacher is like that of the artist; it is the shaping of something that is 'given.'" That statement could be taken as Skinnerian except that Dennison adds, "And no serious artist would say in advance that he knows what will be given."[18] The implication here is that the lives of the children may have some similarity to wax or water, but human life is a much more complicated material to work in. The lives of even very young children already have a complex design woven into their histories and their makeup. All attempts to shape human life are reshapings of past achievements.

When the learner willingly presents his or her body for reshaping, no moral dilemma is evident. For example, a 40-year-old man goes into a health center and says, "I want to shape up by losing twenty pounds and getting rid of this flab around the middle." The shaping up is a matter of learning some exercise techniques, discipline, and dietary helps. The man is shown how to live according to better standards of health, and after a while he can go on as he has been taught; he is now the teacher of himself.

When a 14-year-old boy presents himself in a classroom, he is *not* saying: my mind lacks certain items or qualities; shape up my mind. Two very important differences from the man in the gym have to be noted. First, the child's freedom is always in question. James Herndon said that the only thing you can be sure of when you see a child in a classroom is that he or she prefers that to jail. The statement exaggerates somewhat; most of the time one can presume a little more. If New York City has 100,000 truants each day and two truant officers, the child is not likely to be worried about going to jail for truancy; the 20,000 spaces in the city jails have prior reservations.

Coming to school for most children does express some degree of interest in learning something. Whether the child really wishes to learn anything being taught in the classrooms is another question. Even without compulsory school-attendance laws, the child is under considerable pressure to be at school (family, friends, the lack of a decent job, playing football).

Adults also experience social pressures on their freedom, but usually the person attending an adult-education class feels a greater sense of choice than do millions of young people in school. Even in the universities of the United States this is the case. Fifty years ago, the one in ten persons who attended college usually experienced it as a privilege rather than a restraint of liberty. But the young person in college today cannot be assumed to be there by a completely free exercise of choice.

A second and more important difference between youngsters in school and the man in the gym is that classroom teaching is directed to the mind. One cannot easily take the image of shaping up the stomach muscles and transfer it to shaping up a mind. Even if a person were to say that he or she wished to have the mind shaped, the image would still be of doubtful validity. Does anyone know how to shape another's mind? Some people fear that such a process is possible and that, for example, advertisers are using devious techniques to shape peoples' minds. Further out in that direction are "religious cults" that are thought to be able to stamp beliefs on the mind.

Most acts of intended teaching exist somewhere between the man saying, "Tone the muscle," and the teenage captive of a cult saying, "Take my mind." That is, human teaching involves an embodied mind, a self-conscious organism. As a result, the shaping up of behavior involves mental awareness, response, and a willingness to go with the teaching. If the man really wants to change the shape of his midsection, he will have to change his mental attitude. Conversely, the most highly rational learning involves external bodily movement. Drill, training, and discipline will be either preconditions or integral elements of intellectual accomplishments.

The shaping, therefore, is usually directed to the whole organism. For a human learner, the shaping is of the human organism in relation to its environment. This relation already has a shape so that one can only proceed by reshaping what is given. The reshaping is within the strict limits of the already shaped material at hand. A dance teacher has to work with a particular body in a particular setting. The foot of the ballet dancer, the shoe she is wearing, and the surface on which she is dancing constitute a complex relation. With teaching and constant practice, the relation can be changed, though the change can only be within strict limits.

The title of this chapter goes a step beyond the image of shaping. With the term "design," it attempts to capture both the express intent of the human teacher and the material limits of what can be taught. Design, I wish to suggest, is a more precise image than shape. Impersonal factors in the environment shape the landscape and the living organism, including the human body. A hard rain or a blistering sun may reshape the landscape; factors such as diet, cramped conditions, stress, or accident may change the human shape.

All of these factors shape the conditions of teaching. But change by design implies a concerted attempt of a human teacher with a human learner to work with given shapes. The dance teacher does have to work with the foot, the shoe, and the floor; but there is also the choreography of the dance. The violin teacher has to work with arm, chin, fingers, and musical instrument; but the design of the music incorporates and goes beyond these elements.

The metaphor of design and redesign is therefore more helpful for my purposes than is the metaphor of shaping. Whereas shaping has usually suggested an *object* that is worked upon, design and redesign have to do with an *activity*. The potential learner is doing something; to teach is to change what is being done.

The beginning point for teaching by design is a human in action. The action may be poorly designed for the purpose it has or it may be adequate. But practically always, an activity can be done better. The teacher by design studies the present design and proposes a redesign. Teachers are sometimes attacked with the cynical statement that "those who can, do; those who can't, teach." There is a profound truth hidden under the cynicism: A good teacher need not be able to practice the design; what he or she needs to do is understand a redesign.

For example, in baseball the best hitters are seldom good hitting instructors. A player, who is among the best hitters in the world, inevitably has a slump. The coach, who never hit well but has studied the design of the batter in batting, says, "You are turning your left shoulder a split second too early." The batter tries the new stance and finds out whether it feels right. People who are very good at what they do are usually not averse to learning how to do it better.

Notice the sequence here; it is not teacher gives, student receives. The pattern is student acts, teacher studies design, teacher proposes redesign, student acts differently. This sequence can be repeated indefinitely. The proposed redesign may not fit this student in this place at this time. The student may be skeptical — probably should be skeptical — that the redesign will work. However, if it has a reasonable chance to succeed, the only way to proceed is to try it out.

All teaching-learning is by doing. What exactly is done varies according to the kind of learning at issue. The doing does not always involve a lot of bodily movement, but human action on the part of the learner is the condition of the learning. I quoted Aristotle in the first chapter that there is only one activity in teaching and it is in the learner. Across the whole range of human learning, Aristotle sees a continuity of principle: "Men become builders by building and lyre players by playing the lyre; so too we become just by doing just acts, and brave by doing brave acts."[19] How this principle applies to forms of teaching in which speech predominates will be discussed in the chapters that follow. The intimation of a solution lies here in instances where speech still functions as choreographing the body.

We learn to build by building, starting with the blocks in the infant crib. Later, the child may construct a house from pieces of plaster bought in a store or from branches of a tree for a secret tree house. There is design to such activities; it may be conveyed by instructions for store-bought houses or by a friend's advice on building tree houses. If the toy or machine comes with printed "instructions," the teaching is very limited. If a living teacher provides "instruction," then the teaching still has a precise aim but there is opportunity for more redesign.

The term "instruction" has a central place in the history of teaching. Its directedness worries those who are concerned for the freedom of the learner. However, simply sliding away from clarity, precision, and directedness is not the way to liberation. Those who wish to learn need instruction; if the instruction is precisely directed at the elements of the skill involved, no limitation of freedom is implied. A vague choreography is not the way to teach dance; a musical score that does not indicate each part's notes is not the way to teach music.

As someone masters a skill, he or she will find ways to go beyond the instruction or to work variations within the instruction. Instruction, nevertheless, remains a highly directive act; not "What would you like to do here?" but "Turn at this spot," or "That's an F sharp." Teaching is not equivalent to instruction. As described in chapter 2, many cases of "show how" by human and nonhuman teachers are wordless. Later, we will discuss uses of speech in teaching that are not bodily instruction; but even in these cases there is instruction of another kind.

The one who commands, "Do it now," has to be trusted. This relation of trust is a precondition of the act of teaching rather than an element of the teaching act itself. At the moment of instruction, there is often no time to think, Do I trust this person? Within a context of trust, the learner can concentrate on following the instructions in careful detail.[20] The teacher's concentration is on speaking clearly and simply, with the instruction directed to that precise point at which the design of the situation becomes a redesign.

I asserted in chapter 2 that learning is the proof that teaching has occurred. The teaching-learning continuum does not require speech. However, human learning nearly always includes instructive moments; bodily instruction is where human learners are closest to nonhuman learners ("sit...now bark...good dog"). Instruction within a rich human context is not demeaning; the choreographed instruction for the body will lead into other uses of speech. With young children, crisp, clear instruction is a necessity. Even though the commands to a two-year-old sound similar to animal training ("sit...watch out ...good boy"), they have their meaning within a context of human dialogue.

Take the case of a child learning to walk. Who teaches the child to do that? A plausible starting answer is that the entire human race does so. Walking on two legs is an extraordinary act; as every nonhuman animal knows, it is not quite natural, and the human's lower back often agrees with the other animals. A newborn child comes to this strange activity because other humans have designed the environment that way. If you wish to run with the humans you have to learn to walk.

Most parents have a vivid memory of the exact moment when the infant's ontogeny recapitulated thousands of years of human phylogeny, that is, the child took a first step. A physically safe atmosphere was guaranteed by a trusted parent and perhaps an encouraging entourage. The infant, who had been crawling and who has now stood with the aid of furniture, lets go. The only adult instruction may be, "Come to Mommy." Along with the design of outstretched arms, the words can be a bridge between the fear of falling and the accomplishment of walking.[21] After the child has fallen a few times, a teacher may be able to give it a little more physical/oral instruction. Before there can be that redesign, the child has to get up and walk according to the design it responds to, a design that evolution and millions of human choices have prepared for today's child.

The appropriate design of this chapter is to finish with some extended examples. I will offer three of my own, but I first call attention to one of the best descriptions of teaching by design, found in an essay entitled, "Skiing as a Model of Instruction."[22] The authors break down the complex act of skiing into "microworlds," by which they mean a task that can be performed successfully as a simple version of the whole activity. They identify three elements of a microworld that can be manipulated by the teacher: equipment, physical setting, and task specification.

The teaching of skiing has dramatically improved in recent decades as these elements have been recognized and manipulated. For example, short skis and safety bindings give the novice skier a better chance of succeeding. The instructor has to choose snow conditions that are appropriate for each stage of learning. A downhill slope that feeds into an uphill path helps the beginner to learn how to stop. And the skiing coach has to be precise in specifying the action. The authors distinguish between "executable" commands and just "observable" commands. The teacher has to know exactly what to command as action. It is useless to tell beginners, "Shift your weight," if they do not yet know where their weight is.

I think that the authors' description of teaching a person to ski is an invaluable piece of writing. And they are interested in generalizing from the example to other examples of teaching. They develop a theory of "increasingly complex microworlds" in which the learner faces difficult challenges but also experiences success. In my examples that follow I start with experiences that are more universal and less complex than skiing. Despite the increased popularity of skiing, it will probably never be encountered by most people. And I am not interested in developing a technical vocabulary in these examples, but instead keeping the description as close as possible to ordinary speech.

These descriptions have to be somewhat extended to convey the flavor of the details. The design exists only with detail. Each example has its own unique constellation of detail and requires a separate description. But as a line of T. S. Eliot has it, "Each case is unique; and similar to the others." Each act of teaching requires attention to all the details of the situation. It is in the particularity of human situations that we best glimpse a universal human condition.

The description of teaching by design should include crucial details but not all details. When we watch a great athlete, musician, carpenter, or painter at work, and we ask, "How do you do that?" we are asking for instructional detail. The accomplished person who says, "I don't know, I have never thought about explaining it," is of little help as a teacher. In contrast, what Donald Schön calls a "reflective practitioner" is able to pick out some crucial steps. We get impatient with the explanation because we know that there is much more. However, Schön warns us that we would not be able to absorb an exhaustive explanation of the process. So perhaps the teacher is providing more than we think he or she is doing in a sketched-out design.[23]

The three examples I have chosen are teaching a person to swim, to cook, and to use a computer. Each of these examples involves bodily movement in a context of human response. The instructive element is clear in each case, the physical movement becoming a lesser element in the learning as we go from example 1 to example 3.

To highlight the instructional element, I will describe teaching an adult. Children can be and are taught these three things. In the case of the child, the teaching-learning may be so smooth and effortless that the elements of teach-learn are difficult to pick out. With adults, there is likely to have developed an obstacle to the learning. A design is already fixed; the teacher's design to teach requires a careful redesign.

I cited Aristotle as saying that the way to learn walking, talking, or virtue is to grow up in a walking, talking, or virtuous community. We are not amazed that children who grow up in a Greek-speaking community speak Greek; children who grow up in a Russian community learn to speak Russian. Similarly, the way to swim is to grow up in a swimming community; the way to cook is to grow up in a cooking community; the way to learn computing is to grow up in a computing community.

In the first two cases, to swim and to cook, that is just the way most people learn. However, a sizable number of adults have not learned these skills in that way. They are good cases for examining "to teach:" to show someone how to do something. The third case is even more clearly designed for case study, namely, a generation of grown-ups for whom computers did not exist when they were children, but who now live in a computerized world.

1. *Teaching someone to swim.* Swimming is a natural movement, at least as natural as walking. An infant who is introduced to a body of

water early in life will take to it like a fish. The water does most of the teaching, the arms and legs responding to the water's design. The child does need a little instruction on breathing because a child, in fact, is not a fish. Human beings with the proper equipment can outdo fish at some of their own games. The humans' nature is art; they construct such things as motorboats. However, some humans who can move across the water faster than fish can have never learned to swim.

Millions of people grow up to adulthood without learning to swim. Given the near omnipresence of water, it seems likely that most of these people have a block to swimming. The fear of water is a cause of their not swimming while, in turn, the absence of the skill results in still more fear. For most adult nonswimmers, there is a clear design in the relation of their bodies to ocean, lake, or pool. When circumstances bring them into contact, the design is a lot of thrashing about without efficiency or satisfaction. Watching an experienced swimmer teaches nothing, except frustration.

How does a teacher teach an adult nonswimmer to swim? The first step is to reduce (not likely eliminate) the feeling of threat by some careful choices: the location of the water, the absence of spectators, the shallow depth of the water, the relaxed attitude of the teacher. The learning is a fairly simple set of physical exercises, most of which can be found in a book. The learner will never get that far without experiencing some beginning success and getting some feel for the whole process. That is what an effective teacher on the scene has to make possible and convey.

The nonswimming adult is puzzled at the phenomenon of floating. Such an individual, fearful of sinking, will lift his or her head to be sure of not sinking, which is a sure prescription for sinking. The teacher has to say, "Tilt your head back" and "Relax." Often when we tell someone to relax, it has the opposite effect; the person tenses up in an effort to relax. The nonswimming adult has never once relaxed in the water. One command to do so will not work, though the presence of a trusted teacher and the accustoming of oneself to an all-water environment can over time bring the beginning of relaxation. When that point is reached, then floating on one's back or moving under water produces a moment of victory. A voice will come up out of the center of one's being and say: the water is not the enemy. From that point, instead of fighting the water, one starts to learn from the water and how it interacts with the body.[24]

After running the learner through a sequence of drills, the teacher's job becomes one of watching the design and suggesting redesign. The action is all in the learner; the learning is all in the practice. Small things will be discovered in the doing; they may be small, but relevant to this learner they can be crucial. Two people do not have the same arm movement, kick, or breathing. A good teacher spots some of these particularities and proposes adjustments. The learner is the final judge of whether any redesign is effective.

2. *Teaching someone to cook.* The act of cooking is perhaps as universal as the act of swimming. Anyone growing up to adulthood, one might expect, would learn to cook reasonably well. One learns to cook by growing up in a cooking community; that seems to apply to just about everyone. Cooking does move us a step beyond our animal capacity to swim. Cooking is a specifically human art that is unknown among other animals.

If a person gets to adulthood without learning even the rudiments of cooking, some kind of block must have developed early in life. Like the nonswimmer shying from water, the noncook shies from the kitchen as a place of fear and intimidation. In this case, the block to learning has been reinforced by a cultural assumption. At least until recently, much of the culture conveyed the impression to little boys that they need not cook because someone will cook for them. The culture has shifted rapidly on the point. The present generation of adult men may be an unusual case study in learning to cook. Men who were told a few decades ago that women do the cooking for men now find that this principle is under attack and, in many situations, does not hold. Tens of millions of men are ill-nourished because they do not cook, and eventually Roy Rogers and Wendy's blur into a boring chore.

As with the nonswimmer, much of the attention has to be directed to overcoming the initial block to cooking. Once the fear is dispelled, then learning to cook is largely a matter of following a few simple directions. If you can read, you can cook. But a lot of people cannot in fact read a cookbook because they have not been initiated into that language. For that initiation, one usually needs a trusted friend or family member who shows the learner exactly what to do, and temporarily acts as translator of the cookbook.

I have said that the attempt to teach by design always leads to a redesign of an existing relation between human organism and environment. Similar to the nonswimmer, the noncook may try to avoid the scene of the mysterious power, but he or she still has some kind of thrashing-about relation to cooking. The person may not recognize any existing relation; however, the usual strength to build on is the ability to recognize a well-cooked meal. The person who can do that much is already on the way. In addition, nearly everyone has experiences, at least from childhood, of licking a spoon, watching someone prepare ingredients, or having to scrub a pan.

The person intimidated by the thought of cooking needs to experience some immediate success, like the nonswimmer learning to float. Few people have the talent and the staying power to become great cooks; but everyone has the ability and should get the help to treat food with the appreciative preparation it deserves. For the learner of cooking, someone has to say, "Do this, do this, do this," and the result is a success.

The trick here, as usual, is to contemplate the whole pattern of potential cook, uncooked food, and particular situation. Reducing the threat level is crucial, perhaps by the barring of spectators; that prepares the way for direct commands. Artists of the kitchen, like other artists, are sometimes poor teachers because they cannot state the design in sufficient detail — or are impatient when asked to articulate it. The very good cook may inspire a desire to learn but it is often an inexpert cook who has the feel of what it is like to be bewildered by recipe language and confused by the stove.

The expert cook is liable to end an instruction by saying, "Add a small amount of tomato paste, a dash of thyme and some parboiled noodles. Make sure the oven is hot. Bake it until it looks done." The not-so-expert cook, who understands teaching, might end the same instruction, "Add a tablespoon (the big one) of tomato paste (the small can, not the sauce) and add a half teaspoon (the little one) of thyme (the small box on the spice shelf); add a cup of noodles that you have put in boiling water for five minutes; bake the mixture (that is, put it in the oven) with the temperature dial turned to 350 degrees; take it out after 45 minutes."

The trust between teacher and student will indicate whether these points, and others even more basic, would seem either helpful or condescending. In any case, every question ought to be askable by the learner without feeling stupid. A cardinal rule of teaching-learning is that no question asked in good faith is a stupid question. Once a basic confidence has been gained, the learner does much of the teaching, filling in details of the design, experimenting, and occasionally making mistakes. Tips from friends, the cookbook, and perhaps a television show become one's continuing teachers.

3. *Teaching someone to use a computer.* The human use of computers carries us far beyond the other animals. The very idea of the computer is a work of human genius, and the construction of computers and their gradual miniaturization has been a marvel to behold. Computers in the home have rapidly spread by the tens of millions. They are not yet as omnipresent as the telephone and television but they are on their way to becoming standard home equipment.

The principle, once again, is that we learn by growing up in a community where the quality or skill is taught by its practice. The way to learn computers is to grow up in a computing community. For many children, this condition has already become or is fast becoming a reality. With computers, however, there is human instruction that goes beyond that of swimming or cooking. I am interested in the start of that instruction. For many children the beginning is the "natural" step of playing around with pieces of technology. With just a little coaching, the child can get inside the game and continue to learn from books, friends, and simple trial and error.

The case is very different for a present generation of adults. Only a few decades ago, "computer" and "word processing" were abstract, technical terms that seemed to have nothing to do with personal life. Then, almost overnight, they inundated the world, much to the terror of many 40- and 50-year-olds. The longer the adults wait to confront the machine, the more intimidating it appears. The situation becomes embarrassing when one does not have the language to ask an intelligent question. If one is a university professor, it is humbling to be upstaged by the 17-year-olds in the computer stores or one's 8-year-old daughter. Almost half of the population in the United States has yet to touch a computer.

Is it like understanding cookbooks: if you can read, you can word-process? Perhaps, although reading in this case is a more complicated affair. I find it difficult to imagine that anyone has ever learned to use a computer by reading the 500–page manual (along with the 1000–page supplement) that accompanies the software. These books are a gold mine (or exuberant playground) for those who already know how to use the machine. If one sits down and begins from page 1 on how to do this activity, depression is likely to follow. The manuals do contain some simple and effective drills that have to be practiced. However, one first needs entrance.

The steps parallel the other two cases, starting with a trusted friend who is often not a computer expert, but someone who knows how to do it and knows how to break the learning into manageable parts. The environment has to be one that reduces the threat level; no spectators, please. Every question has to be askable, even the most naive. The teacher has to show how, by providing a few crisp, clear commands of what to do first, second, third. How computers work is material for another time, a distraction for the person who wants to learn to use the machine.

The beginner wants to know what to do after putting in the plug. The teacher has to say, "Push this button, hold down this while pressing that, and this is exactly what will appear on the screen." As with swimming and cooking, some experience of immediate success is indispensable. Untold hours of confusion and frustration may follow the first success as one perfects the learning. The teacher has to see that the design is grasped and that the learner can become the teacher. I think some of the best teachers in the country are the computer people at the end of the toll-free help lines who patiently guide the caller through each step of his or her problem.

In summary, these three extended examples, as well as other examples cited earlier in this chapter, exhibit the same structure. In each case, a human being is acting in a physical environment. To teach that person requires changing the existing design that relates the person's activity and the environment. Much of the effort of both teacher and learner concerns physical behavior that humans share with nonhuman animals. The language in these examples is instruction in physical movement; the words are directly correlated to those movements.

Human beings, however, have learned to use language in ways that increase their ability to learn. Words can be abstracted from immediate relation to the body. The following three chapters describe other forms of speech used in teaching. But the underlying metaphor of design should not be forgotten: to teach is to show someone how to do something, how to choreograph a human body's movement. No matter how abstruse and theoretical teaching becomes, it never severs its roots from the metaphor of design.

Part Two

Chapter 4

Teaching with the End in View

THE NEXT THREE CHAPTERS comprise part 2 of this book. These chapters concern the language of teaching when the verbal part of teaching goes beyond the choreographing of bodily movement. In this case, human language can be examined as a movement in its own right. Each of these three chapters deals with what I call a "family" of languages used in teaching.[1] The teacher is still concerned with choreographing movement, but speech is now used with more self-awareness that speech is at least part of what is being designed.

The moral problem of teaching becomes evident at this juncture, where speech emerges from bodiliness and takes on a life of its own. When a child says, "Teach me to swim," the presenting of the body is evidence for receptiveness to the skill. But when a would-be teacher walks into a room and sees a group of people sitting there, the situation does not provide clear evidence of what, if anything, they are prepared to learn.

Before anyone opens his or her mouth to teach with words, the question has to be asked: Why are these people sitting here? Perhaps in some settings the answer may seem obvious. If they are sitting in a movie theater, they wish to see a film; if at a press conference, they expect a government briefing. The question nonetheless needs to be asked on every occasion. One of the main reasons for a moral problem to exist with teaching is that an inappropriate form of speech is used for the occasion. The teacher must ask, What license do I have from these people? What form of speech is therefore appropriate and justified in this setting?

In response to those questions, chapters 4 and 5 form a contrasting pair. (Chapter 6 will introduce further considerations.) The contrast between the family of languages in this chapter and the family in chapter 5 is based upon a difference in relation to *end*, that is, whether an end is in view. In the discussion up to this point, I have concentrated on situations where intention and its accompanying speech are embedded in bodily movement. As speech can take on a life of its own distinct from the body, so the individual can conceive of ends that move beyond immediate physical behavior to the future, to the spiritual, to the universal. The emergence of such ends, and the language accompanying them, is the great glory of the human race, along with the source of its terrible delusions and violent outbursts.

This chapter's title refers to the language of teaching when the end is in view. John Dewey uses the phrase "end-in-view" as a human guide for action, an end that can be seen and talked about.[2] The human mind can conceive of a good that it wishes to reach (for example, an increase in salary or improved health) and a teacher can have the task of showing how to get from here to there. A danger ever present is that the particular end in view can be misconceived as the ultimate good in life. This danger is offset by the languages in chapter 5 — teaching when the end is *not* in view. I do not wish to choose between these two sets of languages, but rather to hold them together in a healthy tension. If one set acts as corrective to the other, both can be effective — and moral — acts of teaching. Radically split apart, each set is the manifesting of a human weakness that corrupts teaching.

Since the two sets of languages are so wedded, a case could be made either for the present order of the chapters or the reverse order. Depending on circumstances — for example, the age of the learner — one set may seem to take precedence over the other. In actual practice, over a long period of time, each one succeeds the other.

The languages of chapter 5 — removing obstacles to achieving an end — could be argued to have an ontological priority. It would seem that a person first has to remove obstacles (for example, fear or rage) before proceeding toward the end that is seen and desired. In fact, however, people usually discover the obstacles only through their efforts to reach an end in view. I start with the first set both to describe its powerful possibilities and also to note its limitations and the need for other languages. From that context, the set of languages described in chapter 5 has a better chance of being recognized as teaching at all.

My organizing principle largely determines how I name individual cases within both sets. Given that there are hundreds of names and dozens of classification systems, any choice of languages is bound to be somewhat arbitrary. The absence of the name of a particular language does not necessarily mean that it is unimportant; it may simply fall within a different way of classifying language and therefore cut across the names I have chosen. For example, is poetic language a language of teaching? If poetic is the alternative to prosaic, then I would hope for a poetic quality to every example that follows. If, however, the reference is to distinct poems or poetry, then there are several places in the overall description where poetry (or a novel, short story, or play), can be an example, and I will indicate some of those spots.

Along a different line, someone might note the absence of "political speech." If the alternative is apolitical speech, then all of the languages in this chapter are political. However, if what is meant are the speeches of politicians or the discussions of political science, then these forms could be included in several places. Something similar could be said about aesthetic speech, ethical speech, or religious speech; they are *too* important to be embodied in just one of the forms I describe.

A Community Activity

The first family of languages, described in this chapter, arises from a community existence. Every community has a set of beliefs. The family of languages described here is intended to persuade people to act on the basis of those beliefs. The element of command or directive makes this set of languages resemble the choreography of the body. The difference is that the commanding is directed toward the beliefs of the community, rather than toward the body. "We say we believe this [e.g., the good of children]; it follows that we should do that [provide child care]." This family of languages is persuasive of the community. The ancient meaning of "rhetorical" captured the intent of this language. Wayne Booth, describing this meaning of "rhetoric," says it "was practiced when the first mother or father went beyond simple caressing or physical restraint and managed to convey, in sound or picture or sign language, 'No, because . . .' with a reason not present to the senses at the moment."[3]

The teacher in this situation steps forward before the community or, better, steps into the center of the community. The person can be elected, appointed, ordained, chosen by lot, licensed by some trusted group, or be biologically responsible. But this temporary assignment of "teacher" should not mean that some people are teachers and some are not. A group of people who claim to be a community have to consider, as an important criterion of community, Is every member of the group in some way and at some time a teacher to all the rest? If only a small number of people are recognized as teaching, then the likelihood of a mutuality of persons — the hallmark of community — is greatly diminished.

Most groups, whether social, political, religious, or familial, tend to segregate the word "teacher" for a few. It then becomes the task of these few to keep turning the term "to teach" back to the whole community. If other persuasion is to be effective, persuasion as to who are the teachers cannot be overlooked. To teach is to show people how to live; living as a human being includes the act of teaching. "We know a man for a poet by the fact he makes us poets." We know a person for a teacher by the fact he or she makes us teachers.

A teacher in and for the community taps into the memory of the community. The beliefs that are consciously held are a result of a long process of community formation. The process includes forgetting as well as remembering; no set of beliefs can capture the community's most valuable experiences. A teacher with the end in view is someone who can retrieve what underlies community belief, thereby placing the beliefs in a new configuration. Older people in the community have a special place in this kind of teaching; they are linked by personal memory to the vital force that founds the community and provides continuing cohesion. In one sense, nothing new is added in the teaching, no information previously unknown. In another sense, everything is made new as the past is brought to consciousness in the present and everything is seen through the prism of well-articulated speech.

Embodied in the community's existence is the conviction that the end is known, the good to be attained by this group is evident. The teacher does not have the job of discovering the end or proving any scientific hypothesis about it. The teacher's task is to link the past with this end in the future so that the energies of the present are unleashed. This kind of persuasive teacher is in need of *style*, a distinct way of assembling words and delivering them.

The great teacher knows how to touch just those spots of memory so that people are moved to action. It is obvious, of course, that attention to style can be abused. Many political and religious leaders have manipulated masses of people on the basis of style without substance. But that problem arises when community has broken down and left the "mass" of individuals desperate for a leader. In a genuine community, a teacher cannot rely on a style that would be out of touch with memory, faithfulness, hopes, and conviction. The individual teacher realizes that he or she contributes only a small part in that the words arise from the community and are quickly submerged again. The teacher nonetheless seizes the moment to shape the words for their greatest effect.

The teacher tries to become one with the words that are spoken. There is little space for "critical thinking" that would raise doubts about the truthfulness of the teaching. There will be other occasions for self-critical reflection, but this first family of languages is concerned with speech in relation to bodiliness. The speech is interesting, practical, and effective before the reflexive question of truth is raised. Again one can easily see the vulnerability of this teaching to manipulators of truth and falsehood.

For the individual, the community's beliefs are prejudgments; the more common term is "prejudices." Community teaching precedes the individual, encompasses the individual. A person does not simply begin searching for truth at the "age of reason." Instead, a child has already absorbed a world of beliefs. He or she is a prejudiced person at the dawn of conscious reflection: the way his or her family acts is the right way.

The language of the eighteenth century, which we still speak, assumes that prejudices are bad and should be replaced by rational thinking. Education's aim, according to eighteenth-century writers, is to free the child from the prejudices of the father.[4] But if community is to be allowed a place, then the beliefs of the community cannot be assumed to be negative. Some of what is provided to the child may turn out to have some truth. Every prejudice should be open to questioning.

Hans-Georg Gadamer distinguishes between blind prejudice and justified prejudice. We cannot get rid of blind prejudice until we accept the fact of prejudices and begin testing each of them for truth as well as falsehood. "The fundamental prejudice of the Enlightenment," writes Gadamer, "was the prejudice against prejudice."[5] The blind prejudice that each individual should shed whatever beliefs he or she has and invent the world within his or her own private reasoning took deep root in our modern culture.

Because of this prejudice against prejudice, some comments have to be included here concerning the possible charge that all of the languages in this chapter are "indoctrination." One route of defense would be to distinguish two meanings of "indoctrination." What Gadamer does with "prejudice" could be tried with "indoctrination." Leszek

Kolakowski is one contemporary thinker who endorses indoctrination as educationally defensible. He even writes that indoctrination "is included in the acquisition of language itself.... Hence, education without indoctrination is noneducation."[6]

I do not think Kolakowski faces up to the totally negative connotation that the term "indoctrination" has. While there is some foothold for resistance with "prejudice" (and its close relative, "discrimination"), neither history nor contemporary usage offers a realistic basis for what Kolakowski tries to do. I think one has to start with a premise opposite to his, namely, education with indoctrination is noneducation. I would therefore say that the family of languages that presupposes a community and an end in view is not in itself indoctrinative.

Successful indoctrination results in a person so attached to one version of reality that multiple perspectives, ambiguity in language, and the ability to stand at a distance from one's own beliefs have been eliminated. I cannot deny that a use of the first family of languages could lead to indoctrination. The only sure prevention is an effective presence of the other two families. The fact that A can lead to Z does not mean that A is a form of Z.

What the parents and community show to a child is a way of life to which the child responds in his or her own way. Since the community's way of life is bounded by definite beliefs, the child's unique response is within definite limits. Some day those limits must be confronted and in one way or another transcended. But first a world with limits has to be absorbed.

Language, which exists in particular and limited form, is a gift that the child appropriates. Being able to speak a language makes possible a human encounter with all reality. Each particular form has its own restrictions and disadvantages. For example, if you wish to speak French in life, you would best be born in France. If you wish to speak English as a second language, it helps to be born in Sweden rather than in Finland. That is just the luck of the draw in every childhood; Finns have their own advantages. Learning any language does not cut off the possibility of multiple perspectives and self-critical distance.

The testing of the community's prejudices takes place over a long period of time and is finally measured by how the small community contributes to the human community. One of the beliefs of the community may seem to be irrational, but a single belief may derive its intelligibility from its connection to a whole complex of beliefs that has its own human logic. The teacher has to comprehend the connection among the community's beliefs and not merely the beliefs.

The child, for its part, also grasps, in however primitive a fashion, the pattern or structure of belief. For a child, there has to be some kind of world order that provides the security of knowing that someone understands all these confusing pieces and that a benevolent force rules all. The child will fight fiercely for the truth of some propositions because their denial would unravel the fabric of the established world.

The related problems of blind prejudice and indoctrination arise when the mind that was proper to a young child resides in an older child or an adult. In this case, the truth is still dependent on the opinion of a powerful adult; the growing person has not really acquired any beliefs as his or her own. The beliefs have been delivered and accepted. Unless something else happens to the beliefs, they will gradually become more rigid. Paradoxically, they also become more fragile in relation to the external world and therefore in need of greater and greater defense.

The child who is more fortunate is gradually exposed to a plurality of views. There are few places in the world today where plurality is absent. Too much of this plurality too soon could overwhelm the child and lead to a withdrawal from plurality. Parents and other teachers of the young have to gauge the amount of diversity that a child can handle. The child need not be exposed to hundreds of viewpoints on every subject. A good beginning would be two points of view. For a child beyond age 6 (and possibly younger), the teacher has to convey these two views: the truth that the teacher is convinced of and the acknowledgment that another truthful view is possible. This "other view" may turn out to be a dozen, hundred, or thousand views. With other teachers (including the learner as teacher), the learner can continually reshape the overall perception that he or she has of the world.

There are crucial moments in the lives of individuals when the mind breaks through to the recognition that to live the truth one knows does not require attacking anyone else who has a different view. Not all teachers (including schoolteachers) have themselves reached this position. A repressive form of teaching might be perpetuated over generations. The fortunate thing is that one need not have been taught only by very competent teachers. In fact, if a person meets just one or two good teachers in life, that might be enough to break through blind prejudice to receptive listening, respect for others, and an intelligent grasp of complex issues.

At this point it will be helpful to consider three examples of teaching with the end in view: telling stories, delivering a lecture, and preaching a sermon.

Storytelling

The first representative of this family is teaching by storytelling. My intention here is to use a term that can encompass all sorts of oral and literary forms that are siblings within this family. Storytelling extends from a mother telling the tale of "Three Little Pigs Went to Market" to a historian trying to recount the rise and fall of civilizations. What links the many forms is a presumed community that is "on the way." The community has some end in view, although stories at their best do not reduce the end to a simple termination point. The end may be a complex image or metaphor that not only allows but invites a filling in.

Storytelling is a universal human trait, or at least it would be difficult to imagine human lives that do not involve the recounting of tales both for entertainment and instruction. As far back as we can investigate, humans have been telling stories. Earlier and simpler cultures, perhaps, show more evidence of storytelling as a central fact of life. In the contemporary world, people do not sit around a campfire telling stories, though they might sit around the television watching soap operas. Whether this change shows progress is to be questioned. But storytelling certainly does exist in the present in hundreds of forms.

The parent's way of communicating with the small child is largely by story. A great fund of children's stories has been built up throughout history. Some of the best stories are the oldest; they have been tested over time. The "end" they offer is not a moralistic message about good behavior but a complex image of good and evil. Often when people try to invent new tales for children the moral is too obvious and the children see through it. Richly textured stories can be engaged at many levels and allow the listener to take whatever he or she is ready to take. The story needs little or no explanation; the teaching is in the telling.

The great Australian historian Manning Clark, while writing of his own work, could also be describing children's stories: "All the great stories of mankind are told without any comment at all. Perhaps that is why they have outlived their generation, and said something to men at all times and places." Clark goes on to say of these stories, "They make us explicitly aware of what we had vaguely noticed before of what life is like, of what will happen to us if in our folly or in some mad passion we defy the wisdom of humanity."[7]

Traditional fairytales usually deal with the great cosmic struggle of good and evil. The storyline often has frightening elements of child kidnapping, vicious stepmothers, threats of murder, and cannibalism. Adults usually wish to protect children from encountering such horrors. However, if something can be told as a story it becomes bearable, and an artistic story well told is educational. The inner fears of the child find expression in a story of what happened in a land far, far away. The story comes to a resolution and the people live happily ever after. This end is, in fact, an invitation to imagine what follows after the crisis described in the story.

Starting in childhood and continuing throughout life, people adopt storylines with grand designs of where "my people" came from and what we are going toward. It is not an accident that the term "myth" has a double meaning: a story of foundations and a story that is false. We know that the great epic myths that tell of the origin of the world, the human race, or the nation involve fanciful details. But at some level below factual inaccuracy, the great stories of the Book of Genesis, the Iliad, or the Bhagavad Gita provide insight into the human story. Northrop Frye, referring to *Macbeth*, says, "If you wish to know the history of eleventh-century Scotland, look elsewhere; if you wish to know what it means to gain a kingdom and lose one's soul, look here."[8]

The master stories of the world, the human race, or the nation do not always get told directly or explicitly. They may be so thoroughly woven into the texture of ordinary life that the lesser stories are constantly reaffirming them. For example, the master story of the United States is America. From the time of its invention in 1507, "America" has been the name of a great myth, the story of the promised land and the chosen people. The artificially constructed nation known as the United States has from the beginning identified itself with the dream, the ideal, the myth of America. So successful has the identification been that people throughout the world use "United States" and "America" interchangeably. Even more forceful is the calling of U.S. citizens *the* Americans. Every fourth or fifth sentence spoken in the United States reaffirms the story of America, the promised land of freedom, justice, and wealth.

No one can doubt the formative power of this particular story. Many people arriving in the country are disappointed; they expect to find America and what they find is the United States. Those who live under the enveloping myth of America have difficulty getting any critical distance from it. Without using convolutions of language, U.S. people find it impossible to distinguish between their country and a myth; the result is a confusion between politics and religion. With the constant assertion (and diversion) of the "separation of church and state," the politics of the United States is very often the religion of America.

The United States is not alone in having a myth to hold it together. This country is a dramatic example because its nationhood is so precarious. The modern world with its nationalism practically requires that people have a myth of origins, unity, and greatness. Europe, after the passing of "Christian Europe" or the "Holy Roman Empire," depended on the cohesion of nation-states. There is an old European saying, "A nation is a group of people united by a common error concerning their ancestry and by shared hostility to their neighbor." Nevertheless, even as these states warred with each other, Europe exported nationalism to the rest of the world. In some places it took easily, blending in with tribal loyalties; other places resisted. The "Islamic community," for example, cannot really comprehend independent nation-states, but nationalism surfaced even in the Muslim world.

My only interest here is to note the power of master stories that shape the lives of billions of people. They may not know the story, they may even wish to reject the story, but the stories do exist and have overwhelming power. I have intimated that these stories, while inevitable, are not all to the good. Storytelling is often romanticized in uncritical ways. As I have said of this whole family of languages, which includes stories, the only protection against the possibly corruptive influence is the presence of other families. Especially needed is academic criticism of the story when it envelops whole nations, or other ethnic, religious, and racial groups.

At the everyday level, storytelling takes up much of life. Like Molière's Monsieur Jourdain, who was unaware he had been speaking prose, we often do not reflect on the narrative character of ordinary conversation.[9] These brief and often fragmented stories are a continuous form of teaching. Take, for example, gossip. Almost no one would be proud of being called a gossip and yet practically everyone deals in it. Gossip should perhaps have a better reputation than it has. When the gossip becomes malicious, then it needs restraint or criticism. But condemning gossip itself has little effect. As in telling jokes, it is a way of testing out the self in relation to the fabric of community existence.[10]

Among literary forms, consider the mystery/thriller/crime story. It is usually not praised as a literary genre, though it can range from the real potboiler (where the only point is to get to the end) to the textured writing of Elizabeth George or P. D. James. Reading such stories gives people a sense of order in the universe. One is comforted by the fact that by page 250 Commander Dalgliesh will have solved the mystery and a balance of justice will be restored in the world. Everyone knows that the world is not so completely ordered, but that does not lessen our need to discover, affirm, or create order in parts of the world. For some people, to be engrossed in light fiction is a guilty pleasure for four hours on a plane or an afternoon on the beach. However, light fiction or gossipy conversation is better teaching than most of the sensationalistic television that appeals to the same instincts.

Those people who are blessed with native talent and a solid education can have their lives sustained by richer, more complex stories. Most of the teachings of great philosophers and religious figures exist in the form of stories. Plato's myth of the cave or Jesus' parable of the Prodigal Son never lose their force for those willing to enter the story. In the Jewish tradition, the process of *midrash* goes on today, story about story layered throughout the centuries. Biographies and autobiographies, short stories and novels can become lifelong teachers.

At their best, television and film can be a lively complement to written and oral speech. The evidence of five decades suggests that television is really good at two things: soap opera (the bad and the sophisticated) and "live" talk of the day's events, including neighborhood politics, the sporting match, or the weather. Television, together with the computer, is the single greatest potential for educational reform in the present era. Whether that potential is ever realized, and despite the dreary lineup of most evenings on commercial television, the television set is now the background to most human conversation.

Probably for the first time in human history there is worldwide gossip, some of it boring, some of it malicious, some of it inspiring. Television, along with the computer Internet, enables the verbal and nonverbal art of one people to appear in a living room anywhere in the world. The eighteenth century's conception of "humanity" is starting to be filled out with something more than a few white men and their romantic notions of what they supposed primitive people to be.

The film industry, especially in the United States, has a profound effect in shaping the culture. Even people who do not go to the movies live in the environment of the world on film and videotape. Along with rock music, film has become an international language. There is danger in too much of the language coming from one place on the globe that exports fluffy narrative and orgies of violence. Movies of today, just as in the 1930s and 1940s, run the gamut from truly awful to spectacularly good. The same could have been said of eighteenth- and nineteenth-century novels. We have a few hundred masterpieces from the thousands of pieces that were read and tossed aside like today's tabloids. Teaching by story involves not just the profound side of human nature, but the mundane side as well.[11]

Perhaps the greatest difference between today's stories and the traditional novel of the nineteenth century is the disappearance of the omniscient narrator, at least in much of the literature of the second half of the twentieth century. The result is a voice from within the story giving us a fragment of life. There is an absence of trust in someone telling us the whole story and where it all leads. "We trust only the voice of the witness," as William Styron puts it.

In the world of contemporary literature, the language shifts away from "teaching with the end in view" toward the second family, where the end is not in view. Much of modern fiction, poetry, and drama gives up all instructional tendency and mirrors the confusions and uncertainties of a world in which neither divine nor human intelligence is felt to be in charge. The term "story" has not disappeared. People cling to plot lines, even in fragmented form, to get to next year or next week. But more than ever, other forms of language are needed to complement storytelling. Neatly plotted master stories are too rich for many bewildered people. Other languages of teaching need to complement and sometimes precede storytelling.

Lecturing

The second language in the family of rhetorical persuasion is the lecture, a term that means "reading." It usually refers to a particular kind of reading with an instructive or didactic purpose. The typical approach of authors who teach in universities is to attack the form of lecturing and then go right back to using the term for the language of university teaching.[12] A whole set of jokes exists for describing lectures; for example, the lecturer is someone who talks in someone else's sleep; or a lecture is what passes from the teacher's notes to the student's notes without passing through the head of either.

In this section, I wish to take exactly the opposite tack from one that ridicules lecturing as a form and then resignedly accepts its use in the classroom. I think that lecturing is to be affirmed and valued as a form of teaching; I also think it is unacceptable as a description of classroom instruction. On the one hand, I think it is a scandal for professors (and ex-professors) to ridicule lecturing. On the other hand, I think universities cannot examine what it means to teach in their setting until they remove the term "lecture" from center stage.

In a book on university teaching, Kenneth Eble begins the chapter entitled "Lecturing" by saying, "The best general advice to the teacher who would lecture well is still, 'Don't do it.' "[13] Eble does not take his own advice, proceeding to discuss the use of lecturing in the university classroom. On the persistence of the lecture form, Eble says, "As has been pointed out countless times, the lecture was outmoded by the invention of printing and by cheap and easy access to printed works." He then expresses at least partial disagreement with this statement by saying that the book did not sweep out lecturing "for the simple reason that human beings remain responsive to all forms of intercourse with other consenting humans."[14] Although I agree with this conclusion, it does little to match this form of intercourse with the appropriate setting.

When a university installs a person in a chair, the occasion is often marked by an "inaugural lecture." Such a lecture is appropriate so long as it is understood as an inauguration of the professor to his or her colleagues and not the beginning of the daily work in the classroom. Lecturing is a highly ritualized act in which a person addresses a community; the end that the lecture has in view is some rational conception of humanity. Far from becoming outdated in the seventeenth century, lecturing began to come fully into its own about that time. The spread of books and book-ordered learning is the precondition of, not the competitor to, the modern lecture form. What has happened in the twentieth century is a fragmenting of the cultural assumptions of book learning. Books (and lectures) have by no means disappeared, but they need complementing in the contemporary diet.

A person reading from an easily available book is not a very effective form of teaching; a person reading notes that he or she has taken from easily available books does not make much sense, either. However, an author reading his or her own words, particularly if done with dramatic style, can sometimes be effective teaching. For the lecture as appropriate form, a whole set of conditions has to come together.

For teaching by lecture, the speaker and the text need a ritualized setting. The listeners need to be capable of appreciating well-written prose delivered with a forceful style. The author needs to speak words that come from the depth of the self. The aim of a lecture is to change, however imperceptibly, the listener's actions as a human being. A lecture to a three-year-old is pointless; to a seven-year-old, a lecture (no longer, say, than one minute) might sometimes be called for. Listening to a 30- or 45-minute lecture is something most of us are ready for only a few times a year. And most of us are ready to deliver a lecture even less frequently.

Some people have a responsibility to give a lecture on a fairly regular basis. A U.S. president is expected to deliver a State of the Union address each year. Such an occasion should provide an example of careful preparation, clear presentation, and reflective response. It deserves an audience of both Houses of Congress and other important government officials. The speech is delivered in a historic setting. The televising of the event to millions of homes need not interfere, can indeed enhance, the ritualizing of the event.

Neither a U.S. president nor anyone else can churn out lectures daily, weekly, or even monthly. The practices of the election campaign tend to subvert the idea of the thoughtful speech in a ritual setting. Television adds to the destruction of lecturing because the presence of the camera becomes the excuse to produce thirty seconds — or less — of clever attack. Television becomes both cause and devourer of such speech.

Consider two examples of teaching by lecture. The first is a memorable speech that Mario Cuomo delivered in 1984 at the University of Notre Dame.[15] It was a political lecture with moral and religious overtones. Cuomo was trying to make intelligible his position on abortion, primarily to his co-religionists but also to any reasonable person. The text was prepared over several months and involved the speaker in considerable study of history, politics, and theology. The choice of a university to give the lecture was a signal of its rational inquiry, and the fact that the university was Notre Dame suggested a serious religious twist. The evening was a very formal ritual in which Cuomo set out a position that involved his deepest personal beliefs and risked his political future. The lecture was broadcast live on cable systems around the country.

Was this a successful lecture? It presented Cuomo's position on abortion as no other format could have done. Many people were not convinced by the careful line the speaker tried to walk. But even those who disagreed, from left and right, could probably appreciate the attempt to frame an argument with careful thinking and well-articulated speech. For years afterward, people continued to refer to the Notre Dame lecture as the standard source for Cuomo's position on abortion.

My second example is a speech that Vaclav Havel gave in Washington, D.C., in February 1990.[16] He addressed the Congress of the United States from the well of the House. The politicians, I suspect, were startled by his taking out a yellow pad on which he had written his speech. The lecture had immediate urgency for the several hundred people present. Its appeal, however, was to reasonable men and women everywhere. Havel had spent a good part of his adult life in prison, thanks to Soviet officials. Yet here he was urging Congress to give aid to the former Soviet peoples.

Havel's lecture had all the marks that I have cited for teaching by the form of lecture: the ritual setting, the personal involvement in the message, the carefully crafted words, the appeal to rational order. He was appealing to the self-interest of his hearers, but the ultimate basis of his speech was his own particular humanism. The only thing he may have lacked was a sufficiently thoughtful audience. His speech did not succeed in its immediate mission to provide economic aid. On a larger scale of political history, however, the lecture may have given a ray of hope within a depressing world of ordinary wheeling and dealing. Clement Atlee said of Winston Churchill in 1945, "Words at great moments of history are deeds." One could say that great words at any time are deeds. At great moments of history, the deedful quality of careful speech is powerfully demonstrated.[17]

Preaching

Only a thin line divides the lecture and the sermon. In its immediate task, Vaclav Havel's speech could be called a sermon. When politics becomes partisan, when the speech is a rousing call to action directed to the loyal faithful, then politics is more sermon than lecture. Mario Cuomo became an overnight sensation after his keynote address to the

Democratic Party convention in 1984. The response to that sermon was an emotionally charged "amen."

Preaching a sermon is an activity closely identified with the church, and rightly so. The Christian church developed the sermon into an art form. In the fourth century, John Chrysostom ("golden mouth") complained that the congregation expected a performance in church that was proper to the theater. But Chrysostom himself expected cheering and stamping of feet; "What greater disgrace," he writes, "than to walk from the pulpit with blank silence."[18] In the Middle Ages, some of the great rhetoric of the culture is found in sermons. Meister Eckhart's soaring mystical teaching is found not in his Latin treatises but in his German sermons. We have access to his teaching because nuns in the congregation copied down the sermons.[19]

Whereas lectures are written to be read, the sermon is spoken to be heard. Christianity did not begin as a "religion of the book." It resisted literary language and used the spoken language of the day (Koine Greek).[20] In the sixteenth-century Reformation, the call was not to read a book but to hear the word preached. Martin Luther, who wanted the church to be a "mouth house" and not a "pen house," could not have imagined how overwhelming would be the effect of the printing press. The power of the spoken word tended to be eclipsed. In the late twentieth century, however, we may be witnessing a resurgence of the spoken word as what tips the balance of power.

In preaching, there is a text that expresses the community's beliefs. A man or woman steps forward, or steps into the center, to comment on the text. The appeal to understand does not neglect emotion and will. The intention is to move people to do something about injustices of the world. Jonathan Edwards was one of the great preachers in North American history. When Edwards preached a sermon, he was often surprised at the emotional outpouring it sparked. The sermons were learned and intellectual, but deep knowledge, far from being opposed to feeling, is fused with it.[21] The result is that people get up from their seats and engage in political activity.

I have suggested that politicians frequently deal in preaching sermons. They often seem embarrassed by that fact; unfortunately, preachers who are embarrassed to be preachers give terrible sermons. The politician's vocation often calls not only for "discussing issues," but for moving people to action. The focus of belief is tighter than for a lecture; the end sought is more socially oriented. The Gettysburg Address, in Garry Wills's interpretation, was Lincoln's commentary on the Constitution in the light of the need to rethink equality and union. "He came to change the world, to effect an intellectual revolution. No other words could have done it. The miracle is that these words did."[22]

Often it is said that we should not preach to the converted, but that is exactly the group to be preached to. Preaching to the unconverted can be both ineffective and offensive. Here we have the other side of the indoctrination charge: trying to impose a set of practices when the beliefs of a particular community have not been accepted by the listeners. When black preachers on the left get into politics, they are often assumed to be doing the same thing as fundamentalist preachers on the right. The usual difference is, however, that right-wing preachers preach a "Christian America" while the left wing preaches the Bill of Rights. To preach to U.S. people that they should live up to their Declaration and Constitution is entirely fitting; they are already converts.

Journalists in the newspapers or on television are on occasion called to be preachers. Newspapers pride themselves for putting only facts on the front page and reporting stories with objectivity. The editorial and op-ed pages admit to opinion; most writers there would prefer their essays to be called lectures rather than sermons. Nevertheless, the urge to get one's message across in 750 words often pushes the writer toward a sermon. A television reporter often has the camera's picture as the objective fact and is called to offer commentary. Most of the time the language is a form of storytelling. On occasion, the picture is so emotion-laden — in war, famine, storm, or joyful success — that any commentary becomes a small sermon on the human condition.

Journalists might be horrified by the naming of what they do as sermons. Like politicians, they might preach better if they were not embarrassed to be cast into that position. Their journalistic integrity is not compromised if they touch an emotional chord by letting their own emotions be reached when the situation is profoundly moving. No extra layer is laid upon the facts; instead, one can really grasp the facts within the context of an emotion-filled commentary on the obvious text. Edward R. Murrow, a figure of mythic proportions in the history of radio and television, was a young reporter in London during the London blitz. His evening reports to the United States stirred a whole nation. He wrote in a letter to his parents, "I remember you once wanted me to be a preacher but I had no faith, except in myself. But now I am preaching from a powerful pulpit. Often I am wrong, but I am trying to talk as

I would have talked were I a preacher. One need not wear a reversed collar to be honest."[23]

The preacher can and should presuppose a language that has acquired rich association over years or centuries. Those who sit in front of a preacher give license to him or her to so use that language that the listener will be moved to action.[24] There is necessarily a distinction between the inner language of the community and language external to it. Community cannot exist without a language of intimacy that is not entirely comprehensible to the outsider. However, the social relation of outsider and insider need not be hostile.

A test for any preacher is to stir the hearts of the community with its intimate language while not insulting or offending outsiders. I recall going to the synagogue one evening, at the invitation of the local rabbi, to hear the great Talmudic scholar Aidan Steinsaltz. I feared I would not be able to understand his scholarly address, but he spoke in very simple terms of what it means to be a Jew. As the only Gentile in the audience, I could only listen as an outsider. While he spoke the intimate language of the Jewish congregation, he said nothing disparaging of other people. Would that all preaching were so finely tuned.

The main preaching on television is not confined to Sunday mornings. The fifteen-second commercials that blanket commercial television are expensively contrived sermons; they demand that the listener act. If one is not, say, a member of the beer-drinking community, then Bud Lite preaching can be experienced as offensive. The assumption is made by advertisers that the listeners belong to a community that would like to be rich, sexy, and powerful. The challenge is to show and to say something that will convince the viewer that if I use this toothpaste, I will be sexually irresistible; if I buy this car, I will be judged a success in life; if I eat this cereal, I will live forever. The preaching may be very low key, if the reigning theory is that soft-sell works better.

The relentless television advertisements are perhaps a symptom of what happens in a culture when storytelling, lecturing, and political preaching are ineffective. The culture becomes addicted to preaching of the worst kind while thinking it has escaped the preaching of sermons. Because the intellectual leaders do not go to church at 11 A.M. Sundays, they believe they are not enmeshed in sermonizing.

"Preaching is not teaching, except in a church," wrote Philip Rieff to his colleagues.[25] I doubt that he meant preaching really is a form of teaching in churches, but that churches only think that preaching is teaching. Rieff's book, *Fellow Teachers*, like many tracts on politics, education, and economics, is a passionate plea that has the qualities of a sermon. Preaching can be a legitimate form of teaching in and out of church; so also preaching can be completely inappropriate in and out of church. When all the conditions are right, a sermon can be among the most powerful forms of teaching. The fact that sermons are often preached when the conditions are lacking is the reason for the negative connotations of "sermonizing" and "preachiness."

I finish with two examples of preaching, one from 1963, one from 1992. Both sermons were preached by a man named King. At the Washington Monument on August 28, 1963, Martin Luther King Jr. gave one of the most stirring sermons in U.S. history. No one knew what he was going to say that day (perhaps not even he), but everyone knew that the conditions were right for a nation to be moved. The speaker's life and words fused in a dramatic moment that could not be completely predicted or controlled.

As any good preacher does, King started with a text that his hearers knew: "When the architects of our republic wrote the magnificent words of the Constitution and the Declaration of Independence, they were signing a promissory note to which every American was to fall heir. . . . It is obvious today that America has defaulted on this promissory note in so far as her citizens of color are concerned."

The task of the preacher, after establishing the text and the failure to live by the text, is to stir the listeners to carry out the implications of what they claim is their belief: "I still have a dream. It is a dream deeply rooted in the American dream that one day this nation will rise up and live out the true meaning of its creed — we hold these truths to be self-evident, that all men are created equal." The cadence and much of the imagery were biblical, but the text was the equality promised in the founding documents of the United States.[26]

A different situation prevailed, though the underlying problem was similar, when Rodney King stepped forward on May 2, 1992. The city of Los Angeles was burning behind him; the tape that showed King being beaten by police officers and the subsequent trial of those men were the ostensible reasons for the violence. King had no text in hand; he had little sense of what to say. In words wrenched from his obvious anguish, he pleaded for calm. "Can we all get along," he said. "We just gotta, just gotta, you know. I mean we're all stuck here for a while."[27] The sermon, which pleaded for an end to the violence, took less time than the eighty-one seconds of the original tape.

Whatever his past or future, King spoke at that moment from complete conviction and undeniable emotion. His text was the belief that no one wishes to see everything destroyed. He evoked a powerful response in many people. Whether he saved buildings and lives is difficult to say. But he surely put to shame all the politicians who could not summon up a few sentences that were adequate to the situation. To Rodney King's words, one might apply Nietzsche's line, "And if someone goes through fire for his teaching — what does that prove? Truly, it is more when one's teaching comes out of one's burning."[28]

Conclusion

The teaching languages described in this chapter presuppose a precise set of conditions. There has to be present a community receptive to the power of language. Someone from the group is prepared to teach and is accepted for the occasion as teacher. The story is told, the lecture is delivered, the sermon is preached. How the teacher uses the language is as important as what is said. Often, no new information is conveyed; the text is likely to be quite familiar. But the individual, as part of the group, gets a firmer grasp on the good to be attained and is inspired to surmount the obstacles to its achievement. To teach in this first instance is to move people to act by appealing to their understanding of the beliefs of a particular community that is representative of the whole human community.

Chapter 5

Teaching to Remove Obstacles

T HIS CHAPTER, starting with the title, is the most paradoxical one in the book. Can we remove obstacles by teaching? Why should we be trying to do so? What obstacles need removing? The answers to such questions involve some strange twists of language and a refusal to accept things as they first appear. The forms of language described in this chapter may seem to have nothing to do with the act of teaching. Nevertheless, these languages in their proper setting are needed to show someone how to live and how to die.

In recent centuries, teaching has been closely connected to the first family of languages described in chapter 4. That is, to teach has been identified with "to explain." The art of persuading the mind to accept rational explanations has dominated the philosophy of education. I described within this family three representative forms: storytelling, lecturing, and preaching. Not accidentally, I think, the first and third have tended to collapse into the middle. Storytelling is thought to be a helpful softening up for rational analysis, while preaching is anathematized as the opposite of teaching. What remains is lecturing, stripped of its ritual. Teaching becomes telling people the truth backed up by empirical facts and logical reasoning.

For several centuries, hope rose that the success of the scientific method would eventually solve the problem of teaching. Explanations could be logically arranged in books and lecture notes. A reasonable person, by reading books and lectures, would acquire the knowledge to live a rational human existence. However difficult it might be to achieve the aim of education, the aim itself seemed clear: the autonomous individual.

Total confidence in reason and scientific knowledge has been slipping away throughout the twentieth century. From a few artists and philosophers who were skeptical of science's capacity to carry the burden of life's teaching, the attack today is from all sides. The ideal of the "rational man" is charged with being sexist, apolitical, unfeeling, class-biased, and so forth. In response to such criticism, the lecturer may try to incorporate the narrative texture of storytelling or the passion of preaching. The real problem, however, is the absence of the clear end to teaching. And yet the dominance of lecturing is so complete that it remains in place even when its *raison d'être* no longer seems to exist.

The argument of this chapter is that the explanatory lecture needs help not only from other family members but from another family. Unfortunately, this family has suffered an almost total eclipse in discussions of teaching. Far more than the first family, this collection of languages requires ritual, that is, social patterns that continue from one generation to the next. Modern times have been hard on the traditional rituals that surround birth, courtship, marriage, family life, religion, and death. Important rituals cannot be reinvented overnight. What we need to look for are rituals of everyday life that have survived even in fragmentary form. These rituals have to be nurtured and sustained as we await the slow development of new rituals.[1]

I will refer to this second family of languages as "therapeutic." They are the languages that calm, soothe, and heal. Therapy is a central need of human life; it should be recognized as central to teaching. This second family has always been the precondition of the first. For example, if someone is distraught with fear or overcome with grief, a lecture, no matter how well ordered, is not going to succeed. Often the need for this therapeutic family becomes evident only as someone tests the limits of the first family. In whichever sequence the two sets of languages emerge, they have a complementary relation.

The perennial need for therapeutic languages has been rather suddenly enlarged. The end of life and the aim of teaching had seemed securely in place. But the scientific ideal that largely replaced classical philosophy and Christian religion was itself undermined. Science was part of its own undoing. It succeeded in getting rid of "final causes." The question now thrust upon increasing numbers of people is, How do you live in a world where no one knows the purpose of things? People still rely on science to bring them wonderful new technology, but they do not on those grounds accept that science can teach them how to live and how to die.

This feeling of sudden abandonment can lead to skepticism or nihilism. In the flight from all claims to know the truth, therapy can proceed to swallow every other language. People can become addicted to therapy; a whole culture can slide in that direction. In the 1960s, Philip Rieff wrote a book entitled *The Triumph of the Therapeutic*.[2] The intervening decades have seemed to move further in the direction he was describing, namely, the reduction of politics, economics, and education to a massaging of the emotions. And as lecturing took over the meaning of "to teach" in the first family, the reaction against lecturing tends to be a single form of therapy: the bull session. In the world of the classroom, the alternative to the lecture is usually assumed to be "group discussion." In these groups, whether anything is learned or not, everyone is supposed to feel better at the end for having expressed his or her opinion. With radio call-ins, television talk shows, and computer chat rooms, the whole country sometimes seems to be a bull session.

Consider once again the literature on "adult education." I noted in chapter 1 that if teaching is confused with big people telling little people what to think, then to teach an adult is impossible. To try to teach an adult is insulting. The alternative is taken to be adults talking to each other with the aid of a facilitator or group leader. Adult-education theorizing is enveloped in therapeutic language. It opens with "needs assessment:" tell me what you need and I will try to design a program that fits your need. While youngsters are or could be challenged to think about new things by studying subjects they have never imagined, adults are supposedly only interested in solving problems they can readily identify. A low-cost group therapy is the result in many adult-education classes.[3]

This narrowing of education to "facilitation" is a major problem in today's culture. It is particularly deleterious for disempowered people. A culture intent on making people feel good is a comfortable place for the rich but a hopeless place for the poor and the dispossessed. Parallel to what was said in the previous chapter, the cure for the dominance of one therapeutic language is twofold: the acknowledgment of other languages with a family resemblance and the affirming of other families of languages. There is nothing bad about feeling good. It becomes bad only when individuals become obsessed with feeling good to the undoing of their own best selves and to the obscuring of severe injustices that support a feel-good culture.

The Fragmented Community

The therapeutic does not presuppose a well-functioning community in which the goal of teaching is inspiring people to act on their beliefs. On the contrary, the therapeutic assumes a fragmented community in which the individual is trying to find him- or herself. It is the nature of human communities to be imperfect and to have individuals who feel some disconnectedness. However, recent times have cast the individual into a confusing overlay of communities, with doubt arising as to how any particular community relates to a universal human community. The disconnected feeling that has concomitantly increased is likely to include the individual's own bodiliness. The right of people to choose for themselves is more strongly insisted upon, but how that "willing" relates to the bodily organism is not so clear.

One sign of this individual aloneness is the talk of "human rights." No one is sure of the "common good," but individuals should have the right to engage in their own search. Or, since the good is unknown beforehand, the individual may have to will it into existence. Immanuel Kant was, if not the inventor, at least the gatekeeper of this way of conceiving ethics and political philosophy. At the beginning of a book on morality, Kant writes, "Nothing in the world can be conceived of as good, without qualification, except a good will."[4] Kant himself pushed on toward a reunification of "man and nature" but the solitary consciousness trailed in his wake. By the late twentieth century, the feeling of aloneness has spread far and wide. It sometimes manifests itself in outbursts of violence; at other times, the individual withdraws into bouts of apathy and depression.

When these problems become severe enough, society calls upon the prison and the mental hospital to stem the tide. The prison uses harsh, repressive language to cure the problem; however, it would be difficult to find anyone who thinks that prisons cure anything. Similarly, well-staffed mental hospitals can help the sick, but many hospitals are holding areas that return disturbed people to the streets.[5]

Most people are not at these extremes. What most people do need at certain moments of a day, a year, or a lifetime, is the help of restorative language. The help needed is not a complex theory that explains life but ordinary speech that calms and comforts. Speaking is itself a therapeutic process. Violence, terror, anxiety, and depression leave us outside conversation. The person who is sick has to learn to trust in words, using speech to relate to other humans. Part of the strange technique that Freud developed is that people should talk about whatever comes into their minds. The point of the conversation is not to reach any particular conclusion; it is to allow the force of life in the form of the will to reemerge in the context of ordinary life.

The family of therapeutic languages therefore ranges from the most ordinary of expressions to the most paradoxical of twists. At the surface level, we can be taught something by someone saying "uh-huh:" the bond is holding, it is safe to continue.[6] Below the surface, human beings trap themselves in plans and projects that they can neither execute nor let go. Effective speech here has to dart behind and below the obvious; it is, as Buddhists say, speech to destroy speech.

Even if one does not go all the way with Buddhism's search-and-destroy mission, selective strikes on the mind's imprisonment of itself in story, lecture, and sermon can be helpful. All of the main religions have used enigmatic sayings to teach the human mind that it has limits. One needs a technique to stop the mind from chattering on. At the center of speech there has to be a profound silence. Forms of therapeutic speech are constituted more by silence than by sound.

In teaching with therapeutic languages, one tries not to "move the will" but to restore the person to willing. However, there is no direct way to accomplish that; the disempowered cannot be directly empowered. Any direct assault ("pull yourself together") will likely drive the problem deeper. Freud rediscovered what most religions knew, that what we think of as free will is not free. Human freedom is at a deeper level where a yes or no is given to life. One has to be able to act; just as important, one has to be able to *not* act, to stop speech and allow what is not verbal to lead.

Much of twentieth-century philosophy has abandoned the project of explaining reality with a grand theory. Philosophy is turned back on itself and released from its pretension to take up a view that God had before creating the universe. Wittgenstein is most explicit in seeing philosophy as therapy: "The real discovery is the one that makes one capable of stopping philosophy when I want to — the one that gives philosophy place.... Instead, we now demonstrate a method, by examples, and the series of examples can be broken off."[7] In the early Wittgenstein, the silence is found by going up a ladder to the point where speech is surpassed (he contrasted what could be shown to what could be said).[8] In the later Wittgenstein, the silence is found at the

center. Our many games of language show a way but the greatest philosophy is what stops philosophy and leaves us at what Wittgenstein
calls "the mystical" at the center of ordinary life.

The frequent mark of therapeutic speech is the double negative.
When language is negating life, the solution cannot be more of the
same speech. What has to be negated is the negation so that life can
flow. Philosophy or religion can seem negative when it is constantly
nay-saying. The question is whether its nos are single or double. Most
of the sayings and stories in Buddhism deal in double negatives, which
the West has often mistaken for nihilism. A famous Buddhist saying
begins, "Monks, there is a not born, not become, not made, not compounded"; this is offered as the way to overcome the "born, become,
made, compounded." One could miss the point that the negatives are
the "born, become, made, compounded." At least, they are negative insofar as each is a fracture, a split unity. What is presented as alternative
is not a simple image of oneness but a language of nondualism. That is
as far as language can carry us.

Western mystical tradition is just as rich in this kind of nondualistic
speech. When Maimonides asks if God is alive, his answer is that God
is not dead. An image of a living being is still too confining; "not dead"
affirms life with no limiting image. Thomas Aquinas says that "God is
not a being" because for Aquinas being is a limitation of the act of to
be.[9] Of course, simply saying that God is not a being could be miscon-
strued as simple atheism. Aquinas's last word on God is that God is
"not not being." In a similar pattern, many mystics (Meister Eckhart
quite explicitly) deny that God "exists." To exist is to be one among
many, divided from the others.[10] The ultimate healing unity cannot be
expressed in speech as a thing in isolation from other things. One can
only hold out as hope the overcoming of division.

Development

A possible modern way to speak of teaching when there is no end in
view is the term "development." This term began to come into prominence in the economics of the late eighteenth century and part of its
meaning is still weighted in that direction. In the late nineteenth century, "development" came to overlap "progress" and "evolution." By
absorbing psychological meaning, it came to be more comprehensive

than either "evolution" or "progress." For a while, "development" almost became a subset of "psychology" ("child development"), but it is not confined there today.

"Development," meaning "to come out of the envelope," is an alternative to having an endpoint that would predetermine movement. Teaching for "human development" would therefore mean removing whatever object starts acting as endpoint. Of course, within the process of teaching without end we still need the stimulus of short-range goals. The student turns in a paper to receive a grade; the student takes a required number of credits to get a degree. Goals such as these, which are static objects to possess, have the danger of becoming the end of education.

"Development" in educational circles arose in reaction to a form of teaching in which adults had tried to force-feed children and fit children into a preexisting mold. A favorite contrast of educational reformers has been to replace "push in" with "pull out." The latter may be some improvement as educational policy, although it is not clear that it represents an alternate metaphor. The possible etymology of education as "to lead out" does not of itself avoid authoritarianism. A teacher leading out a student still suggests a highly directive process that goes wherever the teacher wishes it to go. If "development" is really the issue, a teacher has to use more indirect means and use a variety of languages, some of which are spelled out below.

The paradox is how to move from knowledge that is in some sense already present to knowledge that is actual and gets dis-covered by the learner. In the story of Alexander the Great's visit to Diogenes, the famous teacher is asked if he needs anything. Diogenes's reply was, "Only stand out of my light." Some people may require a little more help than that, as in Plato's *Republic*, where teaching is understood to be the teacher turning the student's mind toward the light.[11]

Comenius, in the introduction to *The Great Didactic*, says, "While the seeds of knowledge, of virtue, and of piety are naturally implanted in us, the actual knowledge, virtue and piety are not so given. These must be acquired by prayer, education and by action."[12] I would agree, except that I prefer to use "education" in a broader sense so as to encompass prayer and action. Education includes people sitting in seats and being instructed by story, lecture, or sermon. Education also includes both action of a social-political nature and stillness at the contemplative center of life.

Wittgenstein also includes "praying" as an example within the cluster of languages that he associates with ritual. He lists "asking, thanking, cursing, greeting, praying."[13] Although his statement is a major inspiration for this chapter, I do not think he was trying to make a complete enumeration of this cluster. Thus, I do not feel compelled to follow his lead in naming this set. I do not name "praying" as a language because it cuts across several that I do name. Similarly, "asking" seems to me not a distinct language but a grammatical form that shows up in many forms of teaching. "Cursing" is an interesting case, although I prefer a different term for some of its meaning. His other two examples, thanking and greeting, I address directly. Wittgenstein's great contribution is his recognition of the many languages in life and in teaching. Especially important is his calling attention to this ritual cluster that provides a therapeutic effect in teaching.

When these languages are neglected, they tend to collapse at the threshold of the professional psychotherapist, much like explanatory teaching is handed over to the professional schoolteacher. In both cases, the burden is too great. To receive therapy becomes equivalent to putting yourself in the hands of one person, presumed to possess a curative skill. People who really are sick may not have the means for this kind of treatment; those who do have the means to get treatment may be misled about the nature of healing, helping, and therapy. As James Hillman often insists, the analyst is not the one who heals; he or she can at best mediate the healing forces within the person and between people.[14]

The therapist as teacher engages in teaching with the strangest of languages. A therapist saying, "Yes, that's interesting, continue," may not sound like he or she is doing much. However, most of us cannot be still enough to allow the conflicting elements of another's personality to be brought forth and healed. In Albert Camus's novel, *The Plague*, one of the characters says that he is certain only "that there are victims and there is the plague, and as far as possible I do not wish to be on the side of the plague."[15] This stark contrast and choice is softened by another passage where it is suggested that there may be some people who are healers. The rest of us should take notice of people who seem to ameliorate the effects of plague.

As in much of tribal religion, we seem to be returning to the figure of the teacher as healer; not the one who lays claim to the title of healer but the one whose effect on a community is healing. There may come a time when great visionaries arise who can point the way out of the desert night. For the present, we can only help people "to stand fast, with their souls in readiness, until the dawn breaks and a path becomes visible where none suspected it."[16]

Therapeutic Examples

I wish to illustrate this cluster of languages with three paired terms, plus a pair that is presupposed by them. The three pairs are: welcome/thank, confess/forgive, mourn/comfort. I precede these three examples with a discussion of praise and condemn. Why do I list pairs? The format of pairing is not strictly necessary, but it does call attention to the therapeutic as a constant giving and receiving. The person who is teaching can be on either side of the pair, and the teacher and the learner can easily reverse positions. Giving can be understood as a form of receiving, and receiving as a form of giving. The healing occurs because of this flowing back and forth.[17]

This characteristic of the therapeutic cluster contrasts with the operation of the first set of languages in chapter 4. In storytelling, lecturing, and preaching, the teacher is much more clearly on one side. A lecturer might learn something from an audience, but it is nearly impossible for the teaching to flow smoothly in both directions. In the name of democracy some church congregations have tried "dialogue sermons." But without other changes in physical setting, clerical role, and congregational size, such dialogue tends to be awkward square pegs in round holes. When the educational setting invites stories, lectures, or sermons, there is nothing wrong with the teacher using these forms. But in the forms described here, the teacher is never entirely in control of which language and which side of the language is operating.

Praise and Condemn

This first pair of languages is both precondition and continuing theme for the other pairs presented. Praise and condemn form a link with the first family of languages. Praise and condemn may seem more appropriately linked to the sermon. Aren't praise and condemn what preachers do? Indeed preachers, as well as storytellers and lecturers, often do praise or condemn. But these two languages are dangerous on that side of the divide. Both praise and condemn should not be personalized, at least not too quickly. Preachers tend to condemn people, which is not what I have in mind. And even praise is not to be easily assigned to individual people. As *teaching* languages, praise and condemn start from an impersonal or nonpersonal basis. Most of the therapeutic languages have a strongly interpersonal character, but praise and condemn begin with an attitude toward the universe.

At stake in all the therapeutic languages is a freeing of the individual from its egocentric predicament. So long as a man or woman is striving to control the world, the self is not receptive to what the universe is offering. The cosmos is ready to teach, but the individual has to let go in order to learn. Aristotle believed that philosophy begins in wonder, in being awestruck by the miracle of existence. There are technical problems to be solved but why bother unless there is a sense of wonder about it all.

I use "to praise" to describe the language that is evoked by wonder and awe.[18] Praise is often given in the form of poetry or song; one sings a "hymn of praise." Religious people may imagine a definite object to the praise ("the creator of the universe"). However, in the soul of every man and woman lies a song of praise waiting to be brought forth. The praise is directed toward "all," the universe and every marvelous element within it. Why praise? True, it has no end, no function, no good to be attained. It simply is the special response of the human being to being human within a universe of surprise, beauty, and invitation.

Praise is thus concerned with both natural environment and human accomplishment. It is related to people's actions more than to people themselves. Who exactly should get "credit" for an action's good results is often not clear. With communal activity, an individual can take some pride in being integral to the praiseworthy actions. But the motivation for the individual ought not to be the receiving of praise.

Especially with children, praise should be used sparingly. The child has to learn that the reward for doing good is the good action, not the praise that may or may not follow. A child dependent on praise is vulnerable to a confusion of self-identity when the praise is absent. More important, the child who is doing his or her very best may not be able to accomplish much of what is praiseworthy. That may not be the child's fault; various social and environmental conditions may interfere with the child's efforts at successful actions.[19]

Ordinary life can gradually wear away the attitude that expresses itself in praise. The song no longer comes from the heart; all attention is directed to "making a living." Religions have insisted on the need for ritualized times that allow praise to be renewed. Festival days are celebrated annually; some religions set aside one day of the week. Six days may be devoted to making money, one day for being quiet at the center of life. The secularized version of the holy day is the holiday, although being off the job does not guarantee a nourishing of wonder, awe, and praise.

The term I have paired with praise is "to condemn." The relation is one of opposites. If the natural environment and human accomplishment are to be praised, then what destroys these realities should be condemned. The opposite of praise might seem to be blame. However, blaming carries the sense of personal focus. To blame individuals is to assign guilt for their actions. Aside from the imputation of legal guilt that society must use to defend itself, guilt is not for assigning by human beings. If human beings can be taught to recognize the impact of their actions, then they will accept responsibility, which sometimes includes guilt.

Good teachers do not condemn people, but they sometimes are outraged by situations that ought not to be tolerated. The capacity to feel joy that is expressed in praise implies the capacity to feel anger, outrage, and disgust. The two capacities do not have equal shares in life. What is to be condemned should be condemned directly and quickly; what is praiseworthy should be praised at length. The emotions connected to condemnation have to be carefully budgeted. In one direction, they can overrun an individual's life; in the other direction, they can be unworthily exhausted on trivial situations.

Despite the dangers in the act of condemning, there are times when a person has to say, "This is an intolerable situation that needs to be condemned." If young people are destroying their lives with drugs, if the poor are homeless in the streets, if the rivers and seas are being polluted, then a parent or a politician, a schoolteacher or a social worker, an economist or an environmentalist ought to get angry. Who exactly is to blame is of less importance than marshaling whatever forces are available for changing the situation.

There will be need for technical solutions to technical problems. But the motivation for such actions cannot just be reasonable calculation. David Hume thought that the basis for human ethics is "sympathy."[20] He thought that reason needs the drive of a powerful emotion. His point is well taken, so long as sympathy embraces more than the interpersonal. One has to sympathize with the suffering earth and sea, as well as with individual human beings. No human being is in a position to offer ultimate condemnation of another human being. Here again the child is the dramatic case in point. Whatever correcting of a child's behavior may be needed, the child's person is never worthy of condemnation. Even when the situation into which the child has been born is indeed deserving of condemnation, the child remains a being of illimitable potential. Human possibilities deserve to be praised at length. A realistic assessment of human failure has to be distinguished from a mean-spirited perception that does not let itself praise.

One of the most famous intellectual battles of this century pitted Reinhold Niebuhr against John Dewey. Niebuhr saw himself as the "realist," acutely aware of the arrogance and self-delusion that can corrupt the loftiest human projects. Dewey, however, wished to know why Niebuhr had "to believe that every man is born a sonofabitch even before he acts like one, and regardless of why and how he became one."[21] Niebuhr's attitude was based on the Christian doctrine of "original sin." That doctrine ought to be understood as a statement about the social conditions into which people are born rather than the imputation of a fault to the individual. If Christians want to cope with original sin, let them feed the hungry, clothe the naked, and provide shelter for the homeless.

To condemn situations that breed poverty, suffering, and shame says nothing against people having to "take responsibility" for their own actions.[22] Condemning a situation is never the whole story; but it is the initial step in intolerable cases, a release from a cramped rational calculation. If genuinely experienced, the next step can be vigorous action to relieve the intolerable situation.

Welcome/Thank

This pair of therapeutic languages, welcome/thank, are not opposites such as in the manner of praise and condemn. Rather, they are reciprocal and interlocking expressions. One leads to the other and then back again so that one could say thank/welcome or welcome/thank. The sequence is to some degree arbitrary, although I think that welcome/ thank brings out the relation a little better.

Like praise and condemn, welcome/thank can be directed to the universe as a whole and all manner of natural and human greatness. But unlike praise and condemn, welcome/thank deserves to be brought directly and fully to interpersonal exchanges. Welcome/thank exists not primarily in the song of a poet but in the carefully staged rituals of daily, hourly life. Civilized life could not exist without these fragile arrangements that structure the delicate give and take of human life. The other animals can rely on their built-in rituals of instinct; the humans have to maintain rituals of politeness, formalities that some people dismiss as silly and unnecessary.

Television's MTV produces a documentary series, "The Real World," on a group of young people living in an apartment. The program was initially advertised as "life as it really is, beyond the niceties of politeness." The assumption is a strange one that runs throughout much of modern ethics. If you wish to know what humans *really* are, put them in a lifeboat with no food or water for a week and then examine them when they wash ashore.

Teaching by welcome/thank begins from a different assumption. A welcoming receptivity is what greets the universe and all its surprises. The person who welcomes life, taking it in as it reveals itself, is freed from having to try to invent it every day. The human being remains human, not something absorbed into the rest of nature, but nonetheless moving with the rhythms of nature.

If welcoming is a basic attitude to life as a whole, then expressions of welcome to other human beings generally follow with ease. For friends, welcome is expressed in highly individual expressions; for strangers we need formulas that convey respect, lack of hostility, a readiness to be helpful. The formulas have to be simple and clear, though they are bound to cultural particularity. For an outsider to the culture, expressions of welcome may seem forced or silly. Being met at an airport by a stranger who lays some kind of necklace on you may not be your brand of welcome. Nonetheless, one can appreciate the significance of the gesture, and even the words in a language foreign to you.

A homey example is the U.S. custom of replying to "Thank you" with "You're welcome." The reciprocal character of welcome and thank is neatly captured in this exchange. However, for many speakers of British English this U.S. custom seems a bit ridiculous. Perhaps the phrase, "You're welcome," comes across with an ironic or cynical twist. Or perhaps it has the effect of abruptly ending an exchange in which one person has just extended a word of gratitude. This latter objection does have weight. What is a neat closure in one way of looking at things is also the breaking of dialogue. As for the former objection, the danger of cynicism in the phrase, that problem depends on the tone of the person using it. When some people say, "You're welcome," they convey welcome; other people suggest that they wish you had not bothered them.

In the cause of international understanding, I offer the following reflection. Perhaps the two parts are right but would make more sense if they were reversed. If the one person offered "You're welcome" before there was thanks, the cynical twist would largely be eliminated. The "thanks" is directed toward the experience of being welcomed. The first moment is welcome, the second is gratitude, the third is further welcome. Since the movement is a reciprocal and continuing one, the U.S. practice was not all wrong. Welcome is a kind of thanking and thanking is a form of welcome. Whoever says what first is less important than the recognition that we are thoroughly dependent on the kindness of strangers.

I do not expect U.S. custom to change in the direction I have proposed. However, a change has been occurring in recent decades. "You're welcome" seems to be on the wane. Other phrases are sometimes substituted, such as the jaunty "No problem." More often, the word "Thanks" is being met with "Thanks." This development can cause confusion among people who expect closure to the exchange. The nervous interaction sometimes runs, "Thank you. Thank *you. No,* thank you." Although there may be no clear logic in both parties saying, "Thank you," the wish to acknowledge mutual exchange is clear enough. And the scattering of "Thank you" in all directions (similar to Germans with the omnipresent *bitte*) is probably bringing U.S. and British English closer together.

As another example, take the phrase, "Have a nice day." When it arrived rather suddenly and aggressively on the scene, many guardians of the language reacted with horror and ridicule. But the phrase proved to have staying power. The main objection to the phrase was that it seemed to be an order. It replaced polite acknowledgment of gratitude with a command to feel a certain way (the word "nice" being especially grating). However, as the phrase has blended into ordinary speech, the well-intentioned meaning has become easier to accept: "[I wish that you might] have a nice day." A phrase such as "good-bye" probably once sounded a bit pushy: "[I wish that] good be with you as you go." Such expressions are the rituals of speech that carry good will, kindness, and willingness to care.

The thanking that is the correlative of welcome applies to the universe as a whole as well as to individual people. To the extent that someone feels welcome in the universe, the recipient of miraculous gifts, then expressions of gratitude are called forth. In Wittgenstein's statement cited above, thanking follows asking and leads to greeting and praying. In any genuine form of religion, praying is more about thanking than asking. Thanking is a human necessity, a response to being in the universe.

As with praise, religious people say "thanks" to God. For many people, the sudden removal of God from the map of life creates a vacuum. In *The Brothers Karamazov*, what worried Alyosha about the possibility that there was no God was "whom shall we thank, to whom shall we sing our song?" He goes on to ridicule the idea that "humanity" can simply step in as replacement.[23] And this century supplies considerable evidence that our abstract idea called "humanity" cannot bear all of the burden of religious devotion. The human race would have to go through a long process of concretizing gratitude in rituals that mutually relate men and women, humans and nonhumans.

Our ability to think at all depends on a receptive and thankful attitude that presents the world for our thank-ful response. Martin Heidegger playfully relates thinking and thanking, which comes across in English as well as in German's *denken* and *danken*.[24] Thinking is the human way of saying thanks. In our day, Heidegger and other philosophers have feared that thinking is being reduced to one form of calculating, technical rationality. We need a kind of thinking, with praise and embodying praise, that frees us to try out the range of languages.

The sequence and the precise formulas are not most crucial here. The therapy is in the interaction. We should welcome/thank with bodily presence and with whatever words best convey our attitude. Whenever our offer is reciprocated, then we heal and we are healed by the exchange. The language can be as simple as "yes" (or "uh-huh") said at a moment when affirmation is called for. With rituals of welcome and thanks, the human world goes on to the next day without interruption.

Confess/Forgive

The next pair of languages, confess/forgive, become necessary when human life does not flow smoothly. Human beings exist in the context of promises about the future. We all make agreements about how we will act. On occasion, we all fail to keep our promises. Sometimes the culpability is clear; because of fear, laziness, avarice, or other motives, we are guilty of breaking a promise. Sometimes other factors intervene that prevent us living up to the agreement. But very often we are in a gray area where we are not sure of our own guilt. Perhaps we could have kept the promise; perhaps it was too much to expect.

Whether or not we are guilty, humans need a ritual of confession to remove the burden. Hannah Arendt notes that only really bad people have good consciences; that is, they live behind a veil of culpable ignorance that hides them from guilt. The rest of us have at least a partial sense of our failings. Unless we can deal with that feeling, it threatens to become dead weight in all our actions.[25]

Confessing, similar to other therapeutic languages, is as wide in scope as the whole universe and as narrow as an individual saying, "Excuse me," for blocking an aisle. The premise of confession is that there has been a rupture in the life of a community. A balance needs to be restored and the individual needs to be brought back into the community. Traditional religions had elaborate rituals for this restoration, such as the scapegoat carrying away the faults, or the Catholic church's sacrament of penance. Even though the confession was directed to God, the community that suffered the disruption also had to heal its split.

In Jewish history, the symbol that carries the community's promise is "covenant." The people are related to God in being related to each other. One commentator on the story of Moses at Sinai says that there were 503,500 covenants, the supposed number of adult males at Sinai; no, says another commentator, there were 503,500 x 503,500 because the covenant is also between the people. The idea of covenant carries the element of covenant renewal, when the people recall their past failings and promise to do better. Confession of faults is made externally and verbally to the community or its representatives.[26]

The modern era secularized the idea of covenant and came up with the symbol of "social contract." The individual has an implicit agreement to live according to the laws of society. The law court becomes our confessional box and place of exoneration. If an individual throws him- or herself on the mercy of the court ("I plead guilty"), the penance is likely to be lessened. However, our courts are very limited in the kind of behavior they can judge. There is no confession/forgiveness for the daily failings in the interpersonal world. If there are not other rituals for confess/forgive, the professional psychotherapist will soon be needed to heal the splits within family, between friends, and on the job.

The ability to promise is at the heart of human life. Other animals do not make promises; only the humans can contemplate the future and place their lives in their hands. A handshake or a statement on a piece of paper is the foundation for many human ventures. Because we cannot know the future and because we do not fully know ourselves, we are bound to fail sometimes in living up to promises. Our stories, lectures, and sermons often include promises; praise and thanks also imply a world of promise. The restoration of what has been broken needs to be shown by a teacher if other teaching languages are to be effective.

Human trust is fragile; it depends on the trustworthiness of a person's words. A person who regularly tells lies undermines the whole social structure. The United States was founded on the basis of covenant or contract. Every new immigrant has to swear allegiance to that agreement. In this context, lying is considered an especially grievous failing. We often put people in jail for perjury about their crimes, rather than for those crimes. The only thing worse than telling a lie in this country is denying the lie when found out. Richard Nixon probably could have saved his political career in 1973–74 if he had just said, "I'm sorry. I told a lie." Numerous other people in public life could also have saved their souls, if not their powerful positions, by saying, "I'm sorry." And in the intimate exchanges of private life, love often requires (*pace* the line from *Love Story*) the simple statement, "I'm sorry."

The healing effect of confessing depends on its reception in the act of forgiving. The one who has been wronged is the one best able to do the forgiving. The act of forgiving re-creates the world. It "is the only reaction which does not merely re-act but acts anew and unexpectedly, unconditioned by the act which provoked it and therefore freeing from its consequences both the one who forgives and the one who is forgiven."[27] If no one in particular has been hurt, but the fabric of the community has been torn, then a representative of the group may provide a ritualized forgiveness.

What about between peoples or nations? The possibilities for confession and forgiveness become cloudy, especially when the passage of time is involved. Can a religious group confess its persecution of another group many centuries ago? Who exactly is doing the confessing and what exactly is being confessed? Should the European invaders of North America or Australia confess their guilt to the remnant of the native peoples? Perhaps in some cases a ritual asking of forgiveness would not be a bad idea if coupled with specific helps for the surviving population. The legal complications are often staggering.

Should German leaders ask Jews for forgiveness for the Holocaust? Perhaps a ritual of confession shortly after World War II would have helped to overcome the horror. At this point, with most Germans having been born since World War II, a national confession is not as meaningful as efforts to see that any similar horror never occurs again. On the Jewish side, survivors of the Holocaust have to consider their personal feelings of forgiveness toward individual people. The collective Jewish people is not in a position to issue generalized forgiveness.

The standard cliché is, "Forgive and forget," a strangely illogical phrase. If we were to forget, there would be no need to forgive. We forgive what we remember. Our hope lies in "re-membering," the gathering together of members, to forge a new unity. The memories are good and bad; both have to be preserved in the re-membering. Where we have failed, confession is called for; where others have failed, forgiving is called for. The readiness to forgive is acknowledgment that we are vulnerable to failure. The one who teaches by forgiving knows that in another place on another day he or she will have to teach by confessing.

Mourn/Comfort

The final pair of therapeutic languages is directly related to the final experience of life: dying. Unless we can talk about dying, then all of our other talk becomes veiled in illusion. Plato saw philosophy as a meditation on death. Traditional religions were centrally concerned with funeral rituals. Modern philosophy has been, in large part, a flight from death, a distancing of the self from remembrance of mortality. Since the most fundamental meaning of teaching is to show someone how to live and how to die, the flight from death is also a flight from teaching. Conversely, the languages of teaching must include the language of mourning and its correlative, the language of comforting.[28]

Nothing is more certain about human life than mortality. "They give birth astride a grave, the light gleams an instant, then it's night once

more."[29] As to the fact of death, the humans "die like all the animals";
as for meaning, however, the human being alone can foresee death and
can retain death both in memory and in outward results. "The gorilla,
the chimpanzee, the orang-outang and their kind, must look upon man
as a feeble and infirm animal, whose strange custom it is to store up
his dead."[30]

We mourn the death of someone we love; we also mourn our own
deaths in anticipatory ways. A teenager mourns the death of childhood;
a middle-aged man mourns the passing of youth (in more concentrated fashion than women do, it seems).[31] In these and other instances
throughout life, what seems dark and destructive is actually new life
trying to break through.

The feeling of grief and loss needs outward expression lest it turn
against the griever in the form of violence or depression. "Give sorrow
words; the grief that does not speak whispers the o'er fraught heart,
and bids it break." Paradoxically, the absence of joy is the sign of our
inability to mourn. Turned in on our own grief we cannot rejoice in
life or turn our attention to the hurts of others. Thus, the language of
mourning is crucial to all the other languages of teaching.

Like the other therapeutic languages, except more so, mourning requires a ritual. An era impatient with ritual has been especially hard
on the language of mourning. Geoffrey Gorer's study of grief in the
1960s found an almost total absence of ritual for mourning. He compares mourning in the twentieth century to sex in the nineteenth: no
one admits to it in public.[32]

In the last thirty years there has been some change; in fact, on the
surface there has been a lot of talk about death. The books of Elisabeth Kübler-Ross and the historical studies of Philippe Ariès, followed
by the extraordinary success of Sherwin Nuland's book, are a welcome
sign.[33] Courses on "thanatology" have become part of some school curricula. At the national level the Vietnam Memorial in Washington,
D.C., in stark contrast to the thrusting swords and guns of the other
war memorials, is a place of genuine, ritualized mourning. It is unclear,
however, how much has changed in the lives of individuals and groups
concerning their rituals of mourning.

Mourning is mostly waiting; at the most elementary level it consists
of a "no to death" followed by a "yes to death and no to life," and then a
"yes to life inclusive of death." All of that takes time. "Every cell of the
body must be informed of what has been lost." The middle of mourning

is a period of withdrawal in which the acceptance of death is symbolized by not taking part in ordinary life. Each of the religions specified a definite length of time for mourning and detailed prescriptions of dress, food, responsibility of friends, and so forth.[34]

The funeral rite in the past often mixed the living and the dead in ways bewildering to the modern consciousness. Describing nineteenth-century Irish wakes, S. J. Connolly writes, "To outsiders the results may have appeared incongruous and shocking; but they may also have relieved those who took part from some of the burdens of anxiety and guilt with which more modern modes of reacting to death have made us familiar."[35]

The modern cemetery, which dates from the mid-nineteenth century, was conceived as a way of hiding death. So also is the practice of embalming in the twentieth century and much else in the funeral industry. Religious rituals of death that look so strange to the outsider had the effect of holding together the community while the individual was temporarily cut off from life. When all such rituals disappear, we are returned again to the couch of the professional psychotherapist. For teaching to be effective, the remaining rituals of dying need preserving and new developments (for example, in relation to hospital technology) need careful shaping.

Comfort is what the ritual of mourning should bring. The ritual itself in supporting the mourner brings comfort. The words spoken by relations and friends are also comforting. "To comfort" means to bring strength. Death, which is our point of greatest vulnerability, can also be a source of strength. Usually, those who can best comfort are those who have learned to mourn. The comforter can sympathize with the mourner, which is itself strengthening.

The therapeutic languages tend to be fragmentary, indirect, and illogical. Often at funerals, the first thing said is, "I am sorry," which sounds like a confusion of comforting and confession. The point is to express some solidarity with the mourner. We reach for formulas because few people can come up with original and spontaneous statements.

The Book of Job is one of the world's masterpieces on the subject of grief and mourning. Harold Kushner says that Job's friends did two things right: they showed up and they listened. But the mistake they made was in assuming that when Job asked, "Why?" they should answer by explaining.[36] There are many right ways to comfort; there are a few wrong ways. One wrong way is to explain why the loss is for the best; another is to tell people not to feel bad. Both of these mistakes are often made with children.

Comforting is a simple process that greets us as one of the first things in life and, if we are fortunate, it accompanies us in the end. We begin and end life in silence. Comfort is what breaks the silence for the infant; the difficult transition from uterine to extrauterine life is managed with physical embrace and the language of lullaby. Similarly, at the end of life, there may be little to say, except "We are still here" or "I love you." The dying person who cannot converse may still be responsive to physical touch and to song.

Between birth and death we all need comforting for the hurts and crises that constitute the little deaths within life. When the first child goes to school or the last child leaves home, when a career falters or a marriage dissolves, when the body or the mind begins to weaken, then comforting the mourner is called for. A gesture and a few words give the grieving person a chance to heal. The saying, "Time heals all wounds," is not necessarily true but time is an ingredient in whatever healing is possible.

"You're on earth and there is no cure for that" can be a depressing thought if no word is spoken in comfort.[37] But for those who can mourn, it becomes the passage to new life. The young man in Edmund Wallant's *Children at the Gate* experiences the death and mourns the loss of his friend. At novel's end, "a blade twitched into his heart, beginning that slow, massive bleeding he would never be able to stop, no matter what else he might be able to accomplish. He was surprised and puzzled as he walked with that mortal wound in him, for it occurred to him that, although the wound would be the death of him, it would be the life of him too."[38]

Chapter 6

Teaching the Conversation

THE TITLE of this chapter can suggest an activity that encompasses the whole of teaching. Insofar as teaching refers to interaction in the human community, teaching is always a form of conversation. To be taught as a human being is simply to enter the human conversation. As one learns virtue by growing up in a virtuous community and one learns building by growing up in a building community, so one learns to converse by growing up in a conversing community. Or, put more simply, one learns conversation by joining the human race.

This chapter, however, is about a more specific kind of teaching. I have been examining the languages that can be sorted out within teaching situations. The two previous chapters have dealt with contrasting families of languages: the one where the community has a goal in view and helps the individual to move toward that goal; the other where the community is fragmented and the individual needs healing. The third family, to be discussed in this chapter, presupposes the other two. If the other two are imagined to run horizontally parallel, this third cuts across them vertically. In the other two cases, the teaching is in words but the words are still contiguous with bodiliness; in this third case, we have words on their own.

I have argued that choreography is a helpful image to describe the place of speech in teaching. At first, speech has the part of directing bodily action. However, speech itself can be taken as an action; thus one can have the choreography of speech. The teaching in this chapter is speech about speech; language is examined in relation to itself. This kind of teaching, not surprisingly, can be utterly vacuous. Nonetheless, it is the most specifically human form of teaching and potentially the most powerful. Richard Rorty notes that there are three ways to change a person's beliefs: change of perception, change of inference, and change of metaphor.[1] Only the third brings about radical change in people. This chapter is about changes of metaphor, an examination of the language of the language of teaching.

At first sight, the discussion may seem headed for high-level abstraction. Terms such as "second-order language" or "meta-language" are sometimes interjected here. But my aim is not to construct an artificial language above ordinary language. With language, as Hannah Pitkin says, we are sailors out at sea who can never put in to port to fix our boats.[2] Everyday speech is what is available for examining everyday speech. As the words are forced back on themselves, the result is not to abstract from the words but to go deeper down into the words. What are the controlling assumptions in any use of words? What is the meaning of a word and how far can the meaning change?

I said that this third family of teaching languages presupposes the other two. In regard to the first, storytelling, lecturing, and preaching involve a body of beliefs. The third family of languages does not reject those beliefs; neither does it accept them as true. Instead, the main question it raises is what these beliefs mean. The point would seem obvious that you have to have beliefs before you can criticize them. Nevertheless, much of modern criticism has not abided by that principle. Objecting to this modern approach, Peter Elbow says that "mental housecleaning by doubt" is futile.[3] He suggests as alternative that we "sleep around" with a wide range of ideas if only to find out what is in our minds. Then we can ask critical questions about keeping or throwing out an idea.

As for the second family, the therapeutic languages, we also need to have experienced them before we can ask questions about the meaning of the pattern. These languages free us from trying to reach the end of speech and they return us to the giving and receiving found in ordinary life. If we are obsessed with the realization of some future project, we do not have the mental space to attend to the present. I quoted Wittgenstein earlier that the best philosophy is the one that allows us to stop doing philosophy. He goes on in the same passage to say that philosophy consists of dealing with various problems that do not ever come to an end. The conversation of this chapter has no end, no predetermined endpoint that concludes the conversation.

The second family of languages, I argued in chapter 5, is always needed for the individual's healing of a fragmented self. The future is not denied; it is simply bracketed for the time being. What are the deeper implications of this stance? Can we live without an end? Nietzsche warned that "a man would rather will nothingness than not will."[4] A world cannot live on willing alone; neither can it live on not willing. This chapter reflects back on the relation between the first two families, one of willing and one of not willing. It asks about the meaning of their relation to each other.

While this third family draws its material from the first two, the relation is not entirely one way. The analysis of this chapter reverberates back on the previous two. Like therapeutic languages, this third family has no end beyond itself, but by penetrating further below the surface it can unlock more healing power in language. It breaks the chain of language that can interfere with the use of therapeutic languages.

This third family is also like the first in being concerned with reaching understanding. The mind is called into play in its most intense way. In the first family, the question is, What is the meaning of this text for our lives together? In this third family, the question is, What does it mean to ask the meaning of texts? Not this text's meaning or that text's meaning, but the meaning of the search for meaning. A new kind of advocacy emerges here, which does not look to the changing of social structures. The advocacy is linguistic: how to speak so that greater understanding is possible.

In a well-known passage of modern philosophy, Hegel writes,

> One word more about giving instruction as to what the world ought to be. Philosophy in any case always comes on the scene too late to give it.... When philosophy paints its grey in grey, then has a shape of life grown old. By philosophy's grey in grey, it cannot be rejuvenated but only understood.[5]

Hegel's contrast in this passage and its affirmation of understanding led to an even more famous statement by Karl Marx: "Up to now philosophers have only tried to understand the world, the point is to change it."[6]

Marx's opposition of understanding and change is a scandalous one from the point of view of teaching the conversation. At issue are the understanding of understanding and the image one associates with change. True, the understanding is not in the business of "giving instruction to what the world ought to be." Nonetheless, understanding — and its concomitant change of language — is not the alternative to change but a most powerful force of change.[7]

Understanding of this kind may require privileged spaces where other kinds of change are kept at bay. Many people grow impatient with an artificial segregation of "disinterested speech," that is, inquiry that temporarily suspends political and social engagement. Some eras become more insistent than others that all speech, to be genuine human speech, has to be rhetoric persuasive of political and social change. Language is pressed into the service of one overriding purpose.

Consider this comment by Stanley Fish:

> In ordinary contexts, talk is produced with the goal of trying to move the world in one direction rather than another. In these contexts — the contexts of everyday life — you go to the trouble of asserting that "x is y" only because you suspect that people are asserting that "x is z" or that "x doesn't exist."[8]

I have described in the previous chapter the "ordinary life" where a range of languages exist that are not arguments or explanations. Fish's ordinary life sounds exhausting in its contentiousness. Where is the praise, thanks, confessing, or mourning that is not asserted against anyone's assertion that "x is z"? The only point of "good morning" is to be pleasant. Most of ordinary life is speech that celebrates life — its shared sorrows and joys.

Fish's statement that "everything we say impinges on the world in ways indistinguishable from the effects of physical action" is particularly directed at sanctuaries of "free speech." He wants writers and professors to "take responsibility for our verbal performances," which is, I think, an admirable aim.

However, the argument that *everything* said has effects *indistinguishable* from those of physical action seems wildly overstated. The statement lacks precisely those careful distinctions that a reflection on speech — perhaps in a sanctuary of disinterested inquiry — might provide.

Truth and Meaning

One way to elucidate the issue is through the distinction between truth and meaning. The asserting of the truth "x is y" may be held in suspension while we examine the meaning of x. In an algebraic context, x is simply the name of one clear-cut reality; it either is or is not the equivalent of y. However, in ordinary life, the meaning of "love," "free speech," "equal opportunity," or "right to life" raises unsettling questions. Are we certain we know what we mean when we defend (or attack) free speech? Would we know what it meant to get equal opportunity? Could the right to life include a right to die?

As soon as such questions are asked, they reverberate across a web of related meanings. A term does not have its meaning in isolation. Words have their meanings in context; to understand the word is to be able to place it in context. The context or contexts spread out indefinitely to more and more participants in the conversation. If two people are speaking, the ambiguity in the meaning of any statement is held in check by innumerable factors of past history and present environment. The tone of voice and the facial expression are often the key to what is meant by the words. A person saying, "oh oh," can mean at least half a dozen things, but in any particular instance of utterance the meaning is usually clear.[9]

In a written document, especially one from the distant past, fewer guidelines are available for discerning the meaning. When Baruch Spinoza in the seventeenth century introduced the idea of distinguishing truth and meaning into the reading of the Bible, he found himself in a lot of trouble.[10] But an appreciation of the Bible demands an understanding of what the authors were attempting to write in its various books. To read Genesis, Job, and Song of Songs as if all three were the same kind of literature is to distort the meaning of all three. None of them consists of a series of assertions that "x is y." Even to read Paul's Letter to the Galatians and his Letter to the Romans without asking in each case who he was writing to, who he was fighting against, where he was writing from, and a dozen similar questions, will mislead the reader as to what each letter says.

It is amazing that the Bible has survived its defenders as well as its critics. The interpretive questions applied to that document are now widely used for other literature. Spinoza's distinction of truth and meaning can now be seen not as disrespectful of the text or as a flight from truth, but as the way to a deeper appreciation of the text. Frank Kermode, referring to both the Bible and other texts, says, "All modern interpretation that is not merely an attempt at 'recognition' involves some effort to divorce meaning and truth. This accounts for both the splendors and the miseries of the art."[11]

The distinction between truth and meaning allows for a playfulness with language. The truth is not to be toyed with; its opposite is falsehood, which should not be entertained. But meaning invites the play of imagination and the testing out of alternatives. To be sure, meaninglessness is no friend, but it is a threat only when we cannot live in the house of single sense and yet cannot imagine an alternative. We assign "play" to children and it is indeed their metier. Nonetheless, the ability to play is also the mark of a mature attitude. This third family of languages for teaching cannot be grasped — or lightly taken hold of — unless the teacher has an ironic sense of humor. To teach in this instance is to suspend asserting that "x is y," preferring instead to investigate playfully the meaning of x.

The child consciously enters the human conversation as he or she senses the mysteries, the wonder, the simple fun of human speech. When Wittgenstein proposed the metaphor of "game" for language, some people thought this comparison not serious enough. But many games are very serious, calling forth concentration, dedication, and staying power. One has to follow the rules to play the game, but within the rules all kinds of variations can be tried out. A living language is always inventing new words and occasionally bending the rules as life bubbles up and flows over. The guardians of proper speech sometimes take themselves too seriously, instead of moving with the rhythms of the game.

The child who is just learning to speak flows with the structure of the language, plucking out of the air the words that resonate with the soul and awaken consciousness. There are two ways to understand the relation between thinking and talking. Talking can be understood as thinking out loud. Or, thinking can be understood as talking to oneself. The child regularly talks to him- or herself; adults are usually embarrassed to admit that they do also. Talking out loud on the subway to no one in particular is not to be recommended; it is usually indicative that the person's life is empty of other people with whom to converse. But if one has human partners, then conversation with oneself is stimulated.

Knowledge begins not with an isolated consciousness but a conversation. Both Martin Buber's "In the beginning is relation"[12] and the New Testament's "In the beginning was the word" refer to the Book of Genesis where God creates by speaking. Who was God talking to? He was apparently talking to himself, although when he gets to creating humans, one interpretation of his "let us make man in our image" is that God was speaking to the other animals.

The child, in any case, is not averse to taking both parts in a conversation. Why does the child do that? To find out what he or she thinks. Thinking, says Plato, is "the conversation that the soul conducts with itself."[13] Contemporary thinkers, including Dewey and Wittgenstein, pick up this same theme. If the child's sense of play is not suppressed, later he or she will be able to look at language from several directions. Words will be material for thoughtful artistic play rather than vessels that encapsulate thought.

Dramatic Performance

One of the ways that language is played with in adult life is in dramatic performances. Indeed, the staging of drama is sometimes called a "play." The actors step into roles and pretend to be fictional characters who create a whole world within our everyday world. Plays can fall within the first two families of languages. That is, some plays have directly instructive purposes; they intend to convey a message. Plays that moralize by dictating simple solutions to life's heartbreaks do not usually last more than a season. Other plays may have a kind of message but it is about life's complexities. Plays that are great tragedies, Oedipus, King Lear, or Hamlet, do imply some purpose or end to human existence. They warn against destructive obsessions without telling us how we should live our particular lives.

Other plays seem to fit in with the therapeutic family of languages. These dramas are concerned with life's little foibles and how we cope with them. Such plays give us release, let us laugh at ourselves or rejoice in life's triumphs. No struggle toward life's goals is at issue. A comedy of manners by Molière, Chekhov, or Noel Coward provides us with delight, which is of no small importance in life and in teaching.

The play also lends itself to the third family of languages, concerned with teaching human conversation. In fact, the structure of drama is itself designed to fit this form of teaching. Although the play can serve as the vehicle for telling a story or providing therapy, it has the possibility of transcending both kinds of language to become a reflection on language itself. One can perform that reversal in a novel, a short story, or a poem, but in these cases one has to twist the form beyond its shape. Within a play, the play of language is already in place with the adoption of the format. The characters' existence is a play; so it is not surprising when there is a play inside a play.

Much of twentieth-century drama has become fascinated by the structure of the play and its relation to "reality." What happens when the actors on stage break down the wall that creates an audience and the audience becomes part of the play? Or, what happens when the characters in the play start reflecting on what it means to be characters in a play? Such situations are sometimes called Pirandellian (after one playwright who explored these possibilities), but the tendency is found in much of twentieth-century drama.[14]

Shakespeare has his plays inside of plays; in *Hamlet*, "the play's the thing wherein we shall catch the conscience of the king." In the twentieth century, we have Tom Stoppard's lifting out of Rosencrantz and Guildenstern; they then have their own play, within which is *Hamlet*. But now confusion is everywhere, not only in the characters of the play, but in the minds of the audience. We are left with Stoppard's dazzling word play. A typical Stoppard play is a wild sort of physical romp, together with philosophical ruminations on language. Of one of his plays, Stoppard writes, "The first idea I had was I'd like to write a play in which the first scene turned out to have been written by a character in the second scene. That was all I started with."[15] Plays of the twentieth century are not necessarily telling a story; they more often reflect on storytelling and other forms of speech.

A favorite form of this century, not surprisingly, is the comedy routine between a couple of characters who continually misunderstand each other. The pun calls attention to the ambiguities in language. Good routines by Laurel and Hardy or the Marx Brothers work with children and adults, work in the 1930s or the 1990s. The Marx Brothers deserve a linguistic study of their own.[16] Each of the brothers takes a different approach to the undermining of ordinary speech. Harpo reminds us that silence is part of speech, Chico regularly mangles the language, Groucho has the puns that endlessly delight. The worldwide collapse of Marxism suggests that Groucho is ultimately more subversive than Karl. And any course on the analysis of language could use Abbott and Costello's "Who's on first, What's on second, I Dunno's on third."

Perhaps the most revolutionary play of the twentieth century is *Waiting for Godot*. At one level it is a comedy routine in the manner of Abbott and Costello; the play is often acted by comedians. It is filled with outrageous puns and continual misunderstandings between the two clowns and between them and their visitors. The play goes nowhere in that the setting at the beginning and the end of both acts has the characters in the same place. This play and others by Beckett are pure conversation; the characters exist because they are held in by the play of voices. Sometimes it is unclear whether the voices belong to one person or a plurality of persons. The ambiguity is not a failure of the playwright. The characters themselves are often unsure if the voices in their heads are coming from outside. The tape recorder plays a prominent part in several plays. Is the voice on the recording another person or the same person at another time? Is that a meaningful question?

Perhaps the purest form of Beckett's plays is reached in *Endgame*. The text can be read as a conversation within one person's head (the set design of the play appears as a head with the two main characters as eyes) or as a conversation between two people who cannot separate. The content of the play is play, with the two characters commenting on the play they are in. The human race seems to have disappeared. "Why do I stay with you?" asks the character Hamm. "For the conversation," is the answer. Or as Estragon says in *Godot*, we are "incapable of keeping silent." The plays of Beckett and Ionesco in the 1950s were sometimes called "theater of the absurd." In fact, however, they are very rationally constructed plays that force us to reflect on the nature of conversation.[17]

Note that the play is not simply the text that comes from the playwright. The stage directions and the set design become part of the conversation, too. The whole performance is what is choreographed. Beckett was almost fanatical in his demand that directors abide by his directions for the set, lighting, and movement. In a staged play, the "teacher" is not an individual but the interplay of actor with actor, actors with audience.

Dialectical Discussion

For the second language I use the somewhat technical philosophical term "dialectical." My aim is to use a term that can in fact include philosophical thinking but can also embrace ordinary discussions that bend back on the meaning of the terms in use. In the middle of a conversation between friends, the question might be heard, "What do you mean by that?" If not a hostile question, it is likely to engage the speakers in a dialectical discourse. Eric Havelock says that dialectic arose when a speaker in Greece was asked to repeat himself. The very act of repetition — one cannot reproduce exactly a set of statements —

sets up a dialectical exchange within the speaker and disturbs the single strand of speech.[18] Dialectical refers to their being two voices and a movement from one to the other. In that sense, dialectical discussion is just another name for dialogue. I am using "dialectical," however, to indicate a more reflective use of language and a concerted effort to find the meaning of the words in the dialogue.

One might also speak here of debate or argument so long as we are still referring to a quest for meaning rather than the scoring of points against an opponent. In philosophy, as in the rest of life, questions are sometimes a cover and a dodge. The questioner is using language merely as a tool for polemical purposes. When Michel Foucault was asked why he avoided polemics — issuing harsh judgments on other people and their views — his admirable response was, "Questions and answers depend on a game — a game that is at once pleasant and difficult — in which each of the two partners takes pain to use only the rights given him by the other and by the accepted form of the dialogue."[19]

The term "dialectical" is probably best known through its prominence in Marxism. For Marx, dialectical refers not to peaceful discussion but to the conflicts of class warfare. Marx borrowed the term from Hegel, who had posited a movement of history through the dialectical synthesis of opposites. Since Marx claimed to turn Hegel upside down (from philosophy standing on its head to standing on its feet), the relation between the two thinkers is itself dialectical. Thus, Marxism is part of a dialectical discussion about the meaning of "dialectical"; and other disciples and opponents of Hegel (for example, Kierkegaard) also become part of the dialectic.

Many people trace the idea of dialectical back to Socrates (or to a slightly earlier era; Aristotle traces it to Zeno the Eleatic). Socrates engaged people in intense discussions that open into a larger philosophical conversation. Socrates did not have much time for protecting reputations, though he also did not engage in ad hominem attacks. Aristotle carried forward the process in more orderly fashion by arranging the views of previous thinkers on particular topics. Dialectic became the mode of argument in the Middle Ages, starting with Abelard's *Sic and Non*, which showed that the church fathers had contrasting views on many topics. The scholastic method at its best (for example, in Aquinas's *Summa*) was a conversation that encompassed the centuries. The method often involved debate. One of the rules of debate was that you had to state your adversary's position, to his satisfaction, before giving your own.[20] This rule would still be helpful to contemporary debate. One would be forced to see the world from the other's perspective; the debate would likely be more thoughtful.

Political life at its best has some of the qualities that are associated with philosophical inquiry. The first responsibility of the political assembly is not that of passing laws or of making speeches. Rather, it is to be a forum that asks about the meaning of our lives together. In contrast, a politics that is based solely on polls and consumer goods is in danger of being swallowed by therapeutic speech, while being surrounded by ineffective lectures and sermons.

A political official cannot just be out to satisfy the people's needs. What constitutes real need can only surface in reflective discussions. "Human subjects have no privileged access to their own identity and purposes. It is through rational dialogue, and especially political dialogue, that we clarify, even to ourselves, who we are and what we want."[21] And although harsh polemics ought not to be the heart of political dialogue, there is plenty of room for disagreement. A culture is not so much a place of common values as a place that has the means for allowing disagreements that do not destroy political life.

Dialectical discussion proceeds by oral exchange and by reading that is respectful of the otherness of the text. Learning to read so that one learns from opponents is a skill necessary to the survival of a living tradition. In a dialogue, an author's voice may have been silenced by death but his or her text still has power to speak. That power is in turn dependent on the willingness of someone to listen. The living thinker has to be gracious and receptive to the text. If the other person's written statements seem absurd, perhaps we have not yet understood them. Sometimes we will find that letting in a strange voice from the historical record will awaken a strange voice within ourselves.

Dialectical discussion is the immediate preparation for academic criticism, which is the topic to be discussed in the next section. By reading books or by listening to a discussion, a student can observe a play of conflicting ideas. One of the worst things about "textbooks" is that most of them have no texts, that is, original pieces of writing by thoughtful individuals. In what are called textbooks, the differing thoughts of reflective people have been boiled down into a thin soup. Most textbooks are veiled sermons rather than dialectical discussions. They give little sense of minds struggling to get a ray of light on complex matters that may not have solutions.

What the student has to find in genuine texts and in oral debate is the play of ideas, the fact that people of fine intelligence and good will imagine different worlds. John Stuart Mill, a champion of human debate, writes, "What Cicero practiced as the means of forensic success requires to be imitated by all who study any subject in order to arrive at the truth. He who knows only his side of the case, knows little of that."[22] Sometimes in a political debate two individuals simply represent their party's orthodoxies. The result is more sermon than dialectical discussion. The same can happen in discussions between economists, psychologists, or social theorists. The spectator, who is trying to learn, is simply asked to choose sides and then he or she will have the truth.

Even when this attitude structures a debate, there may be moments when a breakthrough occurs. If each party is interested in truth, then the play of ambiguous meaning is liable to peek out. Can the one person simply imagine what it would be like to view the world from the other's point of view? If so, the debate will include dialectical moments, the granting of some truth to a position different from the speaker's.

Paradoxically, this recognition is often easier to get when the two parties have very different positions. A Freudian and a Jungian may be able to recognize that they start from differing assumptions, while spokespersons for two Freudian schools may find it more difficult to grant their opponent's legitimacy. Christians find it easier to acknowledge Buddhism's different truth than to grant Judaism's right to a distinct existence. Protestant and Catholic Christians have at times killed each other over doctrinal differences that to the outsider can look slight.

Academic Criticism

The last language in this last family of languages is academic criticism. As the very last, it incorporates all of the previous ones, which gives it its potential. As the furthest example along a process of turning language back on itself, academic criticism can be the most vacuous of languages. This characteristic is reflected in the frequent reference to something as "merely academic." For much of the population, academic matters are trivial or unreal. It could also be the case that public figures dismiss academic matters as trivial so that they will not have to be challenged by academic criticism. My intention in this section is to show

how academic criticism can be among the most powerful of teaching languages.

As is true of the other languages in the third family, academic criticism presupposes the other two families. Without stories, lectures, sermons, and the like, academic criticism would have nothing to work on. Without a sense of the therapeutic, academic criticism could not achieve the distancing it needs, the suspension of belief and disbelief in stories, lectures, and sermons.

Academic criticism is also different from and similar to the other two languages in this chapter, dramatic performance and dialectical discussion. Academic criticism shares with them the calling into question of language itself. It may have some drama about it but it is not cast into separate roles for several players. It shares with dialectical discussion the conversation with great minds of the human race. But whereas in dialectical discussion the student is a spectator to Nietzsche discussing Kant, or Heidegger's writing on Nietzsche, in academic criticism the student is a participant. His or her words are the focus of the criticism.

Given this contrast to dialectical discussion, academic criticism is in one respect more personal, in another sense more impersonal. By becoming a participant in the conversation, the student is more personally involved. However, a distance is still allowed by the fact that it is not the student but rather the student's written and spoken words that are the direct object of concern. Criticism ought not to be personalized; the student should be able to get out of the way.

In ordinary speech, the term "criticism" usually has negative connotations. When someone offers "constructive criticism," the adjective has to be insisted upon to indicate that the intent is not destructive. This reputation for the negative is not without foundation. Although the ultimate hope is for a positive effect, to criticize is to call into question part of the established world. What up to this time was simple fact or assumed truth has its foundation undermined. The fact or truth in question may survive this challenge but it can never be accepted again in the same way.

Criticism therefore has its dangers both for what is criticized and for the critics. People who criticize should not be surprised to find themselves on the receiving end of criticism, one that is not necessarily restrained by an academic intention. "Let us admit the case of the conservative," writes John Dewey. "If we once start thinking, no one can guarantee what will be the outcome, except that many objects, ends and institutions will be surely doomed. Every thinker puts some portion of an apparently stable world in peril, and no one can wholly predict what will emerge in its place."[23]

Dewey's contrast here between "conservative" and "thinking" is not really fair. Most people, including those who call themselves liberal, would be more cautious today in setting up such an opposition. The act of criticizing may indeed come from the liberal side, but the material for criticism has to come from conserving the past. Another way to make the point is that we cannot live on criticism alone. Michael Oakeshott writes that "*ceaseless* criticism never did anyone or anything any good; it unnerves the individual and distracts the institution."[24]

One way forward out of conservative-liberal stalemates is to tie down criticism to the words of a particular text. One has to engage the texts before criticizing them. And after criticism, texts do not disappear; they often flower in meaning. "Liberal" need not mean rejection of the past in favor of an uninvented future. The impression has sometimes been given that the enemy of a liberal approach to learning is tradition and traditional beliefs. "Liberal" would then mean coming up with new *thoughts.* However, if one attends not to thoughts but *words,* then "the new does not emerge through rejection or annihilation of the old but through its metamorphosis or reshaping."[25]

Academic criticism, like every other language of teaching, presupposes a community. The phrase "academic community" is tossed about as casually as those other "communities" that clamor for public support. The phrase "academic community" is both an assertion of positive cohesion and an opposition to the give and take of most areas of life where academic criticism would be dismissed. The cohesiveness of a particular group of scholars or the world of scholarship is quite fragile. The practice of academic criticism presupposes knowledge, discipline, and care for one's colleagues. When there is no sense of community, then criticism quickly turns cynical and self-serving; it becomes a sharp knife that does harm in ad hominem attack.

As most small communities are, academic community is raised in opposition to the wider society. Those who practice its academic language often feel like a beleaguered few. Outside of some guarded preserves, the language of academic criticism is not often found. But although the larger society may sometimes seem the enemy, society's political and economic arrangements provide those guarded preserves of academic life. An all-out attack on society is neither fair nor gracious. No area of society is exempt from criticism, but the criticism ought to be measured, focused, and fair. It should be a radical questioning of specific policies and institutional arrangements.

As the double negative is the sign of therapeutic speech, so the ironic question is the mark of academic criticism. The teacher wishes the listeners to hear their own questions and bend back on the ambiguities in the words. If a teacher asks a straightforward question, it is likely to draw forth information, *the* answer. If the question is a bit shocking and forces the listener to consider whether the teacher is really serious, then the question forces deeper questioning.

Consider the case of a famous speech by Philipp Jenniger on the occasion of the fiftieth anniversary of Kristallnacht, the beginning of the Holocaust. Jenniger was at the time speaker of the West German parliament. The audience, I imagine, was ready for therapy in the form of confession and mourning, combined with a bit of a sermon. Jenniger did those things at beginning and end, but in the middle he tried some academic criticism, a move with disastrous consequences.

His remarks caused a worldwide uproar. The headline in Italy was "Anti-Semitism in the German Parliament," in the Netherlands "Hitler Worship Causes Mayhem in the Bundestag." His well-intentioned speech turned out to be disastrous because the conditions were not there for academic speech. In proper academic form, Jenniger asked a series of ironic questions that included: "And as for the Jews, hadn't they in the past sought a position that was not their place? Mustn't they now accept a bit of curbing? Hadn't they, in fact, earned being put in their place?"[26] The members of the audience that evening were not ready to be academic students. Jenniger's failure "had been to misjudge the occasion, which called for a memorial, not 'a sober historical speech.'"[27]

The academic dialogue is between teacher and students. This dialogue can and does go on in other places, but the classroom is the established place for this language. Conversely, other languages show up in the classroom but academic criticism should be the centerpiece of classroom instruction. In the following chapter, I will distinguish the school from other educational forms. I will also distinguish the school from the classroom that is within the school. The mix of languages in the school differs from the classroom mix. Most often, classroom speech cannot sustain two hours or even fifty minutes of academic criticism. But a classroom without academic criticism is not functioning as a classroom.

In academic criticism, the main point of reference is to the student's own words. Of course, the exchange will be the more valuable if students are in touch with a variety of sources for the topic at hand. In educational discussions, phrases such as "experiential learning," "student-centered learning," or "self-directed learning" can be slogans for avoiding the hard work of finding out what the human race has said about science, politics, religion, love, family life, literary theory, gardening, diet, animal breeding, or any other topic. In eras of rebellion against any formality to education, and especially against academic knowledge, teachers are supposed to avoid demanding that students actually know something about the topic being discussed. Great hope is placed in the sharing of uninformed opinion.

In previous chapters I have insisted that most learning takes place in educational forms other than schools and classrooms. We mainly learn about family life by growing up in families; we best learn about animal breeding by breeding animals; we best learn gardening in gardens. But in this chapter I am speaking in support of one peculiar language of teaching called "academic criticism." This language cannot succeed unless all the conditions for its use are present. A teacher cannot offer academic criticism unless the student does the work of bringing some kind of formed knowledge to the arena of criticism.

The student who has read books or essays, has listened to stories, lectures, and sermons, will have formed particular views on the subject at hand. The teacher in this setting — the critic — invites the student to bring forth his or her words. "Put your words on the table between us" is the explicit or implicit request of the teacher.

Very likely, the student will initially resist; no one wishes to have his or her views exposed to withering attack. The teacher has to show in practice, over a lengthy period of time, that he or she is trustworthy. The teacher, while offering pointed criticism, will treat the student's words with respect. The teacher's challenge does not go beyond the words on the table. The student's thought world is not directly accessible to the teacher or, for that matter, to the student either. What is out in the open for criticism are the student's words.

The teacher's job is to propose a redesign. As I noted in earlier chapters, the sequence is not teacher gives, student receives. Instead, student acts, teacher studies design, teacher proposes redesign, student tries out the new design; then the process begins again. This sequence holds true in academic criticism. Student speaks or writes, teacher listens, teacher criticizes, student tries out new design. And again, the teacher's design is not in generalities or hesitant suggestions. The teacher says, "I know what I am talking about. Try this out and you will find it an improved design of your speaking or writing."

The teacher does not begin with the premise that "I am knowledgeable and you are ignorant." The premise is, "We both know and we both are limited in our expression of the truth. But I have a better way of speaking and writing than you do. I am not necessarily a better person and there are other areas where you could be the teacher and I the student. Nevertheless, on this academic topic I have spent years learning the language. Where I am convinced you are wrong, I will not let it go by. Where you are right, I will propose distinctions to enrich the meaning of your statements." When two informed people strongly disagree, the issue is not usually truth against falsehood. One side is richer in meaning because the metaphors assumed on that side allow more comprehensive and consistent meaning.

The search is to understand the words between us and to distinguish meanings in a way that leads to greater understanding. The teacher does not try to change the student or the student's thinking, only the student's words. Why should the student be convinced? For two reasons: the history of the words and their geography. The two sources are not entirely separable; history asks how the meaning has changed throughout the past and geography asks how the meaning changes from one group to another in the contemporary world.

For example, to understand "nature" one has to know how the term has shifted in meaning over the centuries and what its various meanings are today. There are things the student can say of nature that are simply false; there are other things that might be true but not revealing. And there are other ways of speaking that have been common but are misleading and unhelpful (for example, continuing to use "nature" or "natural world" as synonymous with the nonhuman world). The teacher's job is to show that some ways of speaking about nature open new understanding and lead to profoundly practical conclusions.

The academic teacher thus is an advocate, an advocate of certain ways of speaking. In the academic world, the most common way to classify speech is description or prescription. The only choice offered in this contrast is between a neutral statement of fact and a statement of how things ought to be. The metaphor is borrowed from the medical profession. Within the assumptions of this language, a person has a problem and goes to a physician. The patient delivers a description of the facts, or even better, a machine measures the problem numerically. The physician then writes out a prescription that gets filled by the pharmacist.

Teaching as linguistic advocacy borrows its metaphor from the legal profession. Within this language, the teacher as advocate of language *neither* describes nor prescribes. Human language, excepting mathematics, will already have cast the issue into language that is not neutral or merely factual. But the teacher's job is not to prescribe a solution; most times there is no solution. The teacher can only advocate a way of speaking, plead a case before the jury. In advocacy, if one approach does not work, another can be tried. At the end, some of the jury may remain unconvinced. Those willing to try the position advocated may find their lives slightly bettered; they are the ultimate judges.

Two last claims must be noted about this process of academic criticism, one concerning age, the other gender. To turn the words back on the words and poke about for underlying metaphors may sound like a teaching strategy fit only for esoteric courses in the university. However, my intention is to describe academic work with any students of any age. Indeed, 6-year-olds may be better at this game than some 26-year-olds. Children are still in touch with the sound and feel of the words; human conversation is still an interesting new discovery. In contrast, the 26-year-old graduate student (or 56-year-old professor) may have become immunized against the excitement of words, their connotations and ambiguities.

People described as "intellectuals" are sometimes good at manipulating ideas but lack attentiveness to the words. If such people teach in schools — whether primary, secondary, or tertiary — their classrooms become places of prescribed ideas. University students find ways to cope with this problem (change courses, be absent, daydream in class). Six-year-olds have less protection; they may be forced to listen to one person all day. It is therefore more imperative for second-graders than for university students that classroom teaching be restricted to examining the words that the student willingly brings forth.

My other point concerns a possible gender bias in the invitation to "put your words on the table between us." Is that a typically male invitation? If the words were necessarily separated from personal investment and feeling, perhaps so. My description of academic advocacy allows for varying degrees of emotional investment in the words. I think there may be gender bias in the assumption that "to teach is to explain" or "to teach is to give reasons for." Not that women teachers or women students are incapable of participating in such a process. However, women have historically embodied a wider and richer meaning of "to teach" than the simple equation of "to teach is to explain."

However one describes the difference between genders, advocacy of linguistic change is at least as important today for women as it is for men. Numerous feminist studies are about women finding "voice," of women having full participation in ethical, political, and academic discussions.[28] The invitation in a classroom to bring forth words may not find equal response in a group of boys and girls. Schools have a responsibility to study this issue. Schoolteachers are only beginning to discover the many biases in the educational system that discourage girls from having equal voice with boys in the classroom.

Three Examples

I finish this chapter with three examples, appropriately drawn from previous chapters. Since academic criticism presupposes the other two families of languages and the siblings within this third family, my examples are a return to previous examples with attentiveness to the ambiguity of the words. The examples are "America" from the first family, "development" from the second family, and "to teach" from all three families.

As one form of storytelling, I cited the myth of America. Practically everyone who grows up in the United States is enveloped in this story, even people who have little share in the freedom and wealth recounted in the story. The story conveys a message of hope, particularly to a person growing up or to a newly arrived immigrant. Most public schools begin the day with the religious ritual of saluting the flag. The history, social science, and literature texts are saturated with talk about "America."

I do not see anything generally wrong with this story. It holds together hundreds of millions of people who have little else in common. As a unifying religion, it can soften the conflict that comes from other religions and ethnic diversity. The story turns bad only when intellectual leaders exercise no academic criticism and unthinkingly interchange "United States" and "America." Academic criticism should be aware of the history and geography of terms. Obviously, America and United States are not co-extensive. In time, America is two and a half times the age of the United States; in its geographical meaning (North, South, Central), America is two and a half times as large as the United States.

Academic writing or university teaching that does not regularly distinguish between the United States and America is enveloped in myth. The myth has been a destructive one for Latin America and for other countries as well. The scandalous fact is that the distinction is very seldom acknowledged in scholarly writing. The failure of the left-wing critics is far more shocking than their right-wing opponents. An endless stream of books attacking America goes nowhere. Unless one criticizes specific policies of the United States and its government, what we have is not academic criticism but preaching.

The second example from the therapeutic language family is "development." It is a way for people to talk about almost any kind of advancement. It is not only a modern term; it helps to define what modernity means. We live in what we conceive to be a modern world because we assume that things progress, advance, or develop. Development has become a backdrop of hope that everything will be fine if we keep out of the way and let things take their course.

I do not think that development is a bad idea. We probably cannot manage without some such metaphor of hope that things will get better. But the idea easily degenerates into mindless ideology unless it is subjected to academic criticism. What is badly needed is to understand the "development of development." The history of the term's rise since the eighteenth century needs to be traced. And its geography includes two fields of usage that almost never intersect: economics and psychology. Academic criticism ought to find out how these two uses are related. The failure to explore the relation of these two worlds of development leaves both uses vulnerable to illusion. Is it possible that economic development is a psychological blindspot? Is it possible that psychological development is a rich person's way of looking at things?

The third example, "to teach," comes from this chapter and the book as a whole. The most detailed example I have of academic criticism is what I have done with "to teach." I have tried to break open a too narrow conventional meaning of "to teach." My route has been both history and geography.

Historically, I have brought in voices on teaching from Greek philosophy and ancient religions. I adverted to the etymology of the term and a thousand years of ordinary usage. I have tried to show a narrowing process since the eighteenth century which has created a moral crisis in the meaning of "to teach." I have referred to philosophers in this century who are allies in my attempt to retrieve the meaning of "to teach."

The geography of teaching is the other main source for resolving the moral crisis of "to teach." I pointed out the great variety of instances of teaching. The universe and all its life forms teach those who are ready to learn. Animals teach each other to behave in certain ways. The human community is always teaching, mostly in ways that are not directly intended. Even when the human individual intends to teach, much of the teaching, for better or worse, is outside the intended effect. Human teaching usually includes a verbal element, although initially the words have the function of directly commanding bodily behavior. To this point, there is seldom a moral problem with teaching. The learner signals what he or she is ready to learn; the teacher shows how to do what the learner wishes to do.

Conclusion

These three chapters, comprising part 2 of this book, have examined language when it takes on a specifically human character of being separated from bodiliness. The teacher now has to choreograph not a movement of body but a movement of language. And the crucial moral decision is to get the appropriate language or languages for the particular occasion of teaching. The learner provides the license, often signaled through an institutional arrangement.

Depending on whether I walk into a chapel, a classroom, or a counselor's office (all three might be in the same school building), I indicate what kind of language I am ready to hear. If I go into a therapist's office, for example, I give permission for questions that intrude on my privacy, a permission that I do not give by crossing the threshold of a classroom. We would recognize a moral problem if a therapist were regularly to say, "That's terrible; don't do that." We less easily recognize the corruption of teaching when taken over by preachers of "feeling good." Or we do not grasp the moral problem of professors telling students what to think about the world.

The first and second families of language are concerned with speech that is separated from bodiliness, but the relation to the body is still immediate. In the first case, the language appeals to the understanding and will that flow from and toward an integral communal existence. In the second case, the appeal is to those forces of life that reestablish a healthy relation of mind and body, individual and community. The success or failure of the teaching can usually be judged by tangible results in bodily activity.

The third family is one step removed from bodily life; its immediate contact is not with the body but with other languages. Its first concern is with meaning, not truth, with intellectual understanding, not physical activity. It is not neutral toward forms of love, work, politics, religion, and every other sphere of life; it is a questioning of every form. It advocates ways of speaking that would let loose better forms of life. Its positions are not demonstrably correct but neither are they merely idiosyncratic. They arise out of conversation with humanity. With no one in principle excluded, the conversation is with whatever part of the human race is available. This form of teaching can never replace the other forms, but with their help it can transform the world.

Part Three

Chapter 7

Educational Forms of Teaching

I N THIS CHAPTER I address a theme that up to this point I have put aside, namely, the meaning of "education." My procedure may seem backwards in that most writing on teaching shows up within what is taken to be the main question: education. It is assumed that if the nature and purpose of education are clear, the meaning of teaching easily follows. I do not think that there is anything necessarily wrong in proceeding from education to teaching; the two meanings are intertwined. Unfortunately, however, debates about education have not led to a richly textured meaning of teaching, but instead have implied one very narrow meaning of teaching.

It seemed worth a try, therefore, to begin with teaching separated from any institutional assumptions about education. At the least, attention to teaching would not be shortchanged. In addition, a richer meaning of teaching might provide a novel perspective on the ambiguities of "education." If someone were to say that I have assumed a meaning of education from the beginning of this book, I would not dispute the claim. But that implied meaning of education can now be articulated better with the help of a comprehensive meaning of teaching.

Jacques Barzun, introducing a collection of his essays, writes, "Forget education. Education is a result, a slow growth, and hard to judge. Let us rather talk about teaching and learning."[1] I can almost agree with his first sentence, except that he does not follow his own advice in the second sentence. Instead of saying, "Forget [for a while] education. Let us talk about teaching and learning," he cannot resist saying in the middle sentence what education is. And the two references he makes, "slow growth" and "result," mirror the confusion of so much writing on education. The two images do not go together and each of them represents a misleading way to describe education.

In the first half of this chapter, I propose a comprehensive and consistent meaning of "education." I wish to argue that education is an interaction of forms of life; this set of relations is the most adequate way to comprehend education in the past and to address the needs of today. In the second half of the chapter, I name the most important forms and describe the pattern of a lifelong and lifewide education.

Meaning of "Education"

There is no single "true meaning" of education. Like "teaching," and any other important word in the language, the meaning is found in use. One has to trace the usage both historically and geographically. Historically, the perspective has to include etymology and the shifts in meaning throughout the ages. Geographically, one has to examine the meaning of education assumed by various groups today. Those groups that most control the definition of the term may be excluding voices that should be heard. While definitions of "education" are all too plentiful, they tend to leave out what is most interesting, what makes "education" a fighting word and a word worth fighting about.

Throughout the world "education" remains a word of almost magical power. No politician makes speeches against education. There appears to be unanimity that education is supremely important.[2] Yet this seeming agreement is accompanied by intense frustration and disappointment. At least since the nineteenth century, education has been the great hope that never seems to fulfill its promise.

During the last century and a half, education has been closely identified with schools for children. Writers on education often use the terms "education" and "school" interchangeably, although if they were challenged they would acknowledge a difference. It is assumed that while education can be acquired elsewhere, school is the place that is deliberately and intentionally set up for education. The "professional educator," therefore, tends to talk of education as what you get in school, or at least what is supposed to be available for the getting in school. It is said that school is a mere means; education is the result. Or, for other writers, education is the process of learning that the school should serve.

One common distinction in the twentieth century, which seems to acknowledge the difference between school and education, is "formal" and "informal" education. But "formal education" tends to be a fancy name for school; every other aspect of education is left formless or amorphous. The school retains all the power by reason of appropriating "formal"; nothing else is given an educational name, except otherness to the one form of school.

Religion provides an instructive comparison here. The religions of the world are not adequately described by naming one's own (form of) religion and then waving in the direction of otherness. There can only be dialogue between different forms of religion, not between form and informality. The world of religion is not adequately described by "Catholic and non-Catholic," "Jewish and Gentile," or "Christian faith and world religions." Caught up in our own language, we might not realize that "non-Catholic" is a Catholic word, or that "Gentiles" exist only for Jews, or that Christians have to join the world's religions before speaking with any particular one of them.

The world of education, like religion, does not consist of one form and amorphous otherness; instead, there is a multiplicity of forms. The language of formal and informal education cannot lead to a serious conversation between several forms of education. The distinction between formal and informal does little to illuminate how people have actually been educated. With only the language of formal/informal, it is simply impossible to explore what *forms* of education have existed and still exist.

When David Elkind wrote, "The idea that there are many different forms of education is one of the most important insights we can glean from the observation of young children," I could not agree more. But his very next sentence is bewildering: "The children described so dramatically by Maria Montessori were engaged in *informal* education, an education in which the materials are self-didactic." Of all people to choose for illustrating "informal," Maria Montessori was almost obsessively attentive to form. Yes, children are taught by the (carefully arranged) things in the environment; the form is the most critical element. Elkind is puzzled that people do not see the importance of informal education, that they think "all education is formal education."[3]

Perhaps people think that "all education is formal education" because the term "education" necessarily connotes formalities: forms of time, place, materials, and the relation of organism and environment. I share Elkind's objection to the idea that education means a classroom with an adult at the front explaining things to children. We need other rooms, other languages, other age groupings, other material than that image conveys. In brief, we need to name and explore other forms of education in addition to classrooms for children.

Before the rise of modern education and the assignment of children to school, education had no single form or clearly defined age range. Its meaning usually did have reference to an immature being in need of guidance toward maturity. The age of the learners was not limited to 6- to 16-year-olds. At the beginning of *Emile*, Rousseau cites the poet Varro for the two Latin words that give us "education:" "Educit obstetrix, educat nutrix." The midwife begins the leading out (*educere*), the nurse continues by nurturing (*educare*).[4] All of that happens before the child is of "school age."

Schools have not always existed; at the times and in the places they have existed, they have been only one of the institutions involved in education. It is also of more interest than historical curiosity that in its early usage the word "education" was not restricted to human life; an animal or a plant could also be educated.[5] Education had to do with forms of life and the relation between those forms.

Education in premodern times operated mainly through traditional family patterns, religious doctrines and rituals, and apprenticeship for one's station in life. With the rise of the modern sciences and a concomitant criticism of religion, educational reform was needed. The teacher as trained expert came to the foreground. What the emerging world looked for was explanations based on laws discernible by reason. For the founders of Western Enlightenment, the school was the new temple; where religion had failed in the areas of personal knowledge, good behavior, and social order, success would come through "education" (that is, the school).

In the North American colonies, the ideal of universal schooling was already enunciated by the middle of the seventeenth century. Every town of fifty families was to establish a school to teach pupils to read.[6] The ideal would take several centuries to fulfill; school as a full-time occupation for children could only be afforded by the rich. Both Rousseau and Locke, with their new educational theories in the eighteenth century, chose as the typical student a boy of the upper classes; they were not describing classrooms for the masses.[7] Nevertheless, their meanings of teacher/teaching led to and were easily assimilated by the modern school.

In modern usage, the teacher is an adult who has studied books; the student is a child who, sent to school for the purpose of absorbing the knowledge available in books, sits before the schoolmaster. The actions of the (school)teacher constitute teaching: to teach is to explain, to teach is to give reasons, to teach is to convince little boys to master their letters.

Whether a certain form of education fixed the meaning of teaching or whether a single meaning of teaching led to a concentration of education into one form, the fit between this teaching and this education is obvious. Other forms of education with their own embodiment of teaching did not immediately disappear, indeed have never disappeared. In the seventeenth-century colonies, even as the school was being affirmed as a necessity, the main business of education was still being carried out by family, church, and apprenticeship. But in the twentieth century it became more difficult for other forms of education to be accepted as serious partners with the classroom.

When John Dewey began his educational writing at the end of the nineteenth century, he looked back nostalgically to a time when home, church, and apprenticeship were real partners with the school. But Dewey concluded — fatefully and prematurely — that these other institutions were now all but impotent.[8] The school was faced with the task of picking up the slack and carrying the whole burden of education: socializing the child by community experience, challenging the child's intellect with a curriculum based on modern science, and preparing the child for a job in the technological world. The overwhelming task required religious zeal and supreme confidence.[9]

The narrowing of education into schools for children was already in process before Dewey. His writing, however, towered above other literature on educational reform. He was a man of great ideas that could be used to support the growth of the school business. Of course, there were protests from the beginning of the school system's ascendancy in the nineteenth century. One potentially fruitful criticism came from the "adult education" movement, first in Denmark and England, later in the United States.[10] I have noted that the adult-education movement grasped the inadequacy of equating education with the schooling of the child. The early leaders of the movement foresaw twentieth-century educational centers where people of any age would learn from a wide range of experiences.

Throughout the twentieth century we have sometimes seemed on the verge of this new educational world, but our language badly trails behind. The very existence of the adjective "adult" (or various replacements, such as "continuing") before "education" is symptomatic of the continuing problem. There is still (real) education and adult education, instead of a use of "education," which if unqualified would include all ages. To this day in towns across the country, no one confuses the educational budget with the cost of adult education; on university campuses, the school of education sits next to the school of continuing education; no one ever suggests that adult education is part of "higher education."

The tragic flaw in the adult-education movement, I suggested in chapter 1, was its willingness to relinquish "to teach" to the one form in which an adult explains things to a child. Instead of fighting to diversify the forms of teaching, the literature of adult education quixotically attacked teaching. The result is that "adult education" took on an image just as narrow as (children's) education. Adults do continue to get educated but most of them do not do so by participating in the industry called "adult education." I have no complaint about discussions lasting six or eight weeks on every conceivable topic so long as such programs do not lay claim to being in charge of the education of adults.

An educational pattern that would truly be lifelong would begin by naming those forms of life in which people are taught how to live. This first step is not inventing something new but retrieving what has clearly existed in the past and has continued to be present during this century, even if shunted to the periphery in the discussions of professional educators.

Educational reform movements often try to broaden the meaning of education. I said above that education in premodern times involved several forms of life and the relations between them. If "education" is contracted into a single institution, then we do not get a narrower meaning; rather, we end up with a different kind of reality. Education becomes an "it," mainly if not exclusively available in one institution. If someone tries to broaden this "it," either "education" stays put in its one clear setting, or else "education" becomes increasingly vague as it is assigned to numerous agencies. When "education" does not mean the "it" available in school, its meaning loses concreteness and practicality. Yes, there is "informal education" without limit, but most books on education address the one clear thing that everyone agrees upon, namely, the school.

One author who tried valiantly to break through this dilemma was Lawrence Cremin. In the early 1960s, Cremin wrote several fine histori-

cal studies of the school. He assumed that the school was the center —
if not the whole story — in the history of education. Then he read a
monograph by Bernard Bailyn entitled *Education in the Forming of American Society* and underwent a conversion.[11] As a result, Cremin tried to
write a history of education that would be much broader than the story
of the school. The project became more and more unwieldy as Cremin
found the need to keep adding pieces and players to the story.[12]

Although Bernard Bailyn's study of seventeenth-century education
is a stimulating book about the *agents of education*, it does not spend
much time on the *meaning of education*. And Cremin took over the
configuration of educational agents that Bailyn described without an
accompanying change in the meaning of education itself. What Bailyn offered was a picture of education much broader than what he
calls "formal pedagogy." More exactly, he added church, family, and
apprenticeship. The procedure seems logical: if school is not the only
institution, add the others. But, as I have noted, the reasoning is flawed.
The school in taking over the meaning of education ceases to be a
"form of education" and becomes an institution to house education.
Adding other houses ("agents of transfer") does not reinstate an interaction of forms. In trying to broaden the meaning of education, the one
thing that seems certain is school. This one thing that seems clear is
where the confusion lies.

The modern school is not a form of education; it is an institution
that contains several forms of education, such as classroom instruction,
community experience, and artistic performance. Of course, the second and third of these educational experiences exist in developed form
outside school. As a result, one cannot discuss the interaction of educational forms by naming the school and then adding other forms. The
task is to name the main forms that shape human existence by a *lifelong*
and *lifewide* interaction. The modern school can be a place where some
of this interaction occurs.

Neither Bailyn nor Cremin can resolve this issue. Bailyn's meaning
of education goes toward vague generality; Cremin's meaning remains
tethered to the school. At the beginning of his historical inquiry, Bailyn
simply notes that education is "the entire process by which a culture transmits itself across the generations."[13] That definition may seem
helpfully comprehensive, but lacking any indication of what constitutes
the teaching-learning process, the term "education" has little meaning
distinguishable from culture. Cremin, in contrast, had a precise defini-

tion, which he regularly used and which he had his students memorize: "The deliberate, systematic and sustained effort to transmit, evoke or acquire knowledge, attitudes, values, skills, or sensibilities, as well as any outcomes of that effort."[14] Despite all the qualifiers, the one word that controls the definition is *effort*. "Education is ... effort ... as well as any outcomes of that effort." The standpoint seems to be that of the individual human teacher: to teach is to intend, to teach is to make an effort and hope for outcomes from the effort. With education as effort, Cremin had set himself an impossible task to write the history of education.

I suggest that the key word for beginning a description of education is *interaction*.[15] How is the organism transformed as it interacts with the environment? How do various forms of life interact with and transform each other? The human efforts in the midst of these interactions can sometimes alter the forms, but if human effort is to be worthwhile, one cannot lose sight of the overall context; one has to gauge precisely how human influence can be exercised.

Education connotes interactions that are not random or mindless. There is "end" in the sense of purpose, design, or meaning. This end is not always obvious nor is it always imposed by a living human individual. The form that shapes life (for example, the family) may include generations of design and redesign. And whatever the contribution of persons and groups today, the process continues. Thus, in the other sense of "end" — termination point — there is no end to education; it is both lifelong and history-long. The particular interaction can have a number of ends internal to the process but no external thing to be acquired that would bring the movement to a conclusion. Education, therefore, is always "with end and without end." The difficulty of education is in maintaining a tension between these two meanings of "end," that is, having direction and accomplishment but never reaching a final product.

The Forms of Education

If education is the interaction of forms of life with end (meaning) and without end (termination), then what remains to be done is to describe the major forms that are lifelong and lifewide. The curriculum of education consists of these social forms with which a person interacts in his or her journey from conception to death. The individual's life is transformed by these encounters; the forms themselves are also changed, although their transformation is usually a very gradual one over the course of centuries.

There are innumerable social forms that human life takes. I will concentrate on four of these forms that cut across the lifespan and also influence the individual's entire life. Every child starts out being cared for and taught in some family pattern. Children then receive some kind of instruction for living in their society; this form of education evolved into the classroom. Every society expects its healthy adults to perform tasks for maintaining and enhancing life. Every society allows its older members to step back from the most laborious jobs to take part in what we now call leisure activity. Thus, family, classroom, job, and leisure activity can be viewed as a lifelong sequence, the simplest basis for a theory of education.

A more fruitful educational theory will see these forms as interacting at every stage of personal life. At any age, any one of the four can be at the center or at the periphery; none should entirely disappear. For example, when a child goes to school, familial teaching is likely to recede but it remains a partner with classroom teaching. For people in their 20s and 30s, family may reemerge as central to education, at least until the last child leaves home. Finally, being a grandparent at 60 or 70 may bring familial teaching to the center once more. The point of so describing the family in education is not to fit each individual's life into a preset pattern but to recognize that a person's life is educationally shaped by familial relations, with variations depending on gender, marital status, parental responsibility, housing arrangements, and many other factors.

What I am saying here of the family can also be said of the other three forms, that is, they are likely to be at the center during one period of life but they continue to be of subsidiary importance at other times. Classroom teaching may be especially appropriate for children and youth, but it can be important at any age. Similarly, having a job is the mark of younger and middle-age adults, but each person is taught by the tasks he or she performs from infancy onward. Leisure activity is most prominent in retirement but it cannot fully blossom there without some cultivation throughout life.

Each of the four social forms that I have named is a partial embodiment of some ultimate value that can stand in for the purpose of education. For example, the family partially embodies the value of community. The family educates to the degree that it is truly communal, that is, to the degree that the person and the group, the group and humanity, humanity and the biotic community are mutually enhanced. Even the best of families cannot be more than an imperfect teaching of community. The familial form of community always has to be complemented by nonfamilial but communal expressions of human life: friendship, neighborhood, religious congregation, athletic team, and so forth. As I note in the following chapter, a school ought to be a nonfamilial, communal form of life that teaches community by its procedures, personal interactions, and system of rewards.

Rather than pursue dozens or even hundreds of social forms that teach every person at every age, I will stick to the more manageable task of describing the four major forms of family, classroom, job, and leisure activity. The attempt to be exhaustive here can end in a shapeless profusion of details where education can mean almost anything and everything. Behind that flow of endless possibility there then emerges the one thing that nearly everyone seems to agree is education, namely, the school. However, approaching this question from the perspective of teaching, I have denied that school is (formal) education. As I describe in chapter 8, a modern school is likely to include many forms of education. Before examining the school, it will be helpful to examine the forms of education that exist both within schools and outside schools.

Family

I choose to use "family" here rather than "home." Although "home" in the English language does have the advantage of rich connotations, it may be too weighted toward architecture and place. Those are elements of the context but "family" emphasizes the individual's interaction with a human form of life, a social pattern that stamps the individual for the course of his or her lifetime. For at least several thousand years, family has clearly deserved to be called a form of education. And for all the bewailing about the collapse of the family and the deficiencies of the contemporary family, there is not even a serious competitor on the horizon.

At least since the time of Plato, there have been proposals for alternate social arrangements to rear children.[16] The proposals and their execution have usually involved a high degree of violence. Unfortunately, these attempts to dismantle the family have often been confused with helpful social experiments that recognize sexual diversity. Many communal experiments that exclude children (for example, the Roman Catholic religious order) are not in competition with the family. In fact, the constellation of relatives, friends, and intimate relations that surrounds the family provides the helpful support system that the family requires. The right wing's terror of gay and lesbian relations is particularly unfortunate because a context of stable homosexual relations would enhance any child's (and adult's) education in friendship, love, and community.

Libraries are full of books on the family, augmented by a daily outpouring of talk in the press and on television. I have no hope here of settling all the disputes or eliminating all the myths. This is a book on teaching and I restrict my comments to three points: the family form teaches, parents and children teach each other, and family uses a balanced mixture of the various teaching languages.

First, the use of "to teach" in literature on education regularly obscures the fact that the composition and activity of the family is one of our earliest and most powerful teachers. We are only occasionally forced to face that fact as, for example, in family systems therapy. I doubt that we will ever get to accepting the parents as teachers unless the notion of teaching is depersonalized, so that an environment or a social form can be understood to teach. Whether with good or bad lessons, the family form is the first great teacher.

The assumption that teaching depends on an individual's intending to teach blinds us to what is taught by the daily interaction of a family. If there are two parents, the child learns much from the parental interaction. We should also attend to what is taught when some families have only one parent, or when in some families a friend exercises parental influence.[17] The reality of a mother working outside the home surely teaches something to her children. What it teaches can vary from a terrible lesson of neglect or poverty to a lesson of responsibility and creative talent. But we will not look carefully at what is happening and try to improve the form (perhaps with government expenditures) if we do not accept the fact that the first teacher in the family is the *form* of family.

The second point to be noted is that parents are teachers of their children and children are teachers of their parents. The first half of that sentence may seem too obvious for stating, but that is precisely what is denied when "teacher" is regularly used for "schoolteacher." Emile Durkheim begins his discussion of education by saying that "education is the influence exerted on children by parents and teachers." In addition to confusing teacher/learner and adult/child relations and assuming that the influence is all in one direction, the statement also excludes parents from the set of people called "teachers."[18] While educational writing is fond of saying that parents are the child's first teachers, that assertion is denied in every use of the phrase "parents and teachers." The parental teacher and the schoolteacher have to be spoken about as cooperating in teaching.[19]

As I noted previously, Jane Martin found that in modern education what mothers do with small children is simply not counted as teaching at all.[20] She attributes much of the blindness to gender bias. No doubt that is interwoven throughout the entire discussion of teaching. But we could still miss the full extent of the problem if it were seen only as bias against women. What men as fathers and grandfathers teach has also not counted as teaching. I agree that what mothers do with infants is especially fruitful for reflection on teaching.[21] But we should also not neglect what spouses teach each other, what a parent's interaction with a grandparent teaches a child, and what an 80-year-old has to offer to both grownup son or daughter as well as grandchild.

I also call special attention to the fact that children teach their parents.[22] Of course, the teaching varies according to the age and the condition of the child. A 16-year-old has very different lessons to teach than a six-month-old; a genius child and a child with severe impediments offer challenges different in kind. The recently invented verb "to parent" (one's child) needs the complementary verb "to child" (one's parents). Once again, it is not a lesson the child usually intends to teach; nonetheless, any parent willing to listen will learn lessons from the child's life.[23]

At the 1992 Democratic convention, Elizabeth Glaser gave a moving speech on her own HIV affliction and the AIDS death of her child: "My daughter lived seven years. And in her last year when she couldn't walk or talk, her wisdom shone through. She taught me to love when all I wanted to do was hate. She taught me to help others, when all I wanted to do was help myself. She taught me to be brave, when all I felt was fear."[24] Glaser's situation was extreme, but every caring parent knows that her repetition of the verb "to teach" in reference to a child who could not walk or speak was no mere rhetorical flourish.

Finally, the third point is to notice the family as unusually rich in its variety of teaching languages. All three families of languages discussed in chapters 4, 5, and 6 show up in ordinary family life. The first and the second have about equal weight; the third is a little less prominent, except when the family becomes very self-reflective.

Each of the languages that make up the first and second linguistic families eventually appears in family education. Storytelling, lecturing, and preaching are there, with the first of those being very prominent; the preaching and lecturing, one would hope, appear only intermittently. Similarly, with therapeutic languages, the family is the main place where people learn to show gratitude, to forgive failure, to comfort hurts. Each of these teaching languages is embodied in the rituals of daily family life.

The examples from the third linguistic family (teaching the conversation) should not be entirely absent from family life. For example, children early acquire an attitude to reading, reflective thought, and conversation. Parents (and grandparents) often succeed in conveying a good attitude even if they are not "academically trained." The adult's taste for learning and an excitement with ideas are usually more important than academic credentials. Many immigrants who never had the chance to get beyond primary school have taught their children to value ideas, knowledge, and the pursuit of academic skill.

Classroom

The classroom represents a form of learning that should go on throughout life but is especially prominent in a young person's life. Another way to refer to this kind of learning is "schooling," but I am particularly interested in clearly distinguishing between "school" (an agency, a building, an institution) and a more specifically delineated form of education that classrooms are established for. Under the aegis of the modern school, several other kinds of activity go on that involve other forms of learning. The school can be a place that houses preparation for a job and actual experience of paid or unpaid work. The school is also a place for artistic and athletic performances that are integral to one's education but have never fit comfortably within the walls of the classroom.

I will be brief about classroom learning here because the next chapter goes into detail on this issue. I simply wish to name this form of learning and to place it within the constellation of the four forms of education. It achieves power by having its distinct time and place, but it effectively uses that power only in interaction with the other three forms. During one period of life it is likely to take center stage; at other times, it recedes to satellite status. However, for some individuals it can have either a more permanent or a recurring centrality. Many people in the modern world have jobs that involve constant study. Many other people at ages 50, 60, or 75 are discovering that they are finally ready to hit the books.

I will make three points here parallel to what was said of the family, namely, that the form of classroom teaches, that every individual in a classroom should experience teaching and learning, that the classroom gives prominence to one family of teaching languages while presupposing (or compensating for) the other two.

First, the existence of classrooms and the composition of any particular classroom teach. I will go into detail and offer many examples in the next chapter. Suffice it to say here that the form sets stringent limits on what can effectively be carried out in the name of education. But if the appropriate things are happening in this setting, the classroom as teacher can be a powerful element in education. "In our schools," wrote Maria Montessori, "the environment itself teaches the children."[25]

Second, most classrooms have only one person called "the teacher." In fortunate circumstances, there may be two such people. If the two work well together, the effect is not a doubling of teaching, but a change in the dynamics of teaching. Two people start a conversation and others ("the pupils") are drawn in. The person (or persons) called the teacher is obviously expected to teach, but one of the tests of good teaching is that sometimes the person called teacher becomes the learner. One need not imagine an obliteration of roles or complete equality of participation in the teacher and learner roles.[26]

Third, the classroom is a deliberately invented setting for one kind of learning — reflection on information that is today available in books, television, newspapers, computers. Unlike the family with its balanced mix of teaching languages, the classroom concentrates on the third linguistic family: teaching the conversation. And within that group, academic criticism has a privileged place. The *school* as a whole has a range of educational languages as wide as the family, but the *classroom* has to be focused at one extreme. In practice, every classroom instructor has to deal with deficiencies in the backgrounds of particular groups of students. But if there is little academic criticism occurring in the classroom, the students are not getting the education the school promises.

Job

As in the previous two cases, the form of education called "job" is a partial embodiment of the educational value at stake; in this case the value is "work." Almost everyone has a job, if we extend the word beyond salaried employment to the tasks people must accomplish. Sometimes the jobs we are required to do have little or no educational value; they are not real work. If people have such jobs "to make a living," then they have to find meaningful work at other times. Every job can be reformed in the direction of its being meaningful work, although some aspects of maintaining human life involve drudgery. Machinery has reduced or could reduce some of the laborious aspects of work. However, the dream of completely eliminating such labor is probably a dangerous dream for bodily creatures.

In this context, Maria Montessori's method places great emphasis on the child learning to work and learning by work. She realistically relates work to discipline and labor, although in doing so she may undervalue the connection of work and play. "I have to defend my method from those who say it is a method of play. Such people do not understand that work is natural to man.... Man's true name should be *homo laborans* rather than *homo sapiens.*"[27]

Montessori was reacting here against followers of Friedrich Froebel, who believed that the child's highest activity is play. Froebel had a kind of mystical sense of the divine presence in children's play.[28] Montessori saw all the talk about children's play as evidence of adult control and the trivializing of the child's activity. The two theorists were perhaps not so far apart as their language suggests. If the child's work *is* play, then one does not have to reject the one in affirming the other.

Of course, Maria Montessori would not have liked that formula. She believed that affirming *homo laborans* was the way to overcome the split between working-class laborers and the new professional class. I agree that many professionals could use some labor experience (for example, in the work of caring for the home or children), but unfortunately that will not do much for the laboring class. The laborers need, among other things, the availability of better classroom instruction throughout life and, to whatever extent possible, more play in their work.

"Apprenticeship" is a common term in educational history. Its standard use was for the kind of teaching provided by a master workman to a young person learning the trade. It fits well the root meaning of "to show someone how to live." Occasionally, writers use the term not only for learning a job but for all kinds of learning that involve an expert showing by example how to do something. This meaning is a helpful one to have. But while apprenticeship for a job needs reappropriation, that meaning needs a wider context.

The assumption in former times was that a master instructed an apprentice; once having learned the job, usually in the teenage years, the apprentice was set for life. The more common pattern today is training for the job, training on the job, retraining for a new job. The job has become a more important teacher today, with each of the jobs teaching lessons to a student who is willing to learn.[29]

Many parents today struggle to combine work outside the home and work within the home. The former neat division of men doing public work and women doing "housework" (which often was not classified as work at all) has suffered what is probably a permanent downfall. We do not yet have a healthy, fair, and efficient system. Ideally, no one should be forced into somebody else's idea of the correct system of dividing work. Whatever the pattern of individual lives, nearly everyone is taught by the tasks they have to perform. And for most people that means how to include more than one job in a balanced life.

The job world is in educational interaction with the classroom, a relation that does get some attention these days. The job is also related to family life and leisure activity. For several decades of a person's life, his or her job may hold center stage. But even then, the striving for money, prestige, power, and status has to be balanced both with other kinds of work and other forms of education.

One way that young people can acquire that balance and insight is by experiencing work that provides a needed service to people. The work is done not for pay but because it is worth doing. Such work can include helping friends with schoolwork, minding younger brothers and sisters, helping out in a nursing home. This pro bono work can begin in childhood and continue throughout life.[30]

The school is a chief agency for organizing service work, especially when youngsters are in junior or senior high school. Business corporations working with schools have a place in education; realistic preparation for employment is part of the young person's education. However, the *meaning* of work is more likely to be found by the young person in donating time and energy to help the very young, the very old, the poor, the disabled, or the stranger in distress. A criterion of the educational value of work is that the work is experienced as worth doing.

As to the forms of language that are found in the job/work world, it is more difficult to draw generalizations here than it was in the previous two cases. Each line of work has its own mix and its own emphasis. If one is a law student or lawyer, then the dramatic performance and the dialectical discussion of the third family have a permanent place. If one is a counseling psychologist, the second family of therapeutic languages predominates. If one is a clergyman, the preaching in the first family may be central. There is no one formula for even these fairly well-defined jobs. Each job has an occupational hazard, that a language central to the job can take over one's life — the clergyperson always sounding preachy, the psychotherapist always talking therapeutically, the lawyer ready to debate everyone. The only protection from this hazard is the interaction of several forms that provides a complementarity of languages.

Some jobs, I have acknowledged, are such laborious drudgery that we should try to replace them with machines; until then, those jobs ought to be distributed equitably.[31] For example, the aspects of caring for the home that are bothersome should be divided equally among family members. The fairness of the split as much as the execution of the job becomes the teacher. An equal sharing of the laborious jobs makes it possible for everyone to have a share in the creative work of the home.

Professional work is of such a nature that it should not be laborious drudgery. If professional people are bored with their work and careless in its performance, we have a shocking situation. Obviously the work is not teaching, perhaps because the professional is not ready to learn. Donald Schön describes what he calls a researcher-in-practice who is continuously taught and therefore finds joy and relaxation in the work itself. "When practice is a repetitive administration of technique to the same kind of problems, the practitioner may look to leisure as a source of relief, or to early retirement; but when he functions as a researcher-in-practice, the practice itself is a source of renewal."[32]

Retirement/Leisure Activity

This fourth and last form of education shows up most strikingly in old age but has to be present throughout life. Schön's reference above to "early retirement" is to suggest that if someone thinks that early retirement is the solution to being bored with work, disappointment is likely to follow. Schön also uses "leisure" in the way it is commonly used today — time off the job or leisure as nonactivity. I have combined "leisure" with "activity" to resist this modern bias that classifies leisure as nonactivity. The modern era, reversing what earlier peoples assumed, takes business (busy-ness) as activity and leisure as emptiness. I am positing an activity called leisure that expresses a deep human experience of completeness. This attitude finds expression in a multitude of ways, ranging from utter stillness to exuberant play.

A drastic shift in the meaning of leisure occurred in the nineteenth century. In the classical and medieval periods, leisure was related to the high value placed on the contemplation of eternal truth.[33] Leisure was the soul's best attitude and the culture's calm center. For Aristotle, leisure was a way to describe the purpose and end of education. The fact that the Greek word we translate as leisure (*skhole*) is the word that gave us "school" indicates that a discussion of leisure belongs within the meaning of education.[34]

It is unlikely that "leisure" can be restored to its pre-nineteenth-century meaning. Too much has happened in the interim, especially in the industrialization of our world. But as one era of machinery made a new meaning of leisure (time off the job) increasingly attractive, so a new era of postindustrial technology is now reshaping our idea of leisure. We could end up by just filling "spare time" with another job or with endless television viewing. But it is possible that an increasing number of people will have the chance to engage in pursuits that are enjoyable and educational, personally fulfilling and socially valuable.[35]

The older part of the population is the chief place to look for how leisure is going. People, on the average, are living longer lives with better health. Those who are finding no great fulfillment in their jobs and can manage to retire at an early age often seize the opportunity. The question, then, is what to do with several more decades of healthy life. I am not suggesting older people have to create a busy schedule of daily events. Having many hours to be present with one's grandchildren is a worthy retirement activity. Getting one's hands dirty in the garden is an activity attractive to many people who have lived young adulthood separated from the soil. Both grandchildren and gardens can be great teachers.

All the talk about leisure in old age can sound obscene to those overwhelmed by poverty or sickness. No doubt there are signs of a dangerous selfishness among well-off older people. "I want my comfortable life; I deserve it. I don't care about anyone else's problems." That is one of the reasons why one must resist the trivialization of "leisure" by travel agencies and other commercial interests. Leisure has to be related to profoundly human activity that links the generations.

Older people do deserve much of the economic benefit that has come their way in recent decades. They have the right to step back from the production and management jobs that are burdensome. But for their own happiness as well as society's well-being, leisure activity has to have human depth.

Education among the elderly need not mean classroom discussion — although that should be available and many older people love it. Education in old age concerns the pattern of activity appropriate for the age, health, and talents of the individual.

As was true of the other three forms of education, leisure activity predominates in one part (the later part) of life but it should also be an educational satellite at each stage of life. If one has not been educated in leisure early in life its meaning is not likely to emerge full blown at age 65 or 70. Leisure has to be cultivated hourly, daily, weekly, annually. Religious rituals were once a help here and for some people still are. For other people, opera or baseball has taken that place; one steps out of ordinary time and place to be immersed in a rich pageant of human emotions. From the standpoint of rational productivity, such leisure activity is a terrible waste of time. For the individual participant, it can be a glorious and transformative experience. The whole culture would be the poorer without such leisure activity.

The child is taught leisure both by times when "nothing is happening" and by times of sheer enjoyment of any activity. The very young can probably best learn leisure from the very old; the two are co-conspirators in a world where everyone else is rushing to get things done. When the child has to settle into work at school and at a job, the relaxation, play, and joy may have to recede but they should not disappear.

Schools, as I shall describe in the next chapter, are places for the teaching of leisure activity. Arts and sports do not fit the classroom curriculum, but they are part of the school curriculum. One way that the classroom can contribute to sport and art is by teaching intelligent spectatorship. Being a spectator may not be as satisfying as being a performer but, especially later in life, it can be a valuable part of leisure activity.

To whatever extent it can, the school should provide for artistic and athletic performances. The amount and variety of both should depend on individual choice, but the activities should be available. These things are not frills on a young person's education; they add a necessary complement to the work of the classroom. The form of a basketball team on the court is a teacher. So are the keys on a piano. The young person will usually need some "coaching" along with the nonverbal teacher. A coach will use a rich mixture of teaching languages. Sometimes a little lecturing and preaching may be needed; sometimes forgiving and comforting are necessary. This metaphor of coaching for the purpose of reflecting on teaching will receive more comment in the next chapter.

Chapter 8

Teaching in School

THE QUESTION of school reform has generated a library full of books. Proposals for change have been constant in the United States since the founding of the public school system in the 1840s. The number of reform packages has probably reached a new high since the early 1980s. The most obvious cause for the intense recent interest is U.S. economic competitiveness with Japan, Germany, and other countries.

This chapter does not attempt to compete with proposals that offer a detailed blueprint of how public schools should operate. Much of the economic, political, social, and racial complexity is beyond my scope here. However, I do think that this chapter might contribute to the discussion by offering several clear distinctions. Clarity can sometimes simplify. Behind all the details of complex proposals to improve schools is someone's assumptions about what constitutes a school and what are its proper activities.

I have approached the question of school by asking, "What is the meaning of 'to teach'?" That journey led up to the previous chapter, which set teaching within four major forms of lifelong and lifewide education. Classroom teaching is one of those four forms. The form of classroom teaching exists in relation to forms of teaching outside the school. In addition, classroom teaching is related to other forms of teaching *within* the school. That is, the task of this chapter is not to describe "schoolteaching," but to describe the configuration of teaching forms that a typical school can house.

Many of the books on school reform have thoughtful, exciting, and detailed proposals. But what usually does not get asked is the nature of teaching. In most of these books, the reader is not likely to find a page, let alone a chapter, asking the question, "What does it mean to teach someone something?" The question and an answer are, of course, implied. I can understand that documents largely political and institutional in nature need not always ask philosophical and linguistic questions. Still, teaching is at the center of the school; teaching is also an act that is regularly obscured in educational discussions. If we come to the question of school reform with some clarity about the nature of teaching, we might be able to have a clearer outline of the school. Debate about school reform would be based on a firmer understanding of the limits of a school and what kinds of activity do and do not belong within those limits.

What a School Is

Any "vision" of a reformed school needs to be grounded in what "school" has been in the past and what it realistically could be in a few years. Reform books are often cast either in utopian programs of progress or in apocalyptic announcements that time is running out. People who work in schools often feel battered by what they perceive to be the latest fad — a new piece of machinery, a new management technique, or a new testing device. The great new reform often comes across in the form of a slogan or an acronym. At the back of the room, someone is usually muttering "we tried that in 1970 (or 1960, or 1950)." But even the schoolteacher who just wishes to close the classroom door and get on with the lesson plan knows that drastic changes have been occurring in the world surrounding the school. How much and in what ways should the school be changing in response?

Schools cannot pretend that videotape, computers, high-tech industries, and an interlocking world economy do not exist. No modern invention or interest should in principle be excluded from the school. But there is a debatable issue of how to incorporate "relevancy" to the contemporary world without obscuring or destroying the fragile institution of school. If "school" is the name of a single place with a limited time, then reformers have to keep in view the simple outline of the school when new things are suggested. If something is being added, what will be subtracted?

Herbert Kliebard, in his excellent history of school curriculum, notes that "one major function of life adjustment education was its emphasis on the indefinite expansion of the scope of the curriculum."[1] The intention was for the school to face "real-life problems," but theorists have to face the fact that the curriculum cannot indefinitely expand. The attempt to add every social problem to the school's curriculum eventually causes the inevitable reaction: Let's get rid of all these frills and go back to the three Rs. Reform movements with too wide a curriculum lead to reform movements too narrow in their concern.

The peculiar cry of educational reformers in the twentieth century has been that the school should deal with "real-life problems." That concern is related to the commonly made contrast between the school and the "real world." To say that the school is outside the "real world" is contemptuous of the school and its endeavors. It is shocking to hear schoolteachers accept and use this language. The fact that the contrast is embedded in common speech is not a good reason for participating in self-degradation.

The school, I have indicated, is a place to step back from many of life's pressing concerns. The school is an extraordinary world but not an unreal world. In fact, the classroom is one of the few places that takes as its concern the entire real world. Theodore Sizer notes that the contrast between school and real world allows society to neglect "the real world found inside the school."[2] For young people who are legally required to be there, the school world is undoubtedly real, often painfully so. The students are not going to respect their world if the school's administrators and teachers do not accept the importance — or even the reality — of school life. We need more research into what is called the "ethnography of schools" to know what the life of the school is and how the reality of schooling shapes individuals.[3]

If school reform starts from the premise that the existing school is outside the real world, it is not surprising that reform proposals go in one of two directions: either make the classroom as painless and entertaining as possible while children are kept segregated from the real world; or else tear down the school walls and put teachers and students to work in reconstructing the real world. One can see these attitudes reflected in two of the most important educational movements in this century: the "child-centered classroom" and the "social reconstructionist movement." Both movements are credited to (or blamed on) John Dewey. The two movements were most prominent in the first half of the century, but they continue to resurface with only slight changes in their language.

At the end of the nineteenth century, the school reformers wished to make the classroom a kinder place for the child. More particularly, they thought that the curriculum should serve the child's development. "Child-centered" was a way of saying that the psychologists should direct the child's education. And very quickly educational language was absorbed into psychological language. By 1900, John Dewey was already trying to correct what he thought was a new misplacement of emphasis. As someone who was identified with the new psychology, Dewey was assumed to be on the side of the child. However, in *The Child and the Curriculum*, he insisted that the center of the school is not the child but the *relation* between child and curriculum.[4] By 1930, Dewey had dissociated himself from the Progressive Education Association's program of child-centered education. In one of his last books on education in 1937 he was still trying to make his point when people were attributing to him whatever was being done in the name of child-centered education.[5]

Dewey never succeeded in extricating himself from the widespread perception that he wished to place the child at the center of the school. The author of a recent book quotes Dewey as saying that "the child is the starting point, the center, and the end. His development, his growth, is the ideal. It alone furnishes the standard." The author then comments on this passage: "In theory, this ideal is unassailable. In practice, it has proved largely unattainable."[6] The words quoted are in fact those of Dewey but they are a description of the theory he was assailing. It is not that our problem has been putting the theory into practice. Dewey's contention was that the theory is wrong.

Why is a position that Dewey was at pains to deny for more than forty years still attributed to him? His express intention was to interrelate "child" and "curriculum," but he could not overcome the limitations of his beginning terms. I think he would have fared much better if he had distinguished among the curriculum of education, the curriculum of the school, and the curriculum of the classroom. In addition, he should not have assumed that "student" and "child" are interchangeable.

John Dewey never developed a theory of teaching. It is amazing that in his major educational treatise, *Democracy and Education*, he seldom uses the verb "to teach." When he does, he nearly always refers to what schoolteachers ("educators") do. Education is assumed to be what children receive in a classroom.[7]

To this day most books on school reform begin by assuming a classroom is a place for older people to instruct children or youth. It is understandable that a writer may wish to concentrate on the high school or the elementary school. But even to analyze either of those settings one is not helped by assuming that a classroom is a place for older people to instruct children. The meaning of teaching is seldom explored when one assumes that the teacher/learner relation is a variation on adult/child. In contrast, the question of the nature of teaching will very likely be raised if the teacher can be the same age or younger than the students.[8]

Within the configuration of educational forms, the classroom has a special, but not exclusive, relation to young people. Classroom learning belongs to every age. Some reflective and literate knowledge is best learned between the ages of 6 and 16. Many other things are better learned later in life.[9] Our university and community college populations now embody a great diversity of age. Nothing helps a classroom discussion by 18-year-olds like the presence of some 40- or 70-year-old students. Beyond the university, tens of millions of people in the United States are involved every day in courses, seminars, and workshops.

The phrase "schools and universities" has the effect of keeping schools equated with children. A preferable way of speaking is to include universities within the meaning of school. Students often do experience a big difference when they move from the twelfth to the thirteenth grade, especially in living arrangements. However, the continuity of the classroom experience should not be overlooked. The United States could profit from a closer relation of primary, secondary, and tertiary schooling. The ones who might learn the most from this relation would be university professors, who often reflect little on the nature of classroom instruction. They do their research and give their lectures, assuming that is what it means to teach. But teaching in a classroom is a special kind of teaching that a university professor ought to learn by watching someone who does it well.

There are places in John Dewey's writings where he suggests that education is not exclusively for children. His test of good education is that it stimulates the desire to get more education. On that basis, education (including classroom teaching) should never cease. Dewey also warns against assuming that adults and children are opposites when it comes to matters of dependence. In that framework, teaching would not be mistaken for a child's dependence on an adult. Dewey also has intriguing comments on teaching by indirection: the teacher influences the student by altering the physical and social environment.[10] But because Dewey has no overall theory of teaching, it is quite possible to read his writings with one's assumption undisturbed that teaching consists in professional educators telling things to children.

The other direction to school reform — social reconstructionism —

is also traceable back to Dewey's writings at the turn of the century. This movement reached a high point during the economic hard times of the 1930s. When Dewey broke from the child-centered movement, he aligned himself with the movement to reform the social order. The phrase "social reconstruction" is not heard much these days, but the school is still often asked to solve the problems of society: AIDS, racism, drugs, war, traffic deaths, pollution. The school is asked to confront "real-life problems."

In his Pedagogic Creed, Dewey wrote, "I believe that education is the fundamental method of social progress and reform."[11] If by "education" is meant a lifelong and lifewide interaction of social forms, then indeed one would look to education, as opposed to violence, for transforming the social order. But if by "education" one really means school, and by school one assumes a place for 6- to 16-year-olds, then burdening "education" with the task of reconstructing society is unrealistic. John Dewey did not invent the equating of education with schools for children, but neither did he free himself from that assumption.

Dewey's comments on the role of teacher are especially revealing and unrealistic. He ends his Pedagogic Creed with the statement: "The teacher is the true prophet, the usherer in of the Kingdom of God."[12] If Dewey really meant teacher here and not schoolteacher, then the statement would be defensible. The great revolutions of history have been brought on by teachers: Moses and Confucius, Jesus and Socrates, Newton and Einstein, Jefferson and Lincoln. However, Dewey regularly refers to "teacher" when he means "schoolteacher." Asking a schoolteacher — of children — to lead a social revolution is to lay an unfair burden on both schoolteachers and schoolchildren. Schools, especially those with students of all ages, can make a definite contribution to social progress, but only if schools are protected from being wielded as political instruments.

Dewey's alignment with the social reconstructionists of the 1930s was short-lived. He was not prepared to go the route of some other reformers in involving the school in social activism. While he regularly refers in *Education and Experience* to "real-life experience," by which he seems to mean a continuity between in-school and out-of-school experiences, he still appreciated the school as a place of academic study.

The conflict between reformers was brought to a head in a provocative little book by George Counts: *Dare the Schools Build a Better Social Order?* The question for Counts was not "Can the schools do it?" but

"Are the schoolteachers daring enough?" For Counts, "Progressive Education cannot place its trust in a child-centered school"; instead, it must "become less frightened than it is today at the bogies of *imposition* and *indoctrination*."[13] For Dewey, that dismissive attitude to the real problem of indoctrination was too much to take. In 1937, he wrote, "It is unrealistic, in my opinion, to suppose that the schools can be a *main* agency in producing intellectual and moral changes . . . which are necessary for the creation of a new social order."[14]

By the end of the 1930s, therefore, school reform had two opposing parties. Both could claim lineage to John Dewey, but he had repudiated both. It is almost the trademark of great thinkers that they are misunderstood in opposite directions. Dewey tried to take down the wall separating school and nonschool worlds. But in the absence of consistent distinctions between school and education, the result is not a dialogue of educational forms but an engulfment of school by the nonschool world. Even more seriously, in the absence of a theory of teaching, the schoolteacher is either told to get out of the way so that children can grow up or else is hectored to tell the whole world how to live.

I have approached the meaning of "school" by describing in previous chapters the forms and languages of teaching. A school is a distinct location where people step back from ordinary concerns to concentrate upon learning something. Almost any kind of learning could be housed within the school's borders, but the most likely candidates are those forms of teaching-learning that are valued by the group and require the leisure of space and time. Schools throughout the centuries have generally provided two forms of learning: first, knowledge of a scientific or philosophical kind; second, a learning how to do the tasks required to sustain the particular society. This latter form of learning refers to "work" in the full range of its meaning, including labor, art, sport, and religion. The modern school is still a place for either or both of these forms of learning.

Forms of Schoolteaching

Before commenting on the division of the school into its two main learning forms, we should notice a form of teach-learn that is the backdrop for these two. The very existence of school, the functioning of the operation as a human assembly, is a teacher. The community and the physical environment are always teaching in a school. No one intends this teaching, or people usually do not think much about it until someone complains. Despite the inattention — or indeed because of the inattention — the influence can be profound. It can make the difference between the two main forms flowing easily and those forms facing impossible odds.

A school need not be one big happy family; it does need some minimum conditions of physical comfort, efficient organization and a nonhostile body of people. Both the teachers and the students deserve some respect for their personal dignity. The school ought to teach decency in being a school.[15]

The metaphor of family should be used sparingly in reference to schools. The school should be a partial embodiment of community, that is, a communal expression that complements the family. Schools need not have father and mother figures, nor obedient children (including grown ups who are treated like children). But when schools abandon the family posture they need not switch to a free market of competing individuals. Schools need to be disciplined communities of people that teach cooperation between students, as well as between students and school staff.[16] Everyone in a school has a stake in seeing that school be a communal experience that keeps bureaucratic procedures at the service of learning. Nothing can guarantee or permanently secure such an atmosphere, but memos, bells, and loudspeakers do not substitute for face-to-face encounters.

The school's influence on behavior, especially on that of young children, is often called "socialization." A lot of not-so-useful discussion concerns whether the school should be in the socializing business. A good part of the argument could be eliminated by clearly distinguishing between school and classroom. If socializing means picking up the ways to act in society, then children, and many adults, acquire some of that in school. The fact that schools socialize the young is not really debatable. But that the intention of classroom instruction is to socialize is an altogether different proposition. The desired effect of the classroom might very well be to challenge society's ways not only outside the school but also inside the school.

Writers who understandably wish to protect the school's forms of learning often state the case poorly by fighting the school's part in socialization. Kieran Egan writes,

Socializing most effectively happens simply by living in societies
day by day, and schools are generally rather ineffective socializing institutions, when they try to teach what is best learned from
out-of-school experience. And further, by attempting to perform
the socializing role at which they are ineffective, schools tend to
undercut their *educational* role.[17]

The last phrase in this quotation points up the confusion: the school's
educational function includes socializing. It is not that schools should
"try to teach what is best learned from out-of-school experience";
rather, they teach by being schools — they teach bad lessons or good
lessons, but powerful lessons. What Egan is rightfully concerned about
is the reduction of the *classroom* to a place for teaching social conformity. However, that concern is not properly stated by denying that the
school has a legitimate educational role in socialization.

If we move now from the backdrop of community and environment
to the kinds of teaching forms designed for schools, there is a single
clear-cut division. On one side should be the classroom with its peculiar form of learning and on the other side should be the performance
area with its less peculiar ways to learn. There should not be a chasm
between the two; in fact, reaching some harmony and balance, if not
complete integration, should be the heart of school reform.

I call these two school forms of teaching by place names: the classroom and the performance *area*. Without disparaging the individuals
who are trying to teach, I am calling attention to the environment
as teacher. The individual teacher is faced with manipulating the
environment to bring about student response.

A distinction between the two physical environments does not necessarily mean their mutual exclusion. A room clearly designated as
classroom might have computers along the wall for one kind of performance or a small theatrical stage for another kind of performance.
Conversely, the sports complex or the dance studio might have sections
for classroom instruction.

Before contrasting these two settings, we should note some continuity in the metaphors that can be used for teaching in school. Three
of the most promising metaphors are apprenticeship, coaching, and instruction. In writing of job-related learning, I said apprenticeship is no
longer comprehensive enough. But as a metaphor for teaching, it lights
up connections between what a teacher does in a classroom and what a

teacher does in an art studio. If the root meaning of "to teach" is to show someone how to live, it is not surprising that the relation of master-apprentice encompasses both the classroom and the performance area. Alan Tom notes that "apprenticeship is verbal and analytic just as much as it is modeling skilled performance."[18] Or one could vary that formula and say that a classroom teacher has to put on a skilled performance with words. When the metaphor is extended this way, the gender bias that has been part of the idea of apprenticeship throughout the centuries is at least lessened; some people would prefer the word "mentor" here instead of "master," which was used for the man guiding the boy.

A person learns to write, in part, by reading someone who writes well. The response ought not to be slavish imitation but inspiration to exercise one's own talents. That is the real mark of the master/mentor: that the apprentice does not imitate but discovers his or her own way. Maria Montessori used to say that two things should be done for the children: show them exactly how something is done, and destroy the possibility of their imitating that.[19] Master teaching is not just showing but showing how. The skilled person manifests the skill along with a few tricks of the trade. Someone who knows how to do something very well often finds it difficult to think along the lines of universal rules. The apprentice will pick up some of these rules, perhaps some that are not consciously known to the master/mentor.[20]

A second metaphor that helpfully connects the two main forms of teaching in school is "coaching." As apprenticeship comes from the world of work, coaching comes from leisure activity, including art and athletics. Many classroom teachers might take offense at being compared to a football coach. But the metaphor of coaching can transcend sports-crazed coaches and their supporters. Classroom teachers might get new insight into their work by watching how a good teacher in art or athletics operates.[21]

As I described in chapter 3, the sequence in teaching is: student acts, teacher contemplates design, teacher proposes redesign, student tries out the new design. A good coach does not have to memorize that sequence; it is the only way he or she could imagine the activity of teaching. Good coaches are not necessarily great players; the advantage of coaching over the master/apprentice metaphor is that coaching does not require genius or some special talent. The coach, by carefully studying bodily movement and suggesting slight changes, may bring out talent and genius in others.

One author who has brilliantly explored the metaphor of coaching in teaching is Donald Schön. Both *The Reflective Practitioner* and *Educating the Reflective Practitioner* provide detailed examples of how expert teachers coach their students in art, industrial design, city planning, or psychotherapy. It is, therefore, surprising to read the comment of Patricia Graham: "As Schön has observed, professional practice, in this case college teaching is both learnable and coachable, but not teachable."[22] An opposition between teaching and coaching is not at all the point of Schön's two books. On the contrary, he is trying to show how a good teacher teaches by using both apprenticeship and coaching methods.

Finally, there is the metaphor of "instruction." In modern educational literature, this term gets identified with the classroom. But as coaching and apprenticeship could move into the classroom, instruction could use some fresh air on stage or ballfield. What instruction connotes is precise, direct verbal commands. Instruction is a natural part of teaching any bodily skill. It can be thought of as a subordinate element within coaching or apprenticeship, but it is often the most crucial element. Every teacher of anything has to know how to give precise verbal commands that imply analytic understanding of a situation.

If instruction consists of precise verbal commands within bodily movement, how did it come to dominate classroom teaching and what should be its legitimate place? The answer is that the classroom instructor is indeed a choreographer. He or she is trying to do with written and spoken language what the dance instructor is doing with arms and legs. But if one loses all connection to bodily movement — for the classroom instructor that means losing a sense of the rhythms of speech and the ambiguities of words — then one is left with giving direct commands to the mind or the memory. In many contexts (for example, legal references to "religious instruction"), the term "instruction" is synonymous with indoctrination. Any metaphor for classroom teaching has to be grounded outside the classroom or else the classroom will be thought of as a place where big people tell little people what to think.

Classroom Teaching

What I have called classroom teaching can and does go on outside the walls of a classroom. However, in this section I wish to draw a portrait of what can and does happen inside the sacred space of classroom walls.

What are the conditions under which this strangest form of teaching-learning occurs?

First, the physical setting needs notice, both the bare physical facts and some of the aids that technology provides. Classrooms throughout the centuries have tended to be bare-walled boxes. The modern classroom arose as part of the modern concern for control embodied in prisons, asylums, and hospitals.[23]

Several specific reforms of the classroom are needed but its basic form should probably remain: a place that conveys a sense of quiet order, dedicated to ear more than eye. There should be fresh air and plenty of light, along with a minimum of distraction from outside the room. Nothing helps a classroom more than does carpeting. Janitors may not like carpets and children are prone to dirty them, but a carpet is often the difference between thoughtful conversation and someone straining to be heard amid reverberating sound. Many classrooms have the chairs nailed to the floor, all in proper rows facing forward. Fixed chairs for some discussions may be useful but the overwhelming choice has to be chairs that can move in all directions. Traditional classrooms have a chalkboard at the front; it is a human piece of technology not wholly replaceable by overheads, slides, video, computers, and the rest. But if there is still to be a chalkboard it should cover the whole front wall and some of the side walls. Chalkboards are for thinking with and working through long trains of speech.

Traditional classrooms, especially in the university, had a platform for the teacher. The idea was not all wrong, but the platform should be a small performance area either within or attached to the classroom. The platform is for students as much as teachers, or more exactly, the students when they act as teachers. Classrooms should not be cluttered with machinery. If a television monitor is helpful to a particular course, the equipment should be readily available and easy to use. If computers are needed, they should surround the main conversation area. Computers are now indispensable to the school's work but they are not necessarily central to the classroom. The clear focus of the classroom ought to remain the spoken word. Classrooms are one of the few places in the world where people might listen carefully to what someone says and change their minds.[24]

Before commenting on the languages of the classroom, I think it is necessary to defend the classroom against the charge that it is merely talk. People who should be sensitive to the issue often pick up a language that denigrates the classroom. To complain, for example, that the classroom is all talk and no action is to accept the modern split between talk and action. If, in contrast, one begins with the premise that action can be verbal or nonverbal, one is more likely to see how classroom action of the verbal kind can change the world. John Dewey and successive waves of reformers have begun with the principle of "learn by doing," a principle never to be forgotten in teaching. But the peculiar action or doing in the classroom is speaking. Failing to grasp this point, reformers are always trying to shove things into a classroom that do not fit there. The pieces of equipment may belong in school (in the library, performance studios or computer center) but they can obscure the *kinds of speech* appropriate for the classroom.

John Dewey often sets up an unwise dichotomy that undercuts the serious conversation in a classroom, as when he writes in *Democracy and Education:*

> That education is not an affair of 'telling' and being told, but an active and constructive process, is a principle almost as generally violated in practice as conceded in theory.... Its enactment into practice requires that the school environment be equipped with agencies for doing, with tools and physical materials, to an extent rarely attained.[25]

Dewey's unfortunate contrast here is between "telling" and "physical materials." Any physical materials should be at the service of the forms of speech appropriate for the classroom. Dewey fails to name forms of language for the classroom other than "telling." The alternative to telling is not physical equipment but the other teaching languages discussed in chapters 4, 5, and 6.

Of the three families of languages I discussed, the third — teaching the conversation — holds a special place in the classroom. All human life can be imagined as conversation or dialogue. The classroom is a dialogue about dialogue, a reflecting upon the preconditions of conversation, the ambiguities of any genuine human speech, the possibilities of organizing large bodies of information. The classroom is no less than an entrance into the conversation of the human race. The professional schoolteacher's job is to mediate between past writing and present situations. None of the languages of teaching is excluded on principle. Over a period of time, a classroom teacher will use almost every imaginable form of speech to spark interest, to probe for understanding, or to clinch an argument.

Here is an appropriate place to reject the assumption that to teach in a classroom is "to lecture." The assumption is perhaps behind Dewey's contrast of "telling" and "using equipment." The rebellion against lectures seldom leads to the naming of alternative languages for teaching. The only term usually paired with "lecture" is "discussion," often conceived to be the application of the lecture. The university is particularly lacking in imagination when it comes to naming the languages of the classroom. I think that the first step in improving university teaching would be a complete moratorium on the use of the term "lecture."

This language of the university filters into secondary and even primary schools. Perhaps it is a (sad) fact that what many university professors do is lecture. But elementary or secondary school teachers, who survive and do a respectable job in the classroom, do not use lecturing as their way of teaching. They use a variety of forms of speech which, if they had help in naming the languages, might help them to understand better what they are already doing and open new possibilities in their work. The alternative to "giving a lecture" is not arranging the students in groups. The challenge for a classroom teacher is to explore the resources of language.

In chapter 4, I defended the form called lecture against its many detractors. But I also said that lecturing does not belong in a classroom, or at least it should not have a prominence there. It should not be any more common than its close relative, preaching. Every classroom teacher gives occasional sermons; students do not mind so long as the sermons are brief and to the point. Similarly, lecturing can sometimes seem an efficient way to convey necessary information. Students do not mind a little of that, too; in fact, they can easily become addicted to the teacher being a substitute for the library. Student and teacher may end up with a comfortable arrangement of information giving and note taking that does not challenge either of them.

The old saying is more true than ever: any teacher who can be replaced by a machine (or a book) should be. Machinery can be a tremendous aid in enriching the environment with the information that is the *precondition*, but not the aim of the classroom. When Chris Whittle announced his ambition to revolutionize schools, he said, "It's amazing to me that we don't bring the best lecturers electronically into schools."[26] Television can be a helpful tool in a classroom but televised lecturers are just what we do not need.

In chapter 4, in addition to lecturing and preaching, I discussed storytelling. Ideally, students come to class with stories from home, stories out of books, the story of the school, the great stories of the human race. Then the teacher can launch into dramatizing, analyzing, comparing, playing with stories, all with the purpose of having stories better shape our lives. In practice, much of classroom time may have to be spent going over stories for the first time. That is not bad, of course; a good story well told is nearly always welcome. The only danger is that telling stories can edge out the third family of languages, which should have center stage in the classroom.

The second family — the therapeutic languages — have to be kept more at bay in the classroom. A school cannot function without them, but a classroom has to be carefully distinguished from therapy treatment. Sometimes people should not be in a classroom because they first need to get past some obstacles to learning. There are, however, therapeutic languages that are always appropriate in the classroom: the rituals of politeness, kindness, and respect. If a sense of self-respect and graciousness is not evident, then the hard work of thinking about academic matters is stymied.

The classroom's main languages are those of the third family. This family includes dramatic performance, dialectical discussions, and academic criticism. Each of these can be a way of shaking up usual patterns of speech that confine our minds. Dramatic performance connotes playing with language and the taking of parts. The drama may be one that tells a story, but instead of the story simply being a vehicle for the deliverance of truth, dramatic performance interjects a distance between speaker and story. A lot of writing in recent years has dealt with "role playing." As a technique for getting a group of students to reflect on the words they use, such reversals are quite effective. In a class that is dealing with sexual practice, an adolescent playing the role of a parent can change the outlook of a whole group.

What is less often spoken about is that the person at the front of the room called "the teacher" is playing a role all the time. Outside this room he or she has a life distinct from classroom instructor. The person who has spent years preparing to teach in a classroom (and is usually paid to do so) has to approach the work with the zest of a stage actor.[27] The fifty or ninety minutes of this class is sacred time, not just time for an ordinary conversation, but for challenging everyone in the room to reflect on their words.[28]

The classroom instructor's lines are not all set beforehand, although a lesson plan is usually helpful. A class meeting that has been carefully planned allows for the greatest feeling of spontaneity and the possibility of redoing the show in the middle of the play. Some contemporary plays that ask "what is a play?" and "who are the players?" get close to the classroom. If a play in a theater tries to break out from behind the proscenium, an audience unprepared for the experience may be left confused and angry. People entering a classroom should be prepared for exploring what eventually arises in every area of study: Who or what teaches? Who or what appointed the teacher? Who or what decided that history or literature or psychology exist as the subject matter? In the end, the people who entered the class as "students" have to demonstrate, preferably both in writing and in oral presentation, that they could play "teacher." That is really what testing and evaluation are.

The second language in the family of teaching the conversation is "dialectical discussion." The somewhat technical adjective is to highlight that the classroom is different from a local bar or the office coffee machine. The sacred time in the classroom is not for endless bull sessions. Discussion of ideas and their assumptions is what has to be structured in classrooms. The careful choice of the topic for discussion, the proper number of people in each group, and the planning of the physical arrangement of the chairs all lead to the most spontaneity and ease in the discussion.

The use of group discussion is highly praised in educational literature. Adult-education writing often assumes that it is practically the only way for adults to learn. However, much of the praise of discussion groups is simply a vote against "lecturing." That is a bad avenue of approach to using group discussion. Some teachers conclude that if they cannot push it into the students (by lecture) then they will pull it out (by discussion groups). This conclusion is often accompanied by a reference to education meaning "to lead out."

Dialectical discussion can better be imagined as leading people *in*, that is, setting them into the middle of the human race's conversation. Ideas are neither put in nor pulled out; they happen in between the speakers. For each of us as learners, the conversation is at first between great minds who have spent years mastering a "discipline" of ideas. We may have to spend a long time listening carefully to the discussion.

Then our three- or four-person group can be a modest embodiment of that human conversation.

Similar to role playing as dramatic performance, discussion is usually spoken of as a technique that the teacher can use. But the teacher, too, is constantly functioning in a group. Within a school, the group ought to include the faculty's interaction. The faculty ought to stimulate the thinking of individual teachers and protect students if a teacher is irresponsible. The school faculty is a representation of the community of scholars that span the human race. The classroom teacher ought never to lose sight of being in a group of searchers or researchers of the truth. The individual teacher can manifest this relation by a classroom reading of a passage from a book or an essay. This is where a lecture — say, about thirty seconds in length — has a place in the classroom. The teacher can then respectfully agree and disagree with the writer's formulation of the truth. "Dialectical" means going back and forth with the end (purpose) of getting closer to the truth, but without end (termination).[29]

Finally, we come to the language most specifically designed for the classroom: academic criticism. In the previous two languages, the meaning of the words is implicitly in question. Here the meaning of words is the question. The grammatical form that academic criticism takes is the interrogative. Who says so? Why? What is presumed? What implications follow? Of course, in the actual practice of teaching one varies the grammar and syntax. For example, ironic statements can lighten the tone, while forcing the questioning of an apparent statement of fact.

We easily identify questions with the students. The teacher finishes speaking and says, "Are there any questions?" The better teacher tries to start with the student's questions. But asking for questions at the beginning of a class or at the start of a course may be no more effective than asking at the end of the class or the course. The more crucial thing is the teacher's manner of using questions in teaching. If the teacher is asking serious questions, that process will unfreeze the students' questions.[30]

By becoming a questioner the student becomes a teacher. In Augustine's essay "The Teacher" (written in the form of questioning), his interlocutor asks, "How in the world do you suppose we learn, if not by asking questions?" Augustine responds, "I think that even then we simply want to teach. Now I am inquiring of you whether you ask a question for any other reason than to teach the person asked what it is you want to know."[31] At the most primordial level of teaching, bodily examples reveal the continuity of teaching and learning; and at the most esoteric level of ultimate questions, the form of questioning reveals that teaching and learning are elements of the same process.

The central element in the classroom is not the idea or the concept but the word. To walk across the threshold of a classroom, whether in second grade or in a doctoral program, is to expose one's words to public scrutiny. The student's thoughts remain private, largely hidden from the teacher and perhaps from the student as well. But words are in between student and teacher with a social and public existence. The teacher's words as well as the student's words are open to questioning. The first question is not, Do you agree? but, What do you mean? or, even more important, What do the words mean? The difference between the intended meaning of the speaker and the lexical meaning of a statement is precisely the space of academic criticism.

The teacher is the one who is supposed to bring the discipline of academic learning to bear on the inevitable disputes about the meaning of the words. The teacher's criticism is not directed at a person but at words. The teacher unendingly asks, "Is there a better way to say what you are trying to say?" As always, the person who deserves the name "teacher" has to show how to do it better. In teaching academically, a teacher has to use a strange style of bending the words back on themselves so that the student begins to hear his or her own words and to recognize their ambiguity.

Where we have descriptions of great thinkers in classrooms, the initial reaction of a student is commonly one of confusion or anger. The description of Wittgenstein's teaching is probably similar to what one would find with any good classroom instructor: "He taught classes not by lecturing, nor yet by what we usually think of as discussion. Wittgenstein thought aloud before his class."[32] The student becomes a participant in this speaking which is thinking aloud. The student's own words are brought into the thinking aloud with the human race. "Midwife teachers help students deliver their words to the world, and they use their own knowledge to put the students into conversation with other voices — past and present in the culture."[33]

Teaching in a classroom never consists of "covering a subject." Books and computers are available for that purpose. What a student should come to a classroom for is to get insight into what has already been read. The amount of the reading is no measure of the insight. Jerome

Bruner describes a course he took with I. A. Richards that began with the teacher writing on the board: "Gray is all theory / Green grows the golden tree of life." Bruner comments, "The reading time for eleven words was three weeks. It was the antithesis of just reading, and the reward in the end was that I owned outright, free and clear, eleven words. A good bargain. Never before had I read with such a lively sense of conjecture, like a speaker and not a listener, or like a writer and not a reader."[34]

The direct object of "to teach" in the classroom setting is usually "a subject." There is a running debate over whether that is the right noun and whether the idea of a school subject is not a false construct. This is a legitimate area for academic criticism. A first question for biology class is "Who says there is such a thing as biology?" The answer will have to include the admission that "biology" is a somewhat arbitrary invention of someone who thought that speaking of a contrast between living things and nonliving things is a helpful way to proceed.

Inevitably, the classroom curriculum has to be broken down into areas of study. Inventing a lot of new names for these areas may seem attractive but it seldom works. The academic world is constantly, though slowly, reshaping these names. Biology can be broken down into smaller areas of study; and biology overlaps other sciences with different approaches. There continue to be people called biologists, chemists, and physicists. That fact does not necessarily mean that high school students should study biology, chemistry, and physics in three different years. A way to get at better questions might be to have biology, chemistry, and physics teachers cooperate in a single curriculum area. The teachers could devise any plan that would stimulate students' thinking about these and other sciences.

P. H. Hirst has proposed that to teach a subject is to deal with a "logical grammar."[35] That is, each school subject to be a subject has to have a particular structure of ideas that can be presented by the teacher. Hirst draws his examples from history, physics, and mathematics. John Passmore has criticized this way of thinking because it seems inapplicable to much of the school timetable; he cites the examples of typing and cooking as school topics that do not have a distinctive logic. He also thinks that to "teach French" is not done by teaching a logical grammar, and that "history" does not have its own logical grammar.[36] That leaves only physics and mathematics for Hirst's explanation of teaching subjects in school.

Passmore raises several interesting questions here. They force one to think in narrower terms (not necessarily a bad thing) of what teaching a subject in a classroom means. Can one teach something in a classroom that is not a "subject"? I think that what we need is to complement the teaching of subjects with another kind of teaching, one that goes on inside the school as well as outside. Topics such as typing or cooking do not belong in the classroom, though they may belong in the performance area described below. Similarly, French or English is not the name of a school subject, but French grammar or British literature can be.

As for history not having its own "logical grammar," I think Passmore is correct. But what this example reveals is that the whole discussion should be about ways of speaking rather than logical structures. A classroom subject is indeed an arbitrary division, but if it is a way of speaking with a long history (and "history," as an example, does have such history), then it may be a serviceable if slightly illogical category. And a new subject can push its way into the curriculum if enough people are convinced that it is an important area around which intelligent discussion is possible. The walls of the classroom curriculum are always being pushed through, moved around, torn down, and rebuilt. That is the excitement and the frustration for anyone whose work is the teaching of subjects in a classroom.

Performance Areas

The previous discussion focused on a single area, the classroom. The classroom is not an essentially different place for girls or boys, 6-year-olds or 60-year-olds, Africans or South Americans. The activity taking place within this space can be described with some precision. However, the second main form of school learning is necessarily in the plural: performance areas. The complexity of performance casts us into bewildering complexity.

One of the many ambiguities surrounding the word *school* is whether it refers to an agency under which a set of activities can be organized or whether it means a separate and quite restricted institution of learning. Especially for younger people, the efficient way to reach them often seems to be under the auspices of the school. Important health and government services are made available in school. For example, many children receive their best meal of the day in the school cafeteria. If a child needs medical first aid or counseling for emotional distress, the school is likely to be a source of help.

As long as costs are contained, few people complain about these additions to the school. However, the process does create a mentality that the school is an agent for all kinds of social assistance. The result is a constant expansion of topics in the curriculum and additional courses in teacher preparation. If there are 40,000 automobile deaths, introduce driver education. If the real estate industry supports racial segregation, integrate society by busing children to school. If AIDS is rampant, distribute condoms in school.

The last example, condoms, has crystallized the problem more than did dozens of other worthwhile concerns that have been installed in schools.[37] The area of AIDS education raises a question about the nature of education and the limits of the school. The importance of the politically volatile issue of condoms is that it forces people to ask theoretically and practically, What is a school? If the relevance to education of AIDS is only discussed under the rubric of the distribution of condoms, many people object that the school is simply aping the vending machines in a typical men's room.

What this issue could spark is a discussion of how the classroom's verbal instruction can be appropriately complemented by another kind of learning, one that I have placed in the performance areas. In the case of AIDS, the performance might include counseling, artistic exhibitions and the availability of materials for the protection of health (all of these approaches carried out with careful attention to the age of students). Nonetheless, because the school is always on the verge of being overwhelmed by society's concerns, it would be desirable to supply many worthwhile services and educational experiences by a means other than the school.

Although there are many services and concerns that are of questionable validity for school to offer, there are performance areas that have rightfully been acknowledged for many decades as part of school. The three main areas are (1) art, (2) job-related work, and (3) sports. For young people, all of these areas should be part of their school education. For older people, a balance of the three need not always be in a school, but the school should not be thought to exclude one or all of these elements.

The arts, as we use the term, are central to anyone's lifelong education. Aesthetic education begins before age 5 and can continue until death. One can learn an art from an individual teacher outside school, but it makes sense to have the school provide organized teaching of various arts. Any school for young people should have designated spaces for laboratory, studio, or audition hall. How much variety a particular school can offer depends upon local conditions, including financial considerations and the availability of teachers. But every school pupil ought to be able to get a taste of some artistic experience.

Many verbal arts have an obvious connection to the classroom and the assessment of classroom learning. I mentioned earlier that dramatic performance is intrinsic to classroom teaching. A natural overflow is into class or school plays. Similarly, a debating team or newspaper staff carries over verbal learning into verbal art. Sometimes the artistic projects are restricted to a small group who engage in extracurriculars. However, learning through group projects should be a regular part of the school (if not the classroom) curriculum. Not everyone is a talented artist; nonetheless, every young person should be able to stand in front of an audience to articulate what he or she knows and to develop a well-shaped argument.

In the previous section, I noted that English or French is not a classroom subject. Learning to speak a language is an art that is not effectively taught in a classroom. For both one's first and second language, the classroom's effective use is after you have learned to speak. The school can supply aids, such as an audiotape library and recorders. Most effectively, the school can be the organizer of travel to a country where the language is spoken. This foreign country may be a few city blocks away.[38]

Other arts, less verbal in character, should have a place in the school distinct from the classroom. When we are not sure whether something belongs in the classroom, we often insist on its place by attaching the word *education* (driver education, physical education, drug education). This peculiar twist of language usually has the opposite effect of certifying that the course is not a serious part of education. Sometimes we attach appreciation to various things that do not fit in the classroom but we think are a part of everyone's education. Thus, we have courses in art appreciation or music appreciation, but such appreciations have often turned students against appreciating anything but the most banal art.

We need serious courses in the classroom that examine the history and nature of art. In addition, if there is to be a growing appreciation of painting, music, sculpture, architecture, pottery, gardening, or wood-working, we need some participation, however amateurish, in the doing of these arts. With some of the arts, one learns solitude and the value of self-discipline. With other arts, one learns the value of teamwork. A band or chorus for children in a school is an invaluable experience of being taught by community, environment, objects, master teacher and fellow apprentices.

The second general area that most schools have some responsibility for is job performance. The classroom instruction for young people needs complementing with the performance of skills that are helpful to holding a job now or in the future. The majority of students in college and even in high school have part-time jobs so that the school's task is not mainly to initiate work programs but to reach a better relation between existing forms of learning.

The high school or college also has to work in cooperation with business institutions, even while being careful to maintain its own autonomy. The business world can sometimes help financially (for example, with computer material); sometimes it can supply specialized teaching. The school has to ask what realistic experiences of the job world are possible within the school's walls. Where a realistic experience of jobs is not possible, then the school must look beyond itself. The school's performance areas may include a factory downtown or a health center in the neighborhood.

Some schools are predominantly this kind of learning. That makes sense for people training to be better at their job or retraining if they are unemployed. A trade school is a place that unashamedly announces what its function is. Many such schools produce what they promise: training for existing jobs. Unfortunately, the jobs are often ones of limited skill for the bottom of the economy. If people are to advance in personal satisfaction and social rewards through work, job performance usually has to be coupled with serious classroom work. This fact is related to the disastrous split in schools for young people.

Since early in this century, there have been academic schools for those headed for the better jobs and vocational schools for those considered not academically talented.[39] What should be two parts of one school became two schools. The two segregated populations were both the poorer for this segregation. Not surprisingly, the students in the vocational schools were financially poorer. Their training was often on outdated equipment and they were prepared for jobs that were either not in the economy or could quickly disappear. The term "vocational," chosen for its religious connotations, was a galling feature of this split that provided power for the rich and a vocation for the poor.

Despite all the limitations of the trade and vocational system, these schools and their dedicated teachers provide important lessons on teaching. The teacher in the classroom, dealing with literature, science, and history, has to ask, In what way is this real work? In what way do I show these students how to perform, not necessarily how to get rich from a job but how to have satisfaction in work? What does hands-on learning mean in a classroom?

The schools that have taught manual trades are still a helpful reminder. However different the future may be, it will still need people who can make things, fix things that are broken, and take care of complicated services to large populations. If the two-tiered school system is gradually integrated, the academic students might get a more realistic taste of the job experience. Learning to use sophisticated machinery to retrieve information should be a part of everyone's education.[40]

I think it should be clear today that an emphasis upon job preparation need not be gender-biased. What Plato envisioned for his upper class is now required for the whole society: equal pay for equal work, and, more important, equal access to all jobs. If the most desirable jobs are to be shared between men and women, then there has to be a more equitable sharing of housework and child care. Plato casually dismisses womanish work in his ideal education for the ideal state.[41] But appreciation of all work and an equitable sharing of the most laborious jobs are necessary for justice between men and women.

In the previous chapter, I called attention to a particular kind of work — service to those in need — as part of education. The performance area here is generally outside the school, but could be organized by the school. The Carnegie report, *High School*, called for a service requirement in each of the four years of high school. The report suggested that an academic credit be given for such work.[42] Perhaps that is the only way to get educational attention, but it muddies the distinction between classroom curriculum and school curriculum. The *New York Times Magazine* published an article on this movement entitled "Soup Kitchen Classroom."[43] That title does not really help either soup kitchens or classrooms, which are complementary forms of education. The classroom needs protection of its fragile boundaries; and the kitchen is not a place to study lessons but to serve soup.

Few people would object to a program of this kind if it is voluntary. But a school requirement, especially if extended to elementary schools, makes people uneasy. Simply requiring a sixth grader to work in a nursing home could have very poor results. But the issue raises interesting questions about having any requirements in schools and how things that are required are designed and carried out.

Schools in the United States have gone in cycles, saying at one time to students, "We know what is best for you, do this," to saying at another time, "We don't know what is best for you, do anything you wish." Today there may be a better environment for the school advising the student, "We know some things that are good for you, so choose courses in these academic areas."[44] Service is another area that should be encountered in everyone's education. The student should be supplied with places to work and invited to design how she or he will do the work. The many schools that have such programs know that this service area is not informal education. The preparation and monitoring of service work involve at least as much form as classroom instruction.

Finally, sport as a teaching-learning activity deserves some comment. Often, the athletic department is seen as a distraction, or something worse, from the serious business of the school. Much of college and high school athletics is a scandal. Some varsity football teams are simply minor-league teams of the NFL. Hundreds of thousands of black students only have eyes for the 300 slots in the NBA. Even high school teams, especially football or basketball but occasionally any sport, can be exaggerated out of all proportion. Nevertheless, when kept under control, sports can teach powerful lessons about living and dying. Often a young person first learns about discipline, motivation, and team effort by sports activity. School people sometimes hate the athletic department because they suspect that it is the only part of the school that really works, where school has a community spirit and players are fully engaged in what they are doing.

The heart of the problem with school sports is not suppressing them but extending them to every student. If basketball is only for twelve people in a school, its effect in the long run is likely to be distortive. But if the basketball program includes everyone who is interested in playing and has a modicum of ability, it deserves to be recognized as an educational force.

Not surprisingly, the segregation of athletes from nonathletes included a strong gender bias. Women were all but excluded from organized sports. Since the passing of Title IX of the Education Amendment Act of 1972, there has been remarkable progress in correcting the terrible bias against girls and women in scholastic sports programs. A long way remains but a fairer, if not equal, attention to women in sports is one of the great educational successes of recent times.

I think there is an interesting parallel here between gender bias in the classroom and in the sports arena. I said that emphasis on language in the classroom is not gender-biased. To have voice in the classroom is at least as important to women as to men. True, the women have been mostly silent and often overlooked in classroom practice. But in every classroom subject women can hold their own, even if the evidence may never be conclusive whether girls are generally better at some subjects, boys at others.

Performance in the sports arena is a similar case. Women have not been present anywhere near as much as men. A call to recognize the importance of sports in teaching may seem biased against women. But the physical education of the human body is at least as important to women as to men. Women may never match men in some highly valued sport's roles (for example, linebacker), but in other sports with criteria of grace and elegance women may be generally superior. In any case, what Plato once again wished for his upper-class guardians — equality of opportunity in sports — may finally be coming about for young people in the near future.

Chapter 9

Teaching Morally, Teaching Morality

THIS LAST CHAPTER returns to the theme of the first chapter: the moral dilemma inherent to teaching. The intervening chapters have laid out the elements for a solution to that dilemma. If one is attentive to the several forms of teaching and the language appropriate to each form, it is possible to teach morally. Only after that is it possible to move on to teaching morality. If teaching were itself an immoral activity, it would be absurd to ask how to teach morality. In this chapter, I summarize the case for teaching morally. I then turn to the teaching of morality in the various forms of education. And for the most challenging test of teaching morality, I offer a final section on classroom instruction in morality.

Before proceeding to the necessary distinctions for teaching morally, teaching morality, and teaching morality in the classroom, I look first at the twentieth century's attempt to deal with morality under the rubric of "moral education." For much of this century, "moral education" has meant a set of techniques that would supposedly facilitate the moral development of children. During the past decade a vigorous reaction has set in, critical of the vacuousness of moral education. This new "moral education" is concerned with character, virtue, and good behavior.[1]

It would be difficult not to feel some sympathy for this recent movement. Who is not in favor of good character and well-behaved children? For more than a decade, Gallup polls have shown 80–90 percent of parents in favor of a moral education that would develop character and encourage the practice of virtues. Schoolteachers, it should be noted, are nowhere near so enthusiastic. Are they just shirking their duty? Or could it be that while the parents are right in thinking that morality is about good character and virtuous behavior, schoolteachers are also right in sensing the limits of the classroom for such education?

The key to progress here is an understanding of the forms and languages of teaching. In the current cries for reform there is very

little evidence that the issue of teaching is being examined. An earlier phase of moral education — typified by the "values clarification"
of the 1960s — tried to avoid anything that would smack of teaching. The recent reaction simply assumes that if character, virtue, and
good behavior are what we want, then we just get someone to teach
these things ("Tell them what is right"). I have argued in this book that
we need a richer meaning of teaching than is usually assumed. At the
same time, we need a carefully limited and precisely focused purpose
for classroom instruction. The question of morality is the great test for
both points.

"Moral education," as a single term with a single referent, was
born at the beginning of the twentieth century. Not that the adjective "moral" was a stranger to the term "education." But for the most
part, the phrase "moral education" would have sounded redundant. Education since the time of the Greek philosophers was assumed to be
a moral undertaking. In the founding of the U.S. public school, for
example, morality was a dominant concern.[2] Toward the end of the
nineteenth century, however, the rise of the sciences and the decline
of religion led to the conviction that education was becoming amoral.
Two opposite corrections were possible. One was to add a remedy called
"moral education"; the other was to rethink the moral character of all
education.

It may seem that because of the complexity and special circumstances of our era we need something called "moral education." Nonetheless, one must also reckon with the possibility that "moral education"
obscures the questions of teaching morally and teaching morality. The
attempt to create an *addition* to education that deals exclusively with
moral problems reinforces the presumption of the amoral character of
education. An adequate reform movement would probably get rid of the
phrase "moral education" so as to examine morality in education itself.
Most of all it would have to examine the possibilities and difficulties of
teaching morally and teaching morality.

A reform movement that is unacquainted with the past is doomed
to be merely reactive. Why did a moral education, dismissive of terms
such as *character* and *virtue*, arise in the first place? The impression is
sometimes given that a few radicals in the 1960s brought about this
whole problem. The story is much longer and more complicated.

The roots of the moral-education movement go back to the early
stage of modernity. In the seventeenth and eighteenth centuries, many

people hoped that science and religion could work together. The division of the work was that the intellectual class would live by science and the masses would continue to believe the myths of religion. The flaw in this arrangement was that education was placed on the side of science. As education advanced along with science, religion was bound to retreat. The foundation of morality in most people's lives was outside or even opposed to education.

At the middle of the nineteenth century, the study of moral philosophy, with its strong Christian overtones, was still the crown of education in many colleges, the course often being taught by the college president.[3] However, moral philosophy was on one side being crowded by its partner, natural philosophy (empirical science), and on the other side it was being shaken by the troubles of moral theology. A crisis in the religious foundations of morality emerged earlier in Europe than in the United States.

Emile Durkheim is one of the inventors of the term "moral education." In his book of that title, published in 1900, Durkheim described the experiment that was underway:

> We decided to give our children in our state-supported schools a purely secular moral education. It is essential to understand that this means an education that is not derived from revealed religion, but that rests exclusively on ideas, sentiments and practices accountable to reason only — in short, a purely rationalistic education.

Durkheim was referring to 1880–1900 for the launching of a purely rationalistic education in France. In contrast, John Dewey during the same period in the United States had plenty of religious elements in his writings.[4]

Durkheim's book itself has some misgivings about a purely rationalistic education. He was aware that people have never lived by reason alone and probably never will. The moral life is shaped by the power of a community to inculcate discipline and provide guidance for attitudes and practices. Durkheim thought that the family is "an inappropriate agency" for a completely rationalistic education; but "the task of the school in the moral development of the child can and should be of the greatest importance."[5]

Durkheim locates the verb "to teach" with the school's reflection on the needs of society: "To teach morality is neither to preach nor to indoctrinate; it is to explain."[6] What he is in flight from is obvious enough in this statement: preaching and indoctrination. While Durkheim wanted no part of that kind of teaching, he was trapped into using these practices as a reference point for his only alternative: explain.

The history of religious bodies reveals many other ways to teach morality than by indoctrination and preaching. The religions teach mainly by story, example, and ritual. Durkheim's reduction of "to teach = to explain" has the unfortunate effect of giving over most of moral education to processes other than teaching. And in moral education subsequent to Durkheim, even the small part accorded to teaching (that is, explaining) morality has often been denied.

Jean Piaget is the other twentieth-century giant in the origin of moral education. Like Durkheim, Piaget assumes the intellectual bankruptcy of religion as a moral foundation. The title of Piaget's book, *The Moral Judgment of the Child*, indicates the clear and narrow focus of his moral education: judgments made by children. At the beginning of the book, he announces in one sweeping statement: "All morality consists in a system of rules, and the essence of all morality is to be sought for in the respect which the individual acquires for the rules."[7] If one accepts that this is the meaning of morality, then the preeminent task is to have children reason and judge properly. The child discovers the rules through interaction with other children, but morality is not mainly a communal affair; it is about the individual and his respect for rules. Moral education thereby moved from the sociologist describing group behavior to the psychologist describing structures of the individual mind.

Piaget expresses strong disagreement with Durkheim for retaining a morality based on "authority." Piaget rejects the preeminence that Durkheim gives to the school community. He particularly objects to the premise that "the schoolmaster is the priest who acts as an intermediary between society and the child."[8] Adults in general and schoolteachers in particular tend to get in the way of the child's development of moral judgment. Experiencing a game with rules intrinsic to the game is the kind of prod that the child's judgment about justice requires. "Teaching," as Piaget uses the term, has little part.

The child who has begun to reason about rules goes through two stages: the first in which rules are thought to be eternally fixed and externally imposed; the second in which rules are seen to be devised by the community for the service of its changing needs. This second stage of autonomous judgment follows upon the capacity to grasp the concept of equality and a concomitant ability to react emotionally to problems of inequity.[9]

After Piaget documents in exquisite detail this movement to autonomous judgment, he admits there may be further stages that are not within his purview. As an individual passes from childhood to adulthood, other moral categories, such as care or compassion, may become central.[10] Piaget quotes a precocious 13-year-old who, when asked why he did not hit back after having been hit, replied, "Because there is no end to vengeance."[11] Some people (and many nations) never grasp that moral insight. It comes from a moral education not restricted to abstract ideas of equality.

Lawrence Kohlberg, whose name became almost synonymous with moral education in the United States, thought that it was logical to try to stretch Piaget's categories beyond where Piaget had firmly anchored them. Kohlberg used to describe his work as "putting patches on Piaget."[12] Beyond the merely conventional morality that Piaget suggests can be reached by most adults, Kohlberg postulated a "postconventional" morality, in which the individual goes beyond the observance of rules to a more universal stand. Like Durkheim and Piaget, Kohlberg begins with the rejection of a "revealed morality" that he assumes to be the Christian basis of moral education.[13] As in Piaget, the alternative lies in discovering the structures of the mind and the way to facilitate passage from one stage to another.

In 1978 Kohlberg wrote a brief essay that expressed doubt about the whole system.[14] His great hope of a decade earlier for moving students up the ladder to "principled reasoning" had not been realized. The simple fact struck him forcefully that little boys are prone to lie and cheat. Perhaps for some of the population, Kohlberg mused, a little indoctrination might not be such a bad thing. After two decades of attacking religions' use of indoctrination, Kohlberg toyed with the enemy's word.

Describing the effect of Kohlberg's musings, James Rest wrote that for a Kohlbergian it was similar to the first mate hearing that "the captain of the ship has just jumped ship and is headed on another boat in the opposite direction."[15] But then everyone, including Kohlberg, seemed to go back to the business of measuring stages. The collections of Kohlberg's papers, published in the 1980s, show few glimmers of doubt that moral education equals moral development, and that moral development equals the child's power to reason about moral dilemmas.

What Kohlberg might have found if he had delved more deeply into religious practice is a richer meaning of education, including education in moral practices. The major religions are very practical and thoroughly realistic about morality. None of these religions has been unaware of the fact that children lie and cheat. Countermeasures are in place from the beginning so that one does not suddenly have to resort to indoctrination when reasoning does not work. Moral education begins neither with doctrine nor reasoning but with discipline, practice, and ritual.

Religion has been one of the sources for the recent reaction against the Kohlberg version of moral education. "Character" and "virtue" are not necessarily religious terms, but many people closely associate such terms with the Christian religion. For the more secular-minded people in the recent movement, the shift is in part from Piaget back to Durkheim: the school has to socialize the child, teach the child the rules of good behavior. An alternative path of reaction to Kohlberg has been feminist criticism, initiated by Carol Gilligan. Moral development is less about abstract reasoning than about care, compassion, and responsibility.[16]

One of the leading writers in "character education" has been Thomas Lickona. At first, Lickona seemed only to be offering a practical guide for applying Kohlberg. But the subtitle of a later work, "how our schools can teach respect and responsibility," conveys a different project than Kohlberg's. While not directly attacking Kohlberg's theories, Lickona has called for a different approach to educating children in morality. He has also gone into considerable detail on the topic. While other writers usually give a paragraph or at most a chapter to parents, Lickona devoted a book to the family's part before writing a book on the school. His books are eclectic attempts to blur the sharp edges of controversy in this area.[17]

Other writers are more inclined to take a polemical attitude toward what they see as the disastrous failure of Kohlberg-style moral education. William Kilpatrick, in *Why Johnny Can't Tell Right from Wrong*, sets up a contrast between two approaches to moral education. The first is character education, in which there are traits that children should learn and practice; the second is "decision making," a phrase that the author uses interchangeably with moral reasoning, the dilemma method, and values clarification.[18] I think that this contrast is badly stated; it compares two different kinds of things: an understanding of the purpose of education over against an approach in the classroom. That is, most schoolteachers would not vote against character education but they need some distinctions for understanding the classroom's contribution to educating character.

Kilpatrick contrasts two possible courses that might be taught in elementary grades. The first course would deal with dilemmas in which there are no right or wrong answers; teachers would be nonjudgmental and allow students to develop their own value systems. The second course would make a conscious effort to teach specific virtues and character traits; the teacher would express strong belief in the importance of these virtues and encourage students to practice them.[19] Kilpatrick expresses disdain that a majority of schoolteachers, when asked to choose between these two courses, prefer the first. As a classroom instructor, I would certainly choose the first over the second — if those were the only two choices. The first would probably have little effect while the second would undermine the work of the classroom. But this choice is a false one; neither the first nor the second describes an academic course. The direct object of instruction in a classroom cannot be "specific virtues and character traits." That is not to deny that education is concerned with virtue, character, and good behavior; but appropriate distinctions have to be observed.

Within the new moral education, the failure to make any precise and consistent distinctions is manifest in the way "teach," "teaching," and "teacher" are used. So long as teaching is assumed to be what schoolteachers attempt to do in classrooms, then morality and education cannot be properly related. Today's reformers persist in giving over the name "teacher" to those who properly do only one limited form of teaching. Looking back nostalgically on the past, Kilpatrick writes, "The idea that the parent is the first and foremost teacher was taken seriously: teachers acted for the parents as trustees of children's education."[20] A moment's reflection shows that Kilpatrick does not take seriously his own statement that the parent is "the first and foremost teacher." The second half of his sentence ("teachers acted for the parents") contradicts the fact that the parent is a teacher at all. In many books the pious claim that parents are the most important teachers is denied in the next paragraph. Kilpatrick's feat is to put the contradiction in one sentence.

The point may seem minor. Doesn't everyone know what "teacher" means in such statements? The answer, I think, is no. Discussions on education (including its moral dimension) get stalled because we do not name teach, teaching, and teachers properly. Behind that confusion is the unresolved moral problem with teaching itself. The recent writing on moral education tends to dump the problem at the schoolhouse door. Aren't we all in favor of virtue and character? Yes. How does one *teach* virtues, character traits, or good behavior? That's the [school]teachers' job. Let them solve the problem.

Teaching Morally

I began this book by referring to feelings of moral uneasiness about the act of teaching. I cited examples of a widespread suspicion that teaching cannot be done morally, that it is an unethical act. The problem is not surprising if one starts consideration from the typical image of teaching that has dominated modern educational theory: an adult schoolteacher, a child learner, and a subject matter between them. The schoolteacher, most often a woman, is seen as the agent of a system that wishes proper truths to be known. The student is seen as an unwilling child, compelled by law and social custom to be on the receiving end. The curriculum or subject matter is taken to be what some group thinks every youngster should know.

The moral conflict inherent to this image leads to endless wrangling over issues that are not likely to relieve the underlying conflict. Students periodically rebel against the oppressive power of their teachers (even though the teachers themselves may feel powerless). In recent years the rebellion has often been against the choice of writers included in the textbooks and the (classroom) curriculum. But even the most determined attempts at curriculum inclusivity leave various groups feeling oppressed.[21]

My own way of addressing the problem of teaching morally has been to step back from classroom teaching to examine what teaching means in more ordinary situations. Unless these other kinds of teaching are taken seriously, schoolteachers will inevitably be asked to do more than is possible and other than what is ethically defensible. The fundamental meaning of "to teach," as to show someone how to do something, does not immediately connote any moral conflict. Teaching is a special kind of gift that calls forth a personal response. If a gift is not received it turns out to be not a gift but an attempted gift. Coercion is a sign that we are not dealing in gift exchange, that is, something both freely given and freely received.

The most comprehensive teacher is the whole universe, which offers gifts each day. The human being can receive the gift of learning from ocean and desert, mountain and tree, sunlight and star; or the human being can refuse to be taught. The individual human can refuse to learn (or be taught), although it is a refusal to accept one's human nature as the preeminently teachable animal. Individuals can diminish their own humanity, but if most of the human race takes this attitude toward air, water, topsoil, forest, and earth, then the human race will eventually discover that a refusal to be taught is not a long-term option. "Liberation from the soil is not freedom for the tree," wrote Tagore. Liberation from being taught is not freedom for the humans.

The potential for moral conflict has its beginnings when we pass from the universe to the human community as the teacher. Here, the individual human being cannot reject being taught, any more than the human race can reject the sun. To be a human being is to be in the relation of teaching-learning with the human community. The difficulty, however, is that "the human community" is never available. At any particular time and place, what we find are incomplete and imperfect representations of community, for example, one's family.

We do not quibble about the limitations of our community when we are born to this mother and this father. Before one can start raising questions about the deficiencies of one's family, clan, tribe, or nation, one has to have received life and the basic skills to survive. The particular community in being itself says, Here is how to eat, how to speak, how to protect yourself from the cold, how to make things. No one complains that he or she was taught to eat food rather than have the freedom to ingest poison.

The moral problem of teaching emerges fully when an individual steps forth and is called "the teacher." The authority on which this step is taken is an issue that can never be fully resolved. No one gets appointed as universal teacher, a teacher of all things to all people. Anyone who wishes to play the part of teacher must examine the conditions under which he or she can legitimately teach. Who did the appointing and for how long? What is this teacher appointed to teach? Who are the prospective students?

The answers to some of these questions depend upon the teacher listening to the prospective students. Most particularly, the teacher has to ascertain whether the potential learners are actually ready to learn. Clear signals have to provide an affirmative answer that the students are ready at this time, in this place, to learn this skill. That is why times and places have been designated to indicate acceptance of the teaching-learning situation. If someone walks across the threshold of a classroom, that is a signal of a willingness to learn in one clearly specified way for fifty minutes or two hours. The classroom consent is no more and no less than to expose to critical examination one's written and spoken words on an agreed-upon topic.

The learner's consent is to one or a few forms of teaching. Each institution has specified limitations that protect the learner's right to privacy. In a classroom, the learner has a right not to be bombarded with speech not generally appropriate for the classroom. The learner in a church congregation or the client in a therapist's office has consented to other forms of speech. A moral crisis arises when institutions overstep their respective boundaries.

Freedom is always a bounded situation. A person exists with a physical body and a psychological makeup that are a precipitate of the past. At each moment the choice is to consent to what is offered or to say no. Sometimes saying no makes available other possibilities; sometimes the no is all that the exercise of freedom means right now. Over against large institutions (banks, business corporations, post office, city hall) the individual can feel powerless. We do not really expect to win individual games with large foreign powers, but we become dispirited if they run up the score. Children feel much of the time that they are being had. Even when adults try to be nice, children are so outgunned that kindness can seem condescending.

Protests against teaching are usually a protest against the unfair distribution of power that many young people (and some older people) feel. They want a say in how their lives flow. The school is a place that often focalizes resentment, even though the school is usually less repressive than many other institutions. With a few basic changes, students in school can come to see that the school is more on their side than against it.

Very few young people really wish to run a school, but most of them do wish to have some choices in school. Those choices involve space, time, and the forms of learning. Why cannot schools allow students to move between the school's two main areas of learning, choosing to concentrate on one or the other? Why cannot every student be invited to contribute to the design of courses? Such suggestions may sound like prescriptions for chaos, but any movement in the direction of increased choice can be cautious and measured. The principle of respect for a student's choice should be immediately and clearly affirmed. Young people are likely to be patient if they know that the adults are serious about moving in the direction of increased freedom.

In school, a teacher should not have to be confronting students daily in a conflict between the right to teach and the freedom to learn. The validation of the teacher's work should not rest entirely on each teacher establishing it. The environment and the community should supply the context for supporting the teacher's role of authority. The professional schoolteacher has a license to teach, the freedom to do whatever seems the best way to go at teaching-learning. This license is the basis for trust, without which no teaching takes place. If a teacher regularly violates this trust, he or she quite literally loses the ability to teach — which is why asking classroom instructors to teach character traits or specific virtues is seriously detrimental. In contrast, the schoolteacher who uses the license responsibly has a right to the support of school administrators, parents, business people, politicians, religious leaders. When the moral authority of a teacher is evident, students learn not by being subservient but by being cooperative.

There are many situations, of course, in which the potential learner cannot foresee what is coming. He or she consents on the basis of trust in the teacher for getting the process started. If the teacher in a classroom, gymnasium, factory, or church turns out to be unreasonably demanding or a total fraud, there need to be escape hatches for the learner. Even the most trustworthy of teachers needs places along the way to renegotiate the learner's original consent to join the process. The moral character of teaching-learning never reaches a place so secure that it is invulnerable to corruption. However, the moral universe of teaching does not have to be reconstituted every day. Unless there is evidence to the contrary in particular situations, to teach is a morally good activity.

Teaching Morality

This section explores what happens when "moral" is moved from a quality of teaching to the object of teaching. I propose that some kind of morality is always being taught in the activity of showing someone how to live. The explicitness of the concern with morality can vary greatly. In the classroom, for example, every academic subject has a moral dimension, though often it is best kept implicit. However, morality itself can be conceived as an academic subject and then morality becomes the explicit object of classroom teaching. This concern of teaching morality in the classroom is the final test of what teaching morality means; it can also be taken as the final test of what classroom teaching is. Both of those aspects of teaching morality in a classroom are treated in a final section below.

The teaching of morality follows a path similar to teaching morally. That is, we can start with the universe as a whole. The world and all of the great forces within the world teach both greatness and limitation to human aspirations. The human race can also take lessons about good and bad activity from their next of kin in the animal world. At another level, the human community has a moral wisdom that the individual must confront in learning morality. A particular human community, however, introduces questions of authority, place, age, and historical changes. Thus, when a human individual presumes to teach morality, he or she is subject to challenge. Does any individual have the right to teach morality? How can anyone claim certainty for the morality that is taught?

I said earlier that the modern flight from religion unfortunately entailed a flight from all but the most rationalistic form of teaching. The resulting loss was especially grievous in the area of morality. If moral principles, standards, and practices are not taught, the moral life suffers. Calls to reverse this trend often appeal to authoritarian strains that in the long run will fail. Trying to hammer home a moral code is not the way to teach morality.

One of the striking things to learn from traditional religions is that the teachings do not constitute morality in our sense of the word. Instead, the teachings are about small rituals and ordinary practices that do not seem to have moral content: how one dresses and wears one's hair, what one eats and drinks, when one is silent and to whom one speaks, when the time is for sleep and when the time to awake. These are the disciplines that create communities of moral people. Describing Jewish religion, Wayne Meeks writes that "the rabbis begin with what good men in stable communities do." That starting point is similar to Aristotle's, but while Aristotle moves toward clear and logical principles, the rabbis pursue individual instances and thinkable exceptions. "They rarely generalize; they exemplify."[22] With only slight variation, that statement could be made of all the religions: they teach morality by exemplifying life in a virtuous community.

A commandment, therefore, is not an abstract principle but a statement of address. The commandment is a boundary within which life goes on. If one regularly lives by the minor commandments, one will not find the major commands burdensome.[23] When "exhortation" is required, it is to a community that already knows what it should be doing but has strayed from its duties. An individual may stand up and do the reminding from within the group or the reminder and correction may have to come from an outside standard of judgment — not usually a universal law, but a more comprehensive tradition.

Each of the forms of education described in chapter 7 teaches morality in its own fashion. Family, classroom, job, and leisure can be examined as teachers of morality.

Family relations teach morality every day. The lesson varies according to whether the learner is a 2-year-old only child, a 16-year-old oldest of seven, a 30-year-old parent of three, or a 65-year-old grandparent. Children, however young, are morally educated by routines of daily existence. Long before a child can reflect upon rules of conduct, the child's moral future is profoundly influenced.

The strange phrase "family values" has achieved widespread use in recent years; it seems to be a code word for one set of political beliefs. There is no package of "values" that automatically comes with a family. What the family almost always provides is the basis of both good and evil in an individual's life; that is, the family is the primary moral teacher. As I have repeatedly pointed out, the customary usage of "teach" and "teacher" denies this fact. Not surprisingly, the economic and social policies of the country (not withstanding the rhetorical flourishes about family values) reflect a belief that families do not teach and that parents do not need support as teachers.

When moral education is equated with moral reasoning, very young children disappear from the map of moral education. John Locke and Jean-Jacques Rousseau had one of their sharpest disagreements over the reasoning powers of the child.[24] Rousseau thought children should be shielded from reasoning as long as possible, experiencing at first the limits of things. In twentieth-century moral education, Rousseau would seem to have carried the day. Young children are assumed to be incapable of moral reasoning. In Piaget's vocabulary, young children are "pre-moral"; they follow rules but are incapable of reflecting on those rules.[25]

It is doubtful, however, that Rousseau would recognize what he helped to create. He would applaud the realization that large doses of reasoning should not be demanded of young children. But Rousseau insists that "the education of man begins at his birth."[26] Everything done to the child has a moral effect. Children are shown a way of life that they absorb very early. Later they may rebel against it and try to change it, but they cannot entirely discard it. Even John Locke, with his belief in the boy's reasoning powers, devotes the first thirty sections of his book on education to the child's health and bodily nurture. In Locke's four main parts of education, virtue comes first; after that comes wisdom and breeding; finally comes learning.[27]

The child is obviously vulnerable to being miseducated. We have lately become more aware of the violation called child abuse, including abuse of a sexual kind. Rousseau — out of his personal experience — was one of the first writers who began the exposé of child abuse.[28] Other writers quickly followed. We might think there was a sudden rash of child abuse in the eighteenth century. On the contrary, that century was the beginning of the end of child abuse, even though we have yet to bring about that end. The eighteenth century's great contribution was to name the reality and so make it visible.[29]

One of the tragic aspects of child abuse is its self-perpetuating character. Those who are beaten up early in life usually learn their lesson well. Surely, breaking the cycle of child abuse should be central to education in morality, but the issue is simply beyond the boundary of what the twentieth century, either earlier or more recently, calls "moral education." Children are taught by what they see, hear, touch, and taste. To care for a child and show love teaches care and love. To abuse a child sexually or otherwise is to teach a devastating lesson in violence.

I will postpone until the end of this chapter the classroom teaching of morality. But I take note here of the way that schools in other ways teach morality. As in the family setting, the school does most of its teaching by example. The school can be looked upon as a moral community that shows how virtue is practiced. The school community differs from the family community by having a wider range of examples. Morality is taught in a school by the example of other children and by the adult lives of administrators, classroom instructors, coaches, counselors, and janitors. The chief barometer of what the adults are teaching the children is how the adults interact with each other.

Even a small school has a degree of impersonality that sets it in contrast to the family. Durkheim and others believed that the impersonal is not always negative. It can be a helpful aspect of moral learning. A child needs the experience of being treated as the most important person in the world; the child also needs the experience of being one among many important beings. School can be a place of fairness, decency, and respect even when hundreds or thousands of pupils are passing through the doors. Providing safe spaces where youngsters are left alone is a way that schools teach a meaning of leisure that has some moral depth. Encouraging and respecting good work, whatever be the school activity, is a way to teach a moral meaning of work.

At least once a year the *New York Times* has a story headlined, "U.S. Schools Put New Stress on Teaching of Moral Values,"[30] or something akin to that. The new stress has been going on for quite a few years. Perhaps there has been progress from the time when values were only being "clarified." If the schools are recognizing a responsibility to teach values, that could be a great improvement. However, I think it is still unclear what it means to teach values.

"Values" is an abstract term that is presumably a name for a collection of desirable qualities: honesty, responsibility, compassion, courage, friendship, and the like. Such lists of values do not generate protest in the name of dishonesty, irresponsibility, or cowardice. Everyone seems agreed on the value of teaching values. But this quick and easy consensus indicates that all the hard questions have been avoided.

I would not belittle an increased awareness on the part of school staff about how their attitudes and practices affect students. The concern is certainly praiseworthy if it translates into schools being places of honesty and responsibility, and school staff being friendly and helpful. In addition, the school should encourage and support students who are helpful to each other or helpful to people in the school's service program. I do not think the recognition has to be with external rewards.

In one *New York Times* piece, "Teaching of Values in U.S. School," an example of instilling values at one school is "secretaries and cafeteria workers pass out coupons worth twenty-five cents in the bookstore to children who are friendly and polite."[31] What the school is actually teaching by such a practice may be something different from friendship and politeness; perhaps how to make money from acting (at least "acting" in the sense of pretending to be) virtuous. Nevertheless, at least the question of "teaching values" is being put in the right arena, namely, the curriculum of the school rather than the curriculum of the classroom. Individuals are taught to be honest by the example of people in honest communities. For children, the school is a central community of their lives, and the school in its total environment of physical space, temporal arrangements, and human interaction is a main teacher of morality.

A person's job is also an important teacher for nearly all people, especially after they leave high school or college. The kind of work we do and the way we do it shape our way of life. It is morally debilitating not to be able to have a job, that is, tasks that involve intelligence, skill, and training, and which contribute to society's functioning. Money does not have to be involved, although money is often a sign that the job is valued and the laborer is respected. Whether or not money is involved, recognition and appreciation of one's efforts are intrinsic elements in the job being real work.

Some jobs wear people down; those jobs that are physical drudgery or mindless repetition teach very little moral sensibility or passion for justice. But most jobs have at least some spark of possibility for being reshaped into work of friendliness, helpfulness, and social improvement. Bank tellers, toll collectors, elevator operators, postal workers, taxi drivers, train conductors and at times anyone else, can turn bitter and crusty at the limitations of their jobs. Or the way the job is done can teach a lesson about human community and service to fellow human beings.

There is often a strong moral fiber to people in the laboring class who do jobs that are inadequately paid but are necessary for society's running. Getting up in the morning and going off to a job (sometimes within the home itself) take a discipline of life that is reinforced by doing the best job one can. The reward looked for is not wealth but a decent life for one's family or for friends whom one is supporting. In almost every job there are both good and bad examples one can learn from. One's moral development depends on how one responds to both teachers.

An increasing number of workers call themselves "professionals." The term sometimes only means the claim to more money and more control of one's work. Both of these benefits are in fact part of modern professions. However, the benefits are granted because of a more stringent morality. Professional people are not necessarily better people, but they are people who profess something about the value of their work. They believe, for example, that in a conflict between client and money, the client comes first; otherwise, they have no right to the term "professional." They are people who claim to have a calling, an idea traceable to religious vocation and vows.

Since professionals have been graced by some knowledge or skill that a community needs, they have to take special pride in doing their work well, not mainly for money but because the work is worth doing. Professional work is usually more complex and personally fulfilling. It ought to give a moral shape to much of one's life. It is the kind of work one need never entirely retire from.

"Retirement" is not a term in simple opposition to *work;* it refers to degrees of disengagement from one or more *jobs*. If you are a quarterback in the National Football League, retirement is early, definite, and permanent. So, too, is retirement from many jobs that require sheer bodily strength or coordination of bodily skills. But if one is a writer, actor, philosopher, economist, psychotherapist, one might not ever retire completely, though elderhood involves accepting a change in one's physical energies to do some aspects of the work.

In Erik Erikson's scheme of psychosocial development, the last stage of life is characterized by "integrity," a word having strong moral connotations.[32] Similarly, in chapter 7 I placed wisdom as the value embodied in retirement and leisure activity. By the time one is old, life should have taught the person some semblance of wisdom and moral integrity. This moral teaching should have begun in the infant's playpen and continued throughout school and job. The trials of old age challenge life's earlier teaching and develop the human individual's receptivity to life, inclusive of death.

The morality of wisdom is the nonattachment to any earthly possession. One is grateful for the day; one enjoys the hour; one lives in the present moment. Morality is often misunderstood to be a kind of higher selfishness: keep the rules and get greater rewards. The person who morally develops into old age recognizes that we came into this world without possessions and we leave the same way. The deaths of people we love remind us of our own mortality. Death is a powerful teacher for those who are ready to learn.

Retirement from a job does not guarantee a sudden surge of wisdom. Not every 70-year-old is a Buddhist sage. But the leisure activities throughout life, and especially in the older years, carry people down one of two moral paths. Either they become more egocentric in their interests, turned in on their own problems. Or else, they turn toward greater compassion for human and nonhuman life. The liberation from means-to-end thinking can release in older lives a care for other older people who are worse off, and a concern for the young who share a similar position of vulnerability.

Older people often share a conspiratorial friendship with both young children and teenagers. The young and the old often find that they can teach each other about transitions into new life. Sometimes parents and children are locked too closely together; the grandparent has a helpful degree of objectivity. For the child the grandparent paradoxically represents vitality, even in the face of approaching death. The quiet center of retirement's leisure activity seems to be almost contentless, but it is really a revelation of the harmony and unity that morality moves toward.

Teaching Morality in Classrooms

In this final section, a separate consideration is needed for the classroom's part in teaching morality. Two challenges are raised by this issue. What light does teaching *morality* in a classroom throw upon teaching anything in a classroom? How does the *classroom's* part in teaching morality relate to the teaching of morality in and by other educational settings?

Contemporary advocates of character and virtue almost never examine how limited classroom instruction is in this area. They seem to treat literature as illustrations of virtue: choose literature on the basis of which virtue is to be "taught."[33] In contrast, throughout much of the academic world there is a widespread belief that it is impossible — or at least academically illegitimate — to teach morality in a classroom. Concerning the teachability of things in a classroom, a spectrum is assumed that has mathematics and physical science at one end; there is no debate that physics and calculus are teachable subjects. Moving away from that end of the spectrum, we can locate literature, history, human sciences as also teachable. But for many people, religion and morality go off the scale. They are thought to be too private, too subjective, too lacking in definite answers.

A first clarification needed is that "morality" is not an adequate name for indicating the academic form of teaching morality. The academic subject is probably best indicated by the term "ethics." In previous centuries, terms such as "moral science" or "moral philosophy" have served this purpose. Today the term "values" seems to be assumed by some people, but I do not think that the case has been made that "values" is the name of an academic subject. "Ethics," like "morality," began as a term to describe human activities, rather than teaching-learning about these activities. However, ethics has a long history as part of philosophical inquiry.

What is worrisome when people dismiss the possibility of teaching morality/ethics in a classroom is not what they assume about morality, but what they think "to teach" means. An understanding of the teaching of morality/ethics might help to clarify what it means to teach anything. If teaching in a classroom consisted of telling people what is so, then teaching morality/ethics would be a violation of the pupil's right to privacy, conscience, and freedom. The question is whether the main confusion pertains to teaching morality/ethics or to teaching mathematics, science, literature, and history.

The classroom, I have previously argued, is not a place for telling people the truth. It is a place for a peculiar kind of conversation — ultimately a conversation about the nature of conversation. The person who is teaching turns the words of the conversation back on themselves. Every question asked, every problem raised has ambiguity built into the formulation. But the ambiguity in the words is not limitless. Through sustained conversation we can hope to narrow misunderstandings even if we cannot reach complete agreement. To teach morality is to be skeptical of any yes or no answer to a complicated problem. The teacher's job is to be certain that there are enough voices in the discussion and that the terms of the dispute are carefully reflected upon. This process bears little resemblance to what is characterized as "value-free inquiry."

In contrast to academic teaching as conversation, consider this statement in Stephen Carter's *The Culture of Disbelief*:

> It is difficult to resist the impression that some educators simply feel uncomfortable with stating a clear and simple value — they seem to believe that in some way, by telling students what they *should* do (instead of telling them how to do what they want to do) they are engaging in a form of pedagogy best avoided.[34]

I think that "telling students what they *should* do" is indeed a form of pedagogy best avoided. The classroom teacher has no business telling people what they should do, beyond stating the rules of civility in classroom behavior.

Carter's alternative to telling them what they should do is contained within the parentheses: "telling them how to do what they want to do." I would guess he intends that phrase to be caricature or sarcasm. Actually, it is close to stating the classroom's task. As formulated, however, I would not accept either of his alternatives. The underlying problem here is the assumption that to teach is to tell, that classroom teaching in particular is the use of a form of speech in which teachers tell students what is true and what is false, what is right and what is wrong.

Carter wants students "to be told that abstinence is a good and desirable thing." I would not tell students in a classroom that (sexual?) abstinence is a good and desirable thing. I agree that teachers should *not* be telling students that abstinence is a bad and undesirable thing. But the academic alternative to both "tellings" is to bring students into the conversation from which the teacher's own opinions and beliefs have emerged. At the end of that conversation, the student may or may not agree with the teacher. The teacher's success is reflected in whether the student has a better understanding of the issue discussed. To teach ethics is to show a student how to use a language of morality that can improve his or her understanding.

A procedure that is sometimes employed with ethics courses is the case study debate in which the student takes sides.[35] As a technique to get students involved, there is some merit to the approach. But if the result is that the pro and con sides simply dig in deeper to defend their respective opinions, the classroom's potential is dissipated. In a few cases (capital punishment, nuclear war), the yes or no is clear-cut. On ideas of euthanasia, abortion, sexual codes, bigotry, there is probably more agreement than is evident in most debates. If the classroom does not supply a better understanding of what these questions mean, our politics will get hopelessly stalemated. Other issues (feminism, multiculturalism, environmentalism) are not case studies at all but complex movements overlaid with various ideologies. Taking sides on these issues is likely to generate more heat than understanding.

The ethics teacher, like all classroom teachers, has to have two points of view: the first is that the position he or she puts forth is true because it draws upon the richest strands of human history and geography. The second is the view that the position stated is deficient because formulations can always be improved. This dual perspective always applies in the classroom: a certainty that one has some hold on the truth and a certainty that one cannot state the whole truth. What the teacher says in conversation is asserted as not false and not empty, but there is always more to learn for the teacher as well as the taught. The ethics teacher is no worse off here than the science or art teacher; perhaps the ethics teacher is a little better off in having to acknowledge the duality.

An individual teacher need not have numerous perspectives; the textbook and the computer should supply these. There are indeed numerous perspectives on feminism, peace, pollution, poverty, and so forth. At some moments in life it may seem distracting to have more than one perspective. There is nothing wrong with "peace now," "a woman's body is her own," or "gay pride" on a banner at a rally. However, when an emotionally charged issue shows up in the classroom, no orthodoxy can be left unchallenged. In a classroom, every formula on every topic is open to criticism.

Take an extreme case. A school curriculum *Facing History and Ourselves* is in wide use throughout the country; it concentrates, though not exclusively, on the Holocaust.[36] In 1986 it was refused funding by a federal agency. The rumor was leaked out that the refusal was based on the fact that the curriculum did not give Hitler's side. This rumor was confirmed in 1995 when Newt Gingrich tried to appoint the evaluator, Christina Jeffrey, to be historian of the House of Representatives. Jeffrey had written in her evaluation, "The program gives no evidence of balance or objectivity. The Nazi point of view, however unpopular, is still a point of view and is not presented."[37] When that statement was made public it was met with scorn and disbelief. Actually, there was a valid point to be made here, but Jeffrey's phrasing of the issue as "balance or objectivity," as well as Hitler's view being "unpopular," was a naive and misleading way to make her point.

A curriculum that would provide moral symmetry to Hitler and to the victims of the Holocaust would be nothing short of obscene. Nonetheless, the classroom is a place to examine every viewpoint, even Hitler's. Otherwise, the mode of discourse is preaching, rather than academic criticism. The classroom's contribution to preventing future holocausts is understanding, which involves getting inside the minds of

everyone involved in the Holocaust. There is a time for memorial services, for protesting bigotry, for preaching love, for legal restraints on
neo-Nazis. When the time for ethics class comes, the relevant question
is, Do you understand?[38]

We can start asking five-year-olds, "Do you understand?" but it
would be unwise to offer an ethics course in elementary grades. Like
religion or psychology, ethics is a very difficult academic subject that
should not be attempted before many other subjects have been studied.
However, ethical questions can surface in every subject of the classroom curriculum. When enough ethical issues have appeared in their
historical contexts and practical situations, the strands can be gathered
together for reflection on the subject of ethics itself. To teach ethics is to
provide the language to think clearly, comprehensively, and consistently
about the moral life.

Simply dealing with language may seem to be an ineffective way
to get at morality. Is not the point of teaching morality to produce
better people? The knock against teaching ethics is similar to the general complaint against classroom instruction: all talk and no action.
With morality the accusation becomes most acute. What is the point
of knowing Aristotle's analysis of friendship if it is no help to making
friends? I have previously cited Aristotle saying that the way to become
virtuous is to grow up in a virtuous community. That might seem to
imply that studying ethics is a waste of time, or at least not a help to
being moral. Yet, Aristotle gave us our word "ethics" in the naming of
two books that provide instruction on the subject.

The key here is not to neglect the rest of education in morality when
one directly attends to the (classroom) teaching of ethics. If the rest
of a person's education is effective, the teaching-learning of ethics will
make a moral contribution to that education. However, if one's education in morality is generally deficient, the teaching-learning of ethics is
not likely to reverse the process or substitute for every defect. Aristotle
produced his books on ethics for people who were already virtuous and
wished to become more so.[39] A classroom environment may counter
some deficiencies but the teacher of ethics cannot expect to produce
care, love, kindness, discipline, and honesty by teaching ethics.

The ethics instructor hopes to contribute to the improvement of the
human race, but signs of moral uplift cannot be demanded of this pupil
at this moment. When classroom instruction is aimed at something
other than the understanding of spoken and written language, it fails

to do what it is set up to do and what usually will not be sufficiently done elsewhere.

As is true of other classroom instruction, the ethics teacher works with the language of the student set within a conversation of the wisest minds available. The choice is not between talk and action. The real choice is what kind of talk? Talking is a kind of action; the most appropriate action in a classroom is academic criticism. The ethics teacher has to insist on this focus. The temptation is to slide the ethics classroom into storytelling, lecturing, and preaching on one side, or else toward therapeutic opinionating on the other side. Either "I know what is right and I will tell them so" or — more likely in U.S. schools — "Let's all express our views and feel satisfied at the end of class." Teaching ethics means finding the formulas or inarticulate fragments that students have, and trying to improve that language.

The teacher of ethics has a modest position in the teaching of classroom subjects. He or she is likely to be left alone with what is assumed to be an innocuous endeavor. Of course, if the ethics teacher starts preaching revolution or carrying out lab experiments in sexual relations, the course will draw attention because of the misuse of the academic setting. It can happen, however, that the ethics class, precisely because it is doing its job, can conflict with the society around it and even the school that houses it. The questions raised in ethics class about power relations, justice, and bias are potentially embarrassing for any institution. Both school administrators and ethics teachers should be aware that conflict is inherent to the situation. Good will on both sides can ameliorate — though not eliminate — conflict.

Take the case of a particularly sharp tension: a military school. John Keegan, our premier historian of warfare, describes teaching in a military college. He calls the vocational side of the student's education "formation," which "aims, if not to close his mind to unorthodox or difficult ideas, at least to stop it down to a fairly short focal length." Keegan says there is also an academic side, "which aims to offer the student not a single but a variety of angles of vision; which asks him to adopt in his study of war the standpoint not only of officer, but of private soldier, non-combatant, neutral observer, industrialist, diplomat, relief worker, professional pacifist — all valid and documented points of view."[40]

Keegan is describing a history course, but the ethical dimension is obvious. The better the historian does his or her job, the more unavoidable are the ethical questions. Keegan's final statement — that all the views are valid and documented — presumably means only that they exist and can be studied. But what happens if the student officer gets persuaded by the viewpoint of the "professional pacifist"? Is being persuaded of the validity of pacifism a proper education for the man whose formation has everything to do with leading soldiers in battle?

The inference one might draw is that if the academic part of the student soldier's education were adequately developed, it might cause a crisis for the profession. This crisis, it should be noted, is not peculiar to the soldiering profession. Suppose law students really examined the value of a lawyer's work from all perspectives? What if land developers started looking at land from a variety of human and nonhuman perspectives?

My concern here is not the morality of soldiering, law or land development. It is rather that we are all in the same position of being trained to act in certain ways before we can think out for ourselves how to act. That *is* our "moral education" when we are very young. Academic instruction can only come later to examine, not necessarily reject, our prejudices.

Ethics has to challenge assumptions in our family life, career, and leisure activities. Teaching ethics, instead of being off the end of the spectrum of academic subjects, is the logical consequence of teaching anything in a classroom. Similarly, in relation to the overall teaching of morality, the classroom teaching of ethics is a modest part of the whole project, but it is what keeps education in morality from becoming either neutral techniques or conformity to rules. Education, with or without the adjective moral, has to improve human life, including the relations of men and women, adults and children, and reshape for the better the human relation to the nonhuman world.

Conclusion

THIS BOOK has tried to answer a single question: What is the meaning of "to teach"? The argument has necessarily been circuitous. I have proceeded by testing out a beginning meaning of "to teach" to find whether it would both open into diverse kinds of teaching and gather that diversity into a consistent whole. There cannot be a definitive proof that the argument is valid.

When describing academic criticism in chapter 6, I said that the most apt metaphor is a legal one: the teacher advocates a case before a jury. The listeners may or may not be convinced by the argument. This book is written in the language of academic criticism (with occasional help from other forms of speech) and the reader is a jury member. In my final summation, I would like to present a comparison between a first meaning of "to teach" that has dominated books in modern education (I will call it Meaning A) and a second meaning that I have argued is preferable (called here Meaning B).

I have not claimed that Meaning A ("to teach is to explain") is false or useless. It has an appealing clarity within a system of modern ideas on education. Meaning B ("to teach is to show how to live") does not contradict Meaning A; it provides a context for understanding how Meaning A became dominant but why it cannot take us far enough. One way to describe Meaning B is to say that it is a wider, broader, or more general meaning. I would resist such a description. I have not so much tried to expand the meaning of the term as to expand the conversation about that meaning. My method has been retrieval rather than invention. My task has not been to broaden the meaning because the meaning is already there, although participants in a particular conversation may not be aware of it.

Meaning B is not a general or abstract meaning that is out of touch with practical realities. On the contrary, my aim has been to start with a particular, precise, and practical meaning, one that is strong enough to bear a variety of forms. The search here has not been for a general meaning abstracted from individual cases, but for a (nearly) universal meaning embedded in the particular, and found by delving more deeply into particular forms.

The most appropriate image, therefore, is not *broader* but *deeper*. Meaning B starts more deeply and in that way is more comprehensive. I started with a *root* meaning rather than a general one. I have tried to ground the meaning of "to teach" in ordinary, earthy, bodily action. A variety of linguistic branches grow from that root meaning. While the root may not be visible in the branches, the vitality of teaching is still traceable to that root.

In the paragraphs that follow, I will set out a point-by-point comparison of Meaning A and Meaning B.

In Meaning A, to teach is to explain; in Meaning B, to teach is to show someone how to do something, most comprehensively, how to live. The agent of teaching in Meaning A is an individual human being who is capable of giving reasons. In Meaning B, no individual human being is capable of accomplishing the full meaning of teaching. The universe of living beings, including the example of the human community, is the most comprehensive agent.

In Meaning A, the necessary note is intention. Where the intent to teach is present, teaching exists; where there is no intention, there is no teaching. In Meaning B, the necessary note is learning. The only proof that teaching exists is that learning exists. Where there is learning, there is teaching; where there is no learning, there is no teaching.

In both meanings, a gap in the continuity of a process exists. In Meaning A, the gap is between teaching and learning. Two different processes exist: teaching is one activity, learning is another. In Meaning B, the gap is between the individual's intention and what is actually taught and learned. In this case, teaching-learning is a single and continuous process, not entirely under the control of an individual.

These two gaps lead to two different interpretations of the problem of teaching. In Meaning A, it will be said: "I taught; they didn't learn." The conclusion to be drawn is: "They have a learning problem." Meaning B, in contrast, leads to the problem statement: "I tried to teach; they didn't learn." The conclusion to be drawn here is: "*We* have a teaching-learning problem."

Meaning A's response to the problem has usually been a search for psychological causes. Meaning B's "we have a teaching-learning problem" is likely to lead to looking for answers in economic, political, social — as well as psychological — concerns. I intend no disrespect for psychology, which has made some contributions to our understanding of learning. Nevertheless, the almost complete absorption of education's language into psychology has severely limited the discussion of education and teaching. Meaning B opens the conversation to all who teach. It looks for obstacles to teach-learn in the mal-distributions of power between adult and child, men and women, rich and poor, sick and healthy, schooled and unschooled.

When teaching appears to fail in Meaning A, the remedy is twofold: develop better explanations that are aligned with the child's style and stage of learning. Furthermore, we cannot trust that people are going to be reasonable; most people need some direction that is coercive. In Meaning B, the remedy is also twofold: Find out who and what *are* teaching. Then undertake a redesign of the situation. It may take a long time to discover the who and the what of teaching, and our redesigns will always be imperfect. But teaching is the best hope of humanity, not to be cast aside for supposedly quicker and more efficient solutions, such as more police and more prison cells. Such coercive power will probably always be with us but should only be used as a protection of the border of teaching, not as a regular substitute for teaching.

Meaning A is reflected in the language of "formal and informal education." Either *the* form is present and we have education, or else we have only something deficient that claims to be education. The dominant image of "formal education" is a school within which there is a classroom in which an adult stands before a group of children seated at desks. Meaning B does not exist in an institution called "formal education"; instead it is found in many forms. Even within the school itself there may be a multiplicity of forms. If to teach is to show someone how to live, that requires many settings in which adults interact with each other and where children gradually enter these exchanges. I proposed as a pattern of educational forms: family, job, classroom, retirement/leisure. To teach is to reshape one of these forms and to reshape the interrelation of these forms.

Finally, Meaning A of teaching is almost entirely restricted to one form of speech: to teach is to tell. Speech has the function of conveying knowledge from one human mind to another, usually from the trained expert to the ignorant child. In Meaning B of teaching, there are several families of languages and numerous cases within each family. Teaching begins and ends in silence; between the silences, speech takes on a variety of forms. Sometimes speech is used to urge people on to their goal; at other times speech is used to restore a sense of purpose. Speech can also be used to puzzle and provoke the mind, forcing the learner to go in search of the right questions before he or she can get answers. One setting of education differs from another by the particular mix of languages used. For example, a school and a family over a long time will include every main form of speech. They will differ in the prominence and the amount of each speech in their respective mixes of teaching languages.

That completes a point-by-point comparison of Meaning A and Meaning B of teaching. Obviously, I think that Meaning B is superior in every point of comparison. So long as Meaning B is not misunderstood as a kind of soft and sentimental generality, there are no drawbacks to affirming Meaning B. It encompasses what most people in the past have meant by teaching and it gives new seriousness to contemporary uses of "teaching" that otherwise receive only passing mention.

If the case for Meaning B is so strong, why is there such difficulty in getting a hearing and what would be necessary for it to reemerge at center stage? In the course of this book, I have suggested two main reasons behind the twentieth century's narrow meaning of "to teach."

1. The meaning of teaching as "to show someone how to live, including how to die" has moral and religious connotations. The twentieth century has been a sea of confusion about both morality and religion, not to mention the relation between them. In philosophical history, as far back as Socrates, and in religious history, including all the world's major religions, the justifying of who teaches and what is taught have been moral issues. The modern world has preferred to avoid the religious and moral as far as possible. If to teach simply means to give people reasons or to explain things, we seem to avoid all the bickerings of religion and the uncertainties of morality.

There is nonetheless a moral assumption here, namely, that reasons and explanations are desirable and that no sane person can object to being given reasons. The ideal of universal schooling is based on this assumption. Children are confined to schools because they are not yet reasonable adults. Schoolteachers are given license to explain things to children until the children can think for themselves. I readily agree that children receiving explanations in classrooms is a better alternative than what most children in history have faced. The problem is in reducing the meaning of teaching to this one, unusual form.

The attempt to avoid all moral and religious issues has not entirely succeeded. Outside a narrowly circumscribed area of mathematics and science, teachers do not rely exclusively on rational explanations based on objective fact. John Dewey in the 1930s could hold out "scientific method" as the ideal against which all teaching had to be patterned.[1] Since then, however, it has become obvious that classroom instructors in any discipline, not excluding physical science, have to rely on interpretation of data, and must appeal to imaginative, aesthetic, and subjective considerations.

Reason has proved to be a powerful instrument for the human journey; reason has also proved to be a dangerous power if it eliminates what precedes and surrounds it. As Martin Buber said of consciousness, reason ought to play first violin but not try to be conductor.[2] Reason is at the service of life; teaching as the giving of reasons should be at the service of teaching how to live. But if living is the more comprehensive object of teaching, where can we find teachers of how to live? Should we turn our classrooms over to gurus and prophets?

My answer has been twofold. We have to protect the classroom against gurus and prophets if these terms connote preaching messages, indoctrinating young minds, and forming disciples. The classroom is a place for thoughtful conversation carried out in measured speech. But that does not mean that religion and morality should be excluded from the conversation. Religion becomes irrational and morality becomes mindless if they are declared unworthy of serious attention in the classroom.

The other part of the response is to recognize that the classroom's contribution to the moral and religious dimensions of education has always been a minor one. The answer to the question "where do we find teachers of how to live" is that they are already here and doing their job: parents, friends, political and religious leaders; if we would recognize them and name them as teachers, we could help them to do their job better.

The assumption in the late nineteenth century that religion was soon to disappear and that "moral education" could be handled with a few new twists has proved to be naive. We need a coalition of teachers — human and nonhuman — to face up to the moral and religious crisis that threatens to tear apart the world.

2. The second underlying issue in the narrowing of teach/teaching/teacher is closely related to the first. I refer to the growth of the school

system and the better preparation of schoolteachers. For the modern school to fulfill its purpose, full-time, "professional educators" were needed. During the last century and a half, the "teacher," it has been assumed, is a member of this group. Teaching is therefore thought to be the work of the "teaching profession." To challenge the meaning of teaching is to run up against a thick wall of professional control.

There is a certain irony, I realize, in complaining about the control exercised by professional educators. Schoolteachers have had a long journey, not yet completed, to be recognized as a profession at all. In the nineteenth century, when schoolteaching switched from being a man's to a woman's job, many writers described schoolteaching as an extension of the one profession for which women were suited: motherhood.[3] Since then, schoolteachers (along with nurses) have struggled to go beyond what Amitai Etzioni called "semi-professions" and enter the full status of professions.[4]

Becoming a profession looks deceptively easy. Numerous groups take on the trappings of a profession (a code of ethics, a set of credentials, an annual conference, a journal, and so forth) and declare themselves to be a profession. It is another thing, however, for the public to recognize that a group has an area of knowledge and skill under its control, and is capable of offering a sustained service to a community.

The difficulty that schoolteachers have had in establishing their professional claim is that most people think they know what teaching a 6-year-old entails.[5] In contrast, most people are mystified by the talk of lawyers, accountants, and civil engineers. Actually, people are correct when they claim some knowledge of how to teach a 6-year-old; a great many people do have that experience. However, very few people have the knowledge, skill, and dedication to teach 6-year-olds in a classroom. For that, one needs talent, training, and dedication. If schoolteachers would name their profession more accurately, admitting its continuity with teaching in ordinary life, they would get both support as professionals in a distinctive work and cooperation from parents and others whose work has some similarity.

For most of the past 150 years, it has been feared that to admit a continuity with ordinary life would weaken the claim to professionalization.[6] And, indeed, the modern professions have depended upon a perception that their work is so arcane that it is beyond the mere layperson's understanding. The medical profession led the way to the top of professional status, paving the way for tax accountants and mortgage closers. However, in the last two decades a turn seems to have been taken, led again by the medical profession. Having succeeded in isolating their esoteric knowledge from the laity, physicians found themselves losing the trust of the public and being hit with malpractice suits.

Physicians today are being pressed to redesign their relation to other professionals and to the (medical) laity. The emerging result is a new configuration, centered on health not medicine, in which the physician is still a central player but is part of a team. Included in that team is the patient who must learn about health and what to do for his or her body. In the health professions, there can be many concentric circles of expert knowledge but there is no room for a laity, that is, people totally ignorant of health concerns.

The schoolteachers who had seemed to trail behind in the modern professional world may turn out to have an advantage. The link to teaching in ordinary life can place the schoolteachers into immediate relation with the adults and children being served. Every profession in the future has to be a teaching profession in which the aim is to share knowledge rather than hide it in impenetrable jargon. Those who are skillful at instruction are a key to the reformation of professional life.

My resistance to the control of "teaching" by professional schoolteachers is not meant as a disparagement of teaching in school. I believe there is no greater profession in the world of work. However, the case for this profession needs strengthening in U.S. society. The language we have inherited from the nineteenth century tends to flowery praise of teachers but not enough economic and political support for the work of schools and their teachers.

I have proposed that schoolteachers let go of the one word they have in their grasp: teaching. They have to stop talking about the "teaching profession." It may seem that I am asking for professional educators to commit suicide, but it is a stronger profession that interests me. If we start with teaching as showing someone how to do something, school people are challenged to examine their special ways of teaching. Both classroom instructors and performance coaches have a fund of experience that needs to be tapped into. They also need linguistic help to draw from that experience and get help for their work. If this were to happen, we would then be on the way to combining the strongest meaning of teaching with a more solidly grounded profession of schoolteaching.

Notes

Introduction

1. Jacques Barzun, *Teacher in America* (Boston: Little, Brown, 1945); Gilbert Highet, *The Art of Teaching* (New York: Vintage Books, 1954).

2. Barzun, *Teacher in America*, 10.

3. Highet, *The Art of Teaching*, 157.

4. Ludwig Wittgenstein, *Philosophical Investigations*, 3rd ed. (New York: Macmillan, 1968), par. 241, 88.

5. Irving Howe, "The Value of the Canon," in *Debating P.C.*, ed. Paul Berman (New York: Dell Books, 1992), 158.

6. Alexander Bickel, *The Morality of Consent* (New Haven: Yale University Press, 1975), 25.

7. Some of the unfair connection of Nazism and Nietzsche is revealed in a study of how Nietzsche's writing and reputation were manipulated after his death: Ben MacIntyre, *Forgotten Fatherland: The Search for Elizabeth Nietzsche* (New York: Farrar, Straus and Giroux, 1992).

8. Gary Shapiro, "The Writing on the Wall: The Anti-Christ and the Semiotics of History," in *Reading Nietzsche*, ed. Robert Solomon and Kathleen Higgins (New York: Oxford University Press, 1988), 199.

9. As an example, see Aristotle's discussion of justice in *Ethics*, 1128a; Martha Nussbaum in *Language and Logic*, ed. Malcolm Schofield and Martha Nussbaum (New York: Cambridge University Press, 1982), 272.

10. Aristotle, *Metaphysics*, 1014b–1015a.

11. R. G. Collingwood, *The Idea of Nature* (New York: Oxford University Press, 1960), 80–82.

12. J. H. Randall, *Aristotle* (New York: Columbia University Press, 1960), 43.

13. Josef Pieper, *Guide to Thomas Aquinas* (New York: Pantheon, 1962), 113.

14. Wittgenstein, *Philosophical Investigations*, par. 31–32; par. 5: Here the teaching of language is not explanation, but training; see also his *Zeitel* (London: Basil Blackwell, 1967), 355: "If we teach a human being such-and-such a technique by means of examples — that he then proceeds like *this* and not like *that* in a particular new case, or that he gets stuck, and thus that this and not that is the natural continuation for him: this of itself is an extremely important fact of nature."

15. Ray Monk, *Ludwig Wittgenstein: His Life and Work* (New York: Free Press, 1990), 537.

Chapter 1. Teaching as a Moral Dilemma

1. Newt Gingrich, *To Renew America* (San Francisco: HarperCollins, 1995), 142. That this contrast is extreme and unworkable is shown by the fact that Gingrich uses the term *education* as a neutral or positive term throughout the remainder of the chapter.

2. Ibid., 143.

3. Ivan Illich, *Deschooling Society* (New York: Harper and Row, 1971).

4. Ivan Illich, *Tools for Conviviality* (New York: Harper and Row, 1973), 60.

5. Barzun, *Teacher in America*, 10.

6. Jaroslav Pelikan, *Jesus through the Centuries* (New Haven: Yale University Press, 1985), 11, 17.

7. Immanuel Kant, *Foundations of the Metaphysics of Morals; What Is Enlightenment?* (New York: Macmillan, 1990), 83: "Self-incurred is this tutelage when its cause lies not in lack of reason but in lack of resolution and courage to use it without direction from another. *Sapere Aude*. Have courage to use your own reason — that is the motto of enlightenment."

8. G. B. Kerferd, *The Sophistic Movement* (Cambridge: Cambridge University Press, 1981); for the statement of Protagoras, see Plato, *Protagoras*, 316, 324–25.

9. Plato, *Apology*, 21b.

10. Aristophanes, *The Clouds* (New York: Oxford University Press, 1968).

11. Plato, *Symposium*, 216d.

12. Plato, *Apology*, 20d,e.

13. Michael Morgan, *Platonic Piety* (New Haven: Yale University Press, 1990), 7–31.

14. Gregory Vlastos, *Socrates: Ironist and Moral Philosopher* (Ithaca, N.Y.: Cornell University Press, 1990), 33; see also Werner Jaeger, *Paideia: The Ideals of Greek Culture* (New York: Oxford University Press, 1971), 2:171–72: "It is true that the new *paideia* is not teachable as the sophists understood teaching: so Socrates was right to say that he did not teach men — not by giving them information. But by asserting that virtue must be knowledge and making his way toward that knowledge, he took the place of those false prophets of wisdom, as the only real educator."

15. W. P. Wees, *Nobody Can Teach Anyone Anything* (New York: Doubleday, 1971).

16. Johann Comenius, *The Great Didactic*, ed. M. W. Keatinge (New York: McGraw Hill, 1931), 51.

17. Friedrich Froebel, *Education of Man: Selections from His Writings* (Cambridge: Cambridge University Press, 1967).

18. Jean-Jacques Rousseau, *Emile* (New York: Basic Books, 1979), 38.

19. Ibid., 37–39.

20. Ibid., 266–313.

21. Ibid., 96.

22. John Locke, *Some Thoughts Concerning Education*, ed. John Adamson (Cambridge: Cambridge University Press, sec. 85, 68.

23. Donald Schön, *The Reflective Practitioner* (New York: Basic Books, 1983), 40.

24. Kurt Lewin, *Field Theory in Social Science* (New York: Harper, 1951).

25. Rousseau, *Emile*, Book 5.

26. I refer here to Rousseau's later novel, *Les Solitaires*, which he never completed. In it, Sophie becomes a prostitute and Emile finds himself living as a hermit. See Maurice Cranston, *The Noble Savage* (Chicago: University of Chicago Press, 1990), 192–93; Susan Moller Okin, *Woman in Western Political Thought* (Princeton, N.J.: Princeton University Press, 1979), 169.

27. Mary Wollstonecraft, *A Vindication of the Rights of Woman*, ed. Charles Hagelman Jr. (New York: Norton, 1967), 233.

28. Jane Martin, *Reclaiming a Conversation* (New Haven: Yale University Press, 1985), 69.

29. Philip Jackson, *The Practice of Teaching* (New York: Teachers College Press, 1986), 104–05.

30. Willard Waller, *The Sociology of Teaching* (New York: John Wiley, 1967), 336.

31. Jean Piaget, *The Moral Judgment of the Child* (New York: Collier Books, 1962).

32. Emile Durkheim, *Moral Education* (New York: Free Press, 1961).

33. Piaget, *The Moral Judgment of the Child*, 352.

34. Malcolm Knowles, *Self-Directed Learning* (New York: Association Press, 1975); and his *The Adult Learner: A Neglected Species* (Houston: Gulf, 1973).

35. S. B. Merriam and P. M. Cunningham, eds., *Handbook of Adult and Continuing Education* (San Francisco: Jossey-Bass, 1989).

36. John Lowe, *The Education of Adults: A World Perspective* (Paris: UNESCO, 1975), 14.

37. Ibid., 35.

38. Peter Elbow, *Embracing Contraries* (New York: Oxford University Press, 1986), 70.

39. Jackson, *The Practice of Teaching*, 3.

40. Brenda Cohen, *Means and Ends in Education* (London: George Allen and Unwin, 1983), 83.

41. Thomas Green, *The Activities of Teaching* (New York: McGraw-Hill, 1971).

42. Ibid., 5.

43. Ibid., 4.

44. Ibid., 23.

Chapter 2. Regrounding the Verb "To Teach"

1. Israel Scheffler, *The Language of Education* (Springfield, Ill.: Charles Thomas, 1960), 62; Durkheim, *Moral Education*, 120.

2. Friedrich Nietzsche, *Beyond Good and Evil* (New York: Penguin Books,

1973), 45. Nietzsche himself did not seem to apply his own teaching to himself when he talked of being a teacher. He seems to have tried too directly to make disciples and was constantly disappointed; for a discussion of Nietzsche as teacher, see Leslie Thiele, *Friedrich Nietzsche and the Politics of Soul* (Princeton, N.J.: Princeton University Press, 1960), 165–82.

3. John Dewey, *Human Nature and Conduct* (Carbondale: Southern Illinois University, 1988), 124: "We may, indeed, be said to know how by means of our habits.... But after all, this practical work done by habit...is not knowledge, except by courtesy."

4. Alan Tom, *Teaching as a Moral Craft* (London: Longman, 1984), 55; for a more positive assessment of this tradition, see Michael Dunkin and Bruce Biddle, *The Study of Teaching* (New York: Holt, Rinehart and Winston, 1974).

5. H. S. Broudy, *Building a Philosophy of Education* (Englewood Cliffs, N.J.: Prentice Hall, 1954), 14.

6. Gilbert Ryle, *The Concept of Mind* (New York: Barnes and Noble, 1949), 149–52; Scheffler, *The Language of Education*, 42; Green, *The Activities of Teaching*, 141.

7. John Passmore, *The Philosophy of Teaching* (Cambridge: Harvard University Press, 1980), 21; similarly in Eliot Eisner, *The Educational Imagination* (New York: Macmillan, 1979), 157–58: The author says that there are two radically different conceptions of teaching; these are a form of achievement directly related to teaching and a set of acts performed by people we call teachers. Like Passmore, Eisner accepts the ambiguity: "We can appropriately conceptualize teaching both ways." The problem is that in *both* of these radically different conceptions of teaching, teaching and learning are separable categories; in the one case, teaching causes learning, in the other case, teaching does not. What I am proposing is a way of speaking that fits *neither* of Eisner's conceptions.

8. John Dewey, *How We Think* (Lexington, Mass.: D.C. Heath, 1933), 34–35.

9. Aristotle, *Physics*, 202b; Thomas Aquinas, *The Disputed Questions of Truth* (Chicago: Henry Regnery, 1952), Question XI: The Teacher.

10. David Elkind, *Children and Adolescents* (New York: Oxford University Press, 1970), 99.

11. Michael Oakeshott, *The Voice of Liberal Learning*, ed. Timothy Fuller (New Haven: Yale University Press, 1989), 44.

12. Marjorie Boyle, *Erasmus on Language and Method in Theology* (Toronto: University of Toronto Press, 1977), 83.

13. Ryle, *The Concept of Mind*, 312.

14. Ludwig Wittgenstein, *The Blue and Brown Books* (New York: Harper and Row, 1964),16.

15. Gary Snyder, *The Practice of the Wild* (San Francisco: North Point Press, 1990), 23; on trees and forests as teachers, see Brian Walsh, Marianne Karsh, and Nick Ansell, "Trees, Forestry and the Responsiveness of Creation," *Cross Currents* 44 (Summer 1994): 149–62.

16. Jacob Needleman, *A Sense of the Cosmos* (Garden City. N.Y.: Double-

day, 1975), 56; John Haught, *The Cosmic Adventure* (New York: Paulist, 1984), 12; for a similar view in Islamic tradition, see Seyed Hossein Nasr, *Ideals and Realities of Islam* (Boston: Beacon Press, 1972), 139.

17. For dogs teaching other dogs, see Elizabeth Marshall Thomas, *The Hidden Life of Dogs* (Boston: Houghton Mifflin, 1993).

18. Sherwin Nuland, *How We Die* (New York: Knopf, 1994), 1; see also Elisabeth Kübler-Ross, *On Death and Dying* (New York: Macmillan, 1969), preface: "We have asked him [the dying patient] to be our teacher so that we may learn more about the final stages of life with all its anxieties, fears and hopes."

19. Locke, *Some Thoughts Concerning Education*, par. 82, 182.

20. For the statement by Charles Barkley and comments on it, see the editorial in the *New York Times*, June 2, 1993.

21. On the inadequacy of role model in this context, see Elizabeth Wolgast, *Ethics of an Artificial Person* (Stanford, Calif.: Stanford University Press, 1992), 40–57; see also James Coleman, *The Asymmetric Society* (Syracuse, N.Y.: Syracuse University Press, 1982), 36.

22. Malcolm X, *The Autobiography of Malcolm X* (New York: Ballantine Books, 1973), 333–34.

23. Page Smith, *Killing the Spirit* (New York: Viking Books, 1991), 203; A. S. Neill, *Summerhill* (New York: St. Martin's Press, 1992), 138: "I have said it many times and say it again, that you cannot teach anything of importance. Math, English, French, yes, but not charity, love, sincerity, balance, or tolerance."

24. Aristotle, *Nicomachean Ethics*, 1103a33.

25. Steven Pinker, *The Language Instinct* (New York: Morrow, 1994), 39.

26. Erik Erikson, *Childhood and Society*, 2nd ed. (New York: Norton, 1963), 247–74.

Chapter 3. Teaching by Design

1. See Allan Janik and Stephen Toulmin, *Wittgenstein's Vienna* (New York: Simon and Schuster, 1973), 182–83.

2. David Burrell, *Aquinas* (Notre Dame, Ind.: University of Notre Dame Press, 1979), 170–72.

3. Carl Rogers, *Freedom to Learn* (Columbus, Ohio: Merrill, 1969), 153.

4. Susan Walker, *Speaking of Silence: Christians and Buddhists on the Contemplative Way* (New York: Paulist Press, 1987), 172.

5. J. Krishnamurti, *Commentaries on Living: Second Series* (Wheaton, Ill.: Theosophical Publishing House, 1958), 83, 138.

6. Leo Tolstoy, *Tolstoy on Education*, ed. Alan Pinch and Michael Armstrong (Rutherford, N.J.: Farleigh Dickinson University Press, 1982).

7. Ibid., 84.

8. Ibid., 246.

9. E. M. Standing, *Maria Montessori: Her Life and Work* (New York: New American Library, 1962.

10. Maria Montessori, *Education for a New World* (Madras, India: Kalak-shetra, 1959), 66.

11. Sylvia Ashton-Warner, *Spinster* (New York: Simon and Schuster, 1959); her *Teacher* (New York: Simon and Schuster, 1963); and her *Spearpoint: Teacher in America* (New York: Knopf, 1972).

12. Ashton-Warner, *Spinster*, 45.

13. Ibid., 45–46.

14. Lowe, *The Education of Adults*, 95.

15. Paulo Freire, *The Pedagogy of the Oppressed* (New York: Herder and Herder, 1970), 59, 67.

16. Ibid., 57–86.

17. B. F. Skinner, "Behaviorism at Fifty," in *Behaviorism and Phenomenology*, ed. T. W. Wann (Chicago: University of Chicago Press, 1964), 90–91.

18. George Dennison, *The Lives of Children* (New York: Random House, 1969), 89.

19. Aristotle, *Nicomachean Ethics*, 1103 a 34

20. Margaret Donaldson, *Human Minds* (New York: Norton, 1994), 261.

21. Margaret Donaldson, *Children's Minds* (New York: Norton, 1978), 32.

22. Richard Burton, John Brown, and Gerhard Fischer, "Skiing as a Model of Instruction," in *Everyday Cognition*, ed. Barbara Rogoff and Jean Lave (Cambridge: Harvard University Press, 1984), 139–50.

23. Schön, *Reflective Practitioner*, 21–69.

24. Adam Phillips, *On Kissing, Tickling and Being Bored* (Cambridge: Harvard University Press, 1993), 30: A sixteen-year-old describing the experience of learning to swim says: "I knew I was safer out of my depth because even though I couldn't stand, there was more water to hold me up." The therapist comments: "For the boy the risk of learning to swim was the risk of discovering that he, or rather his body would float. The heart of swimming is that you can float. Standing within his depth, apparently in control was the omnipotence born of anxiety; the opposite of omnipotence here was not impotence, as he had feared, but his being able to entrust himself to the water."

Chapter 4. Teaching with the End in View

1. I adopt here and in the following chapters the idea of family resemblance for groups of languages. The claim is not that they have some common essence but that there are qualities that link the family members together. See Wittgenstein, *Philosophical Investigations*, par. 66, 31–32.

2. Dewey, *Human Nature and Conduct*, 159: "An end is a device of intelligence in guiding action, instrumental to freeing and harmonizing troubled and divided tendencies."

3. Wayne Booth, *Modern Dogma and the Rhetoric of Assent* (Notre Dame, Ind.: University of Notre Dame Press, 1979), 125. Booth's book was influential in beginning the attempt to recover the positive, rich meaning of rhetoric.

Despite the wealth of historical writing on this theme published during recent decades, rhetoric/rhetorical continues to have the meaning of vacuous or fraudulent in uses outside this literature. Thus, I do not adopt rhetorical as a general description of this family. For a study of the history of this question, see Bruce Kimball, *Orators and Philosophers* (New York: Teachers College Press, 1986); Takis Poulakos, ed., *Rethinking the History of Rhetoric* (Boulder, Colo.: Westview, 1993).

4. Edmund Burke, *Reflections on the Revolution in France* (New York: Holt, Rinehart and Winston, 1959), 103–6.

5. Hans-Georg Gadamer, *Truth and Method* (New York: Seabury Press, 1975), 247.

6. Leszek Kolakowski, *Modernity on Trial* (Chicago: University of Chicago Press, 1990), 126.

7. Quoted in John Thornhill, *Making Australia* (Newtown: Omnibus, 1992), 194.

8. Northrop Frye, *The Educated Imagination* (Bloomington: Indiana University Press, 1964), 64.

9. In Molière's novel, *Le bourgeois gentilhomme* (Paris: Presses Pocket, 1992).

10. On the value of gossip, see John Sabini and Maury Silver, *Moralities of Everyday Life* (New York: Oxford University Press, 1982), 89–106.

11. On nineteenth-century novels, see Ann Douglas, *The Feminization of American Culture* (New York: Knopf, 1977).

12. Smith, *Killing the Spirit*, 210, 215.

13. Kenneth Eble, *The Craft of Teaching* (San Francisco: Jossey-Bass, 1976), 42.

14. Ibid., 43.

15. Mario Cuomo, "Religious Beliefs and Public Morality," *New York Review of Books*, October 10, 1984, 32–37.

16. *New York Times*, February 15, 1990, 1.

17. Robert Hughes, *Culture of Complaint* (New York: Oxford University Press, 1993), 72.

18. Robert Wilken, *John Chrysostom and the Jews* (Berkeley: University of California Press, 1983), 106.

19. Matthew Fox, *Breakthrough* (Garden City, N.Y.: Doubleday, 1980).

20. Robert Pattison, *On Literacy* (New York: Oxford University Press, 1982), 71.

21. Perry Miller, *Errand into the Wilderness* (New York: Harper Torch, 1964), 175–83.

22. Garry Wills, *Lincoln's Gettysburg Address* (New York: Touchstone Books, 1993), 175.

23. Quoted by Nat Hentoff in *The Village Voice*, March 12, 1985, 3.

24. Augustine, "Christian Instruction," in *Saint Augustine* (New York: Fathers of the Church, 1947), 194: On the need for grand eloquence in preaching: "They must be persuaded not that they may know what should be done, but to do what they already know they should do."

25. Philip Rieff, *Fellow Teachers* (New York: Harper and Row, 1973), 2.

26. Martin Luther King Jr., *I Have a Dream: Writings and Speeches that Changed the World* (San Francisco: Harper, 1992), 101–6.

27. *New York Times*, May 2, 1992, 1.

28. Friedrich Nietzsche, *The Anti-Christ* (New York: Penguin Books, 1990), 181.

Chapter 5. Teaching to Remove Obstacles

1. Mary Douglas, *Natural Symbols* (New York: Pantheon Books, 1970), 73.

2. Philip Rieff, *The Triumph of the Therapeutic* (New York: Harper and Row, 1966).

3. Cyril Houle, *Design of Education* (San Francisco: Jossey-Bass, 1972), 29.

4. Kant, *Foundations of the Metaphysics of Morals*, 9.

5. Michel Foucault, *The Birth of the Clinic* (New York: Pantheon Books, 1973), and *Discipline and Punishment* (New York: Pantheon Books, 1977).

6. Bronislaw Malinowski coined the term *phatic communion* for this yes or uh-huh, that is, a type of speech in which ties of union are created by the mere exchange of words. See Bronislaw Malinowski, "The Problem of Meaning in Primitive Language," in C. K. Ogden and I. A. Richards, *The Meaning of Meaning* (New York: Harcourt, Brace, Jovanovich, 1989), 296–336.

7. Wittgenstein, *Philosophical Investigations*, par. 133.

8. Ludwig Wittgenstein, *Tractatus Logico-Philosophicus* (London: Routledge and Kegan Paul, 1971).

9. Thomas Aquinas, *De Potentia*, 7,5 ad 14; *Summa Theologica*, I, a, prologue.

10. Frank Tobin, *Meister Eckhart: Thought and Language* (Philadelphia: University of Pennsylvania Press, 1986), 80, 167; Reiner Schurmann, *Meister Eckhart: Mystic and Philosopher* (Bloomington: University of Indiana Press, 1978), 213.

11. Plato, *Republic*, 518 c,d,e.

12. Comenius, *The Great Didactic*, 52.

13. Wittgenstein, *Philosophical Investigations*, par. 23, 12.

14. James Hillman, *Suicide and the Soul* (New York: Harper, 1975), 124.

15. Albert Camus, *The Plague* (New York: Vintage Books, 1972), 236.

16. Martin Buber, quoted in Maurice Friedman, *Martin Buber's Life and Work: The Middle Years 1923–1945* (New York: Dutton, 1983), 325.

17. The well-known prayer of Francis of Assisi says, "It is in giving that we receive; it is in pardoning that we are pardoned; it is in dying that we are born to eternal life."

18. Hannah Arendt, *The Life of the Mind: Thinking* (New York: Harcourt, Brace, Jovanovich, 1978), 143.

19. Standing, *Maria Montessori*, 310; John Holt, *How Children Fail* (New York: Putnam, 1964), 44: "Do children really need so much praise? When a child after a long struggle, finally does the cube puzzle, does he need to be

told that he has accomplished something? Doesn't he know without being told, that he has accomplished something? In fact, when we praise him, are we not perhaps horning in on his accomplishment?"

20. David Hume, An Enquiry Concerning the Principles of Morals (Chicago: Open Court, 1960), 121.

21. Robert Westbrook, John Dewey and American Democracy (Ithaca, N.Y.: Cornell University Press, 1991), 180.

22. Gabriel Moran, A Grammar of Responsibility (New York: Crossroad, 1996).

23. Fyodor Dostoyevsky, The Brothers Karamazov (New York: New American Library, 1952), 538.

24. Martin Heidegger, Discourse on Thinking (New York: Harper Torch, 1966).

25. Arendt, The Life of the Mind, 5.

26. On covenant and covenant renewal, see Gabriel Moran, Uniqueness: Problem or Paradox in Jewish and Christian Traditions (Maryknoll, N.Y.: Orbis Books, 1992), chapter 4.

27. Hannah Arendt, The Human Condition (Chicago: University of Chicago Press, 1958), 241.

28. Sogyal Rinpoche, The Tibetan Book of Living and Dying (San Francisco: Harper, 1992), begins with the author being taught about death; the term teaching appears on almost every page of the book.

29. Samuel Beckett, Waiting for Godot (New York: Grove Press, 1954), 57.

30. Miguel Unamuno, Tragic Sense of Life (Princeton, N.J.: Princeton University Press, 1972), 20.

31. Daniel Levinson, The Seasons of a Man's Life (New York: Knopf, 1978).

32. Geoffrey Gorer, Death, Grief and Mourning (Garden City, N.Y.: Doubleday, 1965), 111.

33. Kübler-Ross, On Death and Dying; Philippe Ariès, The Hour of Our Death (New York: Knopf, 1981); Nuland, How We Die.

34. Maurice Lamm, The Jewish Way of Death and Dying (New York: Jonathan David, 1989), 78.

35. S. J. Connolly, Priest and People in Pre-Famine Ireland (New York: St. Martin's, 1982), 159.

36. Harold Kushner, When Bad Things Happen to Good People (New York: Avon Books, 1981), 90.

37. Samuel Beckett, Endgame (New York: Grove Press, 1958), 53.

38. Edmund Wallant, Children at the Gate (New York: Harcourt, Brace and World, 1964), 144.

Chapter 6. Teaching the Conversation

1. Richard Rorty, Essays on Heidegger and Others (New York: Cambridge University Press, 1991), 12.

2. Hannah Pitkin, *Wittgenstein and Justice* (Berkeley: University of California Press, 1972), 297.

3. Elbow, *Embracing Contraries*, 267–84.

4. Friedrich Nietzsche, *Birth of Tragedy and Genealogy of Morals* (Garden City, N.Y.: Doubleday, 1956), 163.

5. Georg Hegel, *Philosophy of Right* (Chicago: Encyclopedia Britannica, 1952), 12–13.

6. Karl Marx, "Concerning Feuerbach," in *Karl Marx: Early Writings* (London: Penguin Books, 1992), 423.

7. Monk, *Ludwig Wittgenstein*, 533: "Wittgenstein's remark about philosophy — that it leaves everything as it is — is often quoted. But it is less often realized that, in seeking to change nothing about the way we look at things, Wittgenstein was attempting to change *everything*."

8. Stanley Fish, "There's No Such Thing as Free Speech and It's a Good Thing, Too," in *Debating P.C.*, ed. Berman, 237.

9. Ludwig Wittgenstein, *On Certainty* (New York: Harper Torch, 1972), par. 433: "The philosopher must give the circumstances in which this expression functions"; par. 229: "Our talk gets its sense from the rest of our actions." *Philosophical Investigations*, par. 489: "Ask yourself: on what occasion, for what purpose, do we say this? What kind of actions accompany these words? (Think of a greeting)."

10. Benedict Spinoza, *A Theologico-Political Treatise* (New York: Dover, 1951), 101: "We are at work not on the truth of passages, but solely on their meaning. . . . In order not to confound the meaning of a passage with its truth, we must examine it solely by means of the signification of the words, or by a reason acknowledging no foundation but Scripture."

11. Frank Kermode, *The Genesis of Secrecy* (Cambridge: Harvard University Press, 1979), 122.

12. Martin Buber, *I and Thou* (New York: Scribner's, 1970), 69.

13. Plato, *Theatetus*, 189e.

14. Steven Cavell, *Must We Make Sense?* (Cambridge: Cambridge University Press, 1969), 157.

15. Mel Gussow, conversation with Tom Stoppard, *New York Times*, August 8, 1992, 2:8.

16. See Peter Farb, *Word Play: What Happens When People Talk* (New York: Knopf, 1974), 24–26.

17. Richard Gilman, *The Making of Modern Drama* (New York: Farrar, Straus and Giroux, 1974).

18. Eric Havelock, *Preface to Plato* (Cambridge: Harvard University Press, 1963), 208; Kerferd, *The Sophistic Movement*, 59–67.

19. Michel Foucault, *The Order of Things* (New York: Pantheon, 1970).

20. Fernand van Steenberghen, *Thomas Aquinas and Radical Aristotelianism* (Washington, D.C.: Catholic University of America Press, 1980); Pieper, *Guide to Thomas Aquinas*, 83.

21. Ronald Beiner, *Political Judgment* (Chicago: University of Chicago Press, 1983), 152.

22. John Stuart Mill, *On Liberty* (New York: Norton, 1975), 36; see also Aristotle, *Topics*, 101a35: "The ability to raise searching difficulties on both sides of a subject will make us detect more easily the truth and error about several points that arise."

23. John Dewey, *Characters and Events* (New York: Holt, 1929), xi.

24. Oakeshott, *The Voice of Liberal Learning*, 115.

25. Leo Straus, preface to *Spinoza: The Jewish Expression* (New York: Macmillan, 1950).

26. *New York Times*, November 12, 1988, 8.

27. Ian Buruma, *The Wages of Guilt: Memories of War in Germany and Japan* (New York: Farrar, Straus and Giroux, 1994), 239; for a summary of the whole episode, 239–49.

28. Carol Gilligan, *In a Different Voice* (Cambridge: Harvard University Press, 1982); Mary Belenky, Blythe Clinchy, Nancy Goldberger and Jill Tamle, *Women's Ways of Knowing* (New York: Basic Books, 1986).

Chapter 7. Educational Forms of Teaching

1. Jacques Barzun, *Begin Here: The Forgotten Conditions of Teaching and Learning* (Chicago: University of Chicago Press, 1991), 3.

2. Leo Tolstoy, "On the Education of the People," in *Tolstoy on Education*, 66: "How can this be? The demand for education is present in every human being; the people love and seek education as they love and seek air to breathe. The government and society have a burning desire to educate the people, and in spite of all the force, the cunning devices and obstinacy of governments and educated classes, the common people constantly declare that they are not content with the education offered to them and, step by step, give in only to force."

3. David Elkind, *The Child and Society* (New York: Oxford University Press, 1979), 107.

4. Rousseau, *Emile*, 42.

5. *The Compact Edition of the Oxford English Dictionary* (New York: Oxford University Press, 1971), 1:833: Education: "the process of nourishing or rearing a child or young person, an animal."

6. Edmund Morgan, *The Puritan Family* (New York: Harper, 1966), 88.

7. Locke, *Some Thoughts Concerning Education*, 51, says that he is writing for "an ordinary Gentleman's Son"; Rousseau, *Emile*, 357, chides Locke: "I do not have the honor of raising a gentleman"; however, at the beginning of the book he says, "I will not be distressed if Emile is of noble birth" (52).

8. John Dewey, *School and Society* (Chicago: University of Chicago Press, 1990), 6–29.

9. John Dewey, "My Pedagogic Creed," in *John Dewey on Education*, ed. Reginald Archambault (Chicago: University of Chicago Press, 1974), 32.

10. See N. F. S. Grundtvig, *Tradition and Renewal* (Copenhagen: Danish Institute, 1983); Basil Yeaxlee, *Lifelong Education: A Sketch of the Range and Significance of the Adult Education Movement* (London: Castile and Co., 1929); C. Grattan Hartley, *American Ideas about Adult Education, 1760–1951* (New York: Teachers College Press, 1959).

11. Bernard Bailyn, *Education in the Forming of American Society* (New York: Vintage Books, 1960).

12. Lawrence Cremin, *American Education: The Colonial Experience, 1607–1783* (New York: Harper, 1970), *American Education: The National Experience, 1783–1876* (New York: Harper, 1980), and *American Education: The Metropolitan Experience, 1876–1980* (New York: Harper, 1988).

13. Bailyn, *Education in the Forming of American Society*, 14.

14. Lawrence Cremin, *Public Education* (New York: Basic Books, 1976), 27.

15. John Dewey and Arthur Bentley, *Knowing and the Known* (Boston: Beacon Press, 1949); in this book Dewey prefers the term *transformation* to *interaction*, the word he used throughout his earlier writings. I think both terms can be helpful rather than the first replacing the second.

16. Plato, *Republic*, Book V.

17. Shoshana Alexander, *In Praise of Single Parents: Mothers and Fathers Embracing the Challenge* (New York: Houghton Mifflin, 1994).

18. Emile Durkheim, *Education and Sociology* (Glencoe, Ill.: Free Press, 1956), 91.

19. For a description of the positive relation of schoolteacher and parental teacher, see Deborah Meier, *The Power of Their Ideas* (Boston: Beacon Press, 1995), 26–27, 51–53.

20. Jane Martin, "Excluding Women from the Educational Realm," *Harvard Educational Review* 52 (May 1982): 133–48.

21. See Sara Ruddick, *Maternal Thinking* (Boston: Beacon Press, 1989), 72–73.

22. Hillary Rodham Clinton, *It Takes a Village* (New York: Simon and Schuster, 1996), only occasionally addresses the theme of its subtitle: lessons children teach us. "Parents discover that this modeling behavior is a two-way street. How many times have you watched a child and thought: If only I could bottle that energy.... Spending time with children elevates our perceptions and energizes us" (108).

23. Eliot Daley, *Father Feelings* (New York: Morrow, 1978), 65: "There are a variety of ways to child one's parents"; Michael Lewis and Leonard Rosenblum, *The Effect of the Infant on Its Caregiver* (New York: John Wiley and Sons, 1974).

24. *New York Times*, July 14, 1992, 18.

25. Maria Montessori, *The Child in the Family* (Chicago: Regnery, 1970).

26. Paulo Freire and Ira Shor, *Pedagogy for Liberation* (Granby, Mass.: Bergen and Garvey, 1987), 172.

27. Quoted in Standing, *Maria Montessori*, 345.

28. See Irene Lilley, *Friedrich Froebel: A Selection from His Writings* (Cambridge: Cambridge University Press, 1967).

29. Howard Gardner, *The Unschooled Mind* (New York: Basic Books, 1991), 55; for a skeptical view of the enthusiasm for apprenticeship, see Oakeshott, *Voice of Liberal Learning*, 92.

30. For some examples, see Clinton, *It Takes a Village*, 193–201.

31. Plato, *Republic*, 536c.

32. Schön, *Reflective Practitioner*, 299.

33. Josef Pieper, *Leisure, the Basis of Culture* (New York: Mentor Books, 1952).

34. Hannah Arendt, *Human Condition*, 131.

35. Witold Rybczynsk, *Waiting for the Weekend* (New York: Penguin Books, 1991); Juliet Schor, *The Overworked American: The Unexpected Decline of Leisure* (New York: Basic Books, 1991).

Chapter 8. Teaching in School

1. Herbert Kliebard, *The Struggle for the American Curriculum, 1893–1958* (Boston: Routledge and Kegan Paul, 1986), 254.

2. Theodore Sizer, *Horace's School* (Boston: Houghton Mifflin, 1992), 11.

3. See George Spindler, ed., *Doing the Ethnography of Schooling* (New York: Holt, Rinehart and Winston, 1982); Peter Woods, *Inside Schools: Ethnography in Educational Research* (New York: Routledge and Kegan Paul, 1986); Mike Rose, *Possible Lives* (Boston: Houghton Mifflin, 1995); Meier, *The Power of Their Ideas*, 161–73.

4. John Dewey, "The Child and the Curriculum," in *Dewey on Education*, ed. Martin Dworkin (New York: Teachers College Press, 1959), 96–106.

5. John Dewey, *Experience and Education* (New York: Collier Books, 1963).

6. Sylvia Farnham-Diggery, *Schooling: The Developing Child* (Cambridge: Harvard University Press, 1990), 95.

7. John Dewey, *Democracy and Education* (New York: Free Press, 1966); the index to the book supports my statement that Dewey seldom uses the verb "to teach." The occasional use of "teacher" is almost always as the equivalent of professional educator; for example: "When the parent or teacher has provided the conditions which stimulate thinking" (160).

8. Passmore, *Philosophy of Teaching*, 26; Gardner, *Unschooled Mind*, 127.

9. Plato's view in *The Republic* is that philosophy is best studied after the age of 50. Aristotle and Thomas Aquinas agreed with this view.

10. Dewey, *Democracy and Education:* on environment as teacher, 18–19; on lifelong education, 51; on the interdependence of the adult and the child, 44, 50.

11. Dewey, "My Pedagogic Creed," 30.

12. Ibid., 32.

13. George Counts, *Dare the Schools Build a New Social Order?* (New York:

Arno Press, 1969), 9–10; on the problem of indoctrination in the writings of George Counts, see Gerald Gutek, *The Educational Theory of George S. Counts* (Columbus: Ohio State University Press, 1970), 115–34.

14. Westbrook, *John Dewey and American Democracy*, 506.

15. Theodore Sizer, *Horace's Compromise* (Boston: Houghton Mifflin, 1985), 120–30.

16. Herbert Kohl, *Growing Minds: On Becoming a Teacher* (New York: Harper and Row, 1984), 80: "Most students in our foolishly competitive schools feel that they are in a battle with their teachers and that when students fail teachers succeed, and when students succeed they do it despite their teachers. Teaching well implies the opposite — our only success lies in how well our pupils do."

17. Kieran Egan, *Teaching as Story Telling* (Chicago: University of Chicago Press, 1986), 49. The italics are mine.

18. Tom, *Teaching as a Moral Craft*, 142; see also Harold Stevenson and James Stigler, *The Learning Gap* (New York: Touchstone Books, 1992), 158: "Curiously, we deny our teachers the apprenticeships that are commonly accepted as effective means for other professionals."

19. Standing, *Maria Montessori*, 216.

20. Michael Polanyi, *Personal Knowledge* (Chicago: University of Chicago Press, 1958), 53.

21. On the metaphor of coaching applied to teaching, see Sizer, *Horace's Compromise*, 99–108.

22. Patricia Graham, *S.O.S.* (New York: Hill and Wang, 1992), 118. She provides no page number in her footnote for this reference. I presume she is referring to 17 of Donald Schön's *Educating the Reflective Practitioner* (San Francisco: Jossey-Bass, 1987), where Schön is describing a section of John Dewey's work.

23. Foucault, *Order of Things*, and *Discipline and Punishment*.

24. Ernest Boyer, *High School: A Report on Secondary Education in America* (New York: Harper and Row, 1983), 201.

25. Dewey, *Democracy and Education*, 38.

26. *New York Times*, July 20, 1992, 35.

27. J. Katz and M. Henry, *Turning Professors into Teachers* (New York: Macmillan, 1988), 128, quoting one professor: "To speak as though someone is listening is something teachers may not do. They may present facts and give a list of information but they are not speaking as if someone is out there. I know from my theater background that you can't get away with that — when you are playing to an audience you have to appeal to them. You can't just get up there and give some information."

28. Northrop Frye, *The Great Code* (New York: Harcourt, Brace, Jovanovich, 1982), xxi: "Information does have to be conveyed in teaching, of course, but for the teacher the imparting of information is again in a context of irony, which means that it often looks like a kind of game."

29. Alasdair McIntyre, *Three Rival Versions of Moral Enquiry* (Notre Dame, Ind.: University of Notre Dame Press, 1990), 233: "Knowing how to read antag-

onistically without defeating oneself as well as one's opponent by not learning from the encounter is a skill without which no tradition can flourish."

30. Frye, *The Great Code*, 15; see also Wittgenstein, *Blue and Brown Books*, 451: "In philosophy it is always good to put a *question* instead of an answer to a question. For an answer to a philosophical question may easily be unfair; disposing of it by another question is not."

31. Saint Augustine, "The Teacher," in *The Fathers of the Church* (Washington: Catholic University of America Press, 1967), 59:7.

32. Pitkin, *Wittgenstein and Justice*, 241; for another description of Wittgenstein teaching, see Monk, *Ludwig Wittgenstein*, 289; see also the description of John Dewey teaching in Westbrook, *John Dewey and American Democracy*, 378–79: The student, Irwin Edman, says that on first impression Dewey "seemed to be saying whatever came into his head next, and at one o'clock on an autumn afternoon to at least one undergraduate what came next did not always have a very clear connection with what had just gone before." Eventually, however, Edman concluded: "I had been listening not to the semi-theatrical repetition of a discourse many times made before — a fairly accurate description of many academic lectures — I had been listening to a man actually *thinking* in the presence of the class. To attend a lecture of John Dewey was to participate in the actual business of thought."

33. Belenky et al., *Women's Ways of Knowing*, 219.

34. Jerome Bruner, *Toward a Theory of Instruction* (Cambridge: Harvard University Press, 1967), 104.

35. P. H. Hirst, "The Logical and Psychological Aspects of Teaching a Subject," in *The Concept of Education*, ed. Richard Peters (London: Routledge and Kegan Paul, 1967), 59.

36. Passmore, *Philosophy of Teaching*, 32.

37. Explaining the policy of the New York City public schools in providing condoms, Joseph Fernandez with John Underwood, *Tales Out of School* (Boston: Little Brown, 1992), 245: "My course, I thought was clear. The school system has a moral responsibility to its children. Its children were dying, and although many would die no matter what we did, if we did nothing the numbers would be apocalyptic."

38. Henry Perkinson, *Teachers without Goals, Students without Purposes* (New York: McGraw-Hill, 1992), 26: "Teachers and schools should never claim that they will teach students how to read, or how to write, or how to speak French, or to perform any skill. The only logical, practical and moral claim educators can make is that they will help students become better readers, better writers, better speakers of French, or better performers of some specific skill."

39. Michael Katz, *Class, Bureaucracy, and Schools*, 2nd ed. (New York: Praeger, 1973), 164–65; for John Dewey's argument against this split, see "Education versus Traditional Training," *New Republic*, May 8, 1915, 8–14.

40. Harvey Kantor, "Managing the Transition from School to Work: The False Promise of Youth Apprenticeship," *Teachers College Record* 95 (Summer 1994): 442–61, is very suspicious of the new enthusiasm for apprenticeship ex-

pressed by politicians. If the new apprenticeship is simply a redoing of the old vocational school for the academic castoffs, then apprenticeship would be a false hope. John Dewey was on the right track early in the century in talking about vocational aspects of education rather than vocational schools; see Dewey, *Democracy and Education*, 316.

41. Plato, *Republic*, 455c.
42. Boyer, *High School*, 202–15.
43. *New York Times Magazine*, September 27, 1992, 37–42.
44. Sizer, *Horace's School*, 183.

Chapter 9. Teaching Morally, Teaching Morality

1. Gertrude Himmelfarb, *The De-Moralization of Society* (New York: Knopf, 1995); William Bennett, ed., *The Book of Virtues* (New York: Simon and Schuster, 1994).

2. See Michael Katz, *The Irony of Early School Reform* (Boston: Beacon Press, 1968); Carl Kaestle, *The Evolution of an Urban School System: New York City, 1750–1850* (Cambridge: Harvard University Press, 1974).

3. Westbrook, *John Dewey and American Democracy*, 6–7.

4. Dewey, "My Pedagogic Creed"; see also the influential educational historian, Ellwood Cubberley, speaking at the beginning of this century: "I am in the strongest sense a harmonizer of Religion and Science; there is no conflict in my mind between the two." Jesse Sears and Adin Henderson, *Cubberley at Stanford* (Stanford, Calif.: Stanford University Press, 1957), 33.

5. Durkheim, *Moral Education*, 18–19.

6. Ibid., 120.

7. Piaget, *Moral Judgment of the Child*, 191.

8. Ibid., 361; Durkheim, *Education and Sociology*, 87–90.

9. Piaget, *Moral Judgment of the Child*, 191.

10. Ibid., 309, 324.

11. Ibid., 323.

12. Lawrence Kohlberg in his speech before the American Psychological Association in 1978; see *Psychology Today*, February 1979, 57.

13. Lawrence Kohlberg and F. Clark Power, "Religion, Morality, and Ego Development," in *Toward Moral and Religious Morality*, ed. Christiane Brusselmans (Morristown, N.J.: Silver Burdett, 1980), 343–72.

14. Lawrence Kohlberg, "Moral Education Reappraised," *The Humanist* 38 (November 1978): 13–15.

15. James Rest, "Basic Issues in Evaluating Moral Education Programs," in *Evaluating Moral Development*, ed. Lisa Kuhmerker and others (Schenectady, N.Y.: Character Research Project, 1980), 5–6.

16. Gilligan, *In a Different Voice*.

17. Thomas Lickona, *Raising Good Children* (New York: Bantam, 1987); and his *Educating for Character* (New York: Bantam, 1991); for a survey of the move-

ment, see Roger Rosenblatt, "Teaching Johnny to Be Good," *New York Times Magazine*, April 30, 1995, 36–74.

18. William Kilpatrick, *Why Johnny Can't Tell Right from Wrong* (New York: Simon and Schuster, 1992), 35–36.

19. Ibid., 93–94.

20. Ibid., 255–56.

21. For a detailed description of the battle over "inclusive" school curricula, see the case study of Oakland's reaction to California's revised curriculum in Todd Gitlin, *The Twilight of Common Dreams* (New York: Metropolitan Books, 1995), chap. 1.

22. Wayne Meeks, *The Moral World of the First Christians* (Philadelphia: Westminster, 1986), 90.

23. Judith Goldin, ed., *The Living Talmud* (Chicago: University of Chicago Press, 1957), 155: "Ben Azzai says: Be quick in carrying out a minor command as in the case of a major one, and flee from transgression. For one good deed leads to another good deed and one transgression leads to another transgression; for the reward of a good deed is another good deed and the reward for a transgression is another transgression."

24. Rousseau, *Emile*, 89; James Axtell, ed., *The Educational Writings of John Locke* (Cambridge: Cambridge University Press, 1968), 181.

25. Piaget, *Moral Judgment of the Child*, 85.

26. Rousseau, *Emile*, 79.

27. Axtell, ed., *Educational Writings of John Locke*, 253, 240.

28. Philip Greven, *Spare the Child* (New York: Vintage Books, 1992), 184–85.

29. Richard Sennett, *The Fall of Public Man* (New York: Knopf, 1977), 94.

30. This is the headline from the *New York Times*, September 15, 1986; perhaps a shift over the years is reflected by the front-page article "Curriculum or Not, Teachers Teach Values," *New York Times*, February 1, 1995.

31. *New York Times*, December 12, 1990, 8.

32. Erikson, *Childhood and Society*, 268–69.

33. See the collections of readings edited by William Bennett: *The Book of Virtues* and *The Children's Book of Virtues* (New York: Simon and Schuster, 1995). See also Colin Greer and Herbert Kohl, eds., *A Call to Character* (San Francisco: HarperCollins, 1995).

34. Stephen Carter, *The Culture of Disbelief* (New York: Basic Books, 1993), 201; see also Amitai Etzioni, *The Spirit of Community* (New York: Crown, 1993), 205: "Educators, however, regularly require students to attend all kinds of classes, from foreign-language courses to math. Why not require them to attend classes that will teach them civility?" The answer to Etzioni's question should be obvious. Math and foreign-languages can be studied in school as school subjects; civility is not the name of that kind of thing. I strongly suspect that "civics" (a word invented in the 1890s for schoolchildren) has never had academic substance. If the issue were to be confronted, it would be found that civics can only be preached in the fifth grade, not academically taught.

35. See Steven Satris, ed., *Taking Sides: Clashing Views on Contemporary Moral Issues*, 5th ed. (Guilford, Conn.: Dushkin, 1996).

36. My comments are not a criticism of this curriculum. The authors are aware of the need to provide multiple perspectives. The principle of criticism discussed here is valid, prescinding from its applicability to this curriculum. See Margaret Strom and William Parsons, *Facing History and Ourselves: Holocaust and Human Behavior* (Watertown, Mass.: Intentional Education, 1982).

37. *New York Times*, January 10, 1995, A8.

38. Sometimes writers who understandably wish to call attention to the Holocaust do not see that their way of insisting on this in schools is self-defeating. Robert Goldman, in an essay entitled "Don't Be Calm about the Holocaust," addresses "teachers, preachers, parents" with the admonition: "Boredom, calm, understanding are not for the Holocaust. Deep anger, disgust and rejection are what it generates among decent people." Boredom does not belong in the classroom, but calm usually does, and understanding is the indispensable goal." See *International Herald Tribune*, August 17, 1994, 6.

39. Aristotle, *Ethics*, 1180a: "In order to be a good man, one must first have been brought up in the right way and trained in the right habits . . ."; 1095a: "For those who regulate their impulses and act in accord with principle, a knowledge of these subjects will be of great advantage."

40. John Keegan, *The Face of Battle* (New York: Viking Books, 1976), 23–24.

Conclusion

1. John Dewey, *Experience and Education* (New York: Collier Books, 1963), 88.

2. Martin Buber, *Eclipse of God* (New York: Harper Torch, 1952).

3. Redding Sugg, *Motherteacher: The Femininization of American Education* (Charlottesville: University of Virginia Press, 1978).

4. Amitai Etzioni, *The Semi-Professions and their Organization* (New York: Free Press, 1969); for the history of the profession of schoolteaching, see Donald Warren, ed., *American Teacher: Histories of a Profession at Work* (New York: Macmillan, 1989).

5. Meier, *The Power of Their Ideas*, 139: "We think we know all about teaching; after all, by the time we become adults we've had prolonged contacts with more teaching situations than those of any other occupation."

6. R. K. Kelsall and Helen Kelsall, *The Schoolteacher in England and the United States* (London: Pergamon, 1969), 147: "One obvious moral to be drawn from the experience of other professions is that, if status is to be maintained or enhanced, practitioners must not be seen to be engaged on any duties which less highly trained people could perfectly easily perform."

Index

Abelard, 133

Abstraction, Aristotle's definition, 10–11

Academic criticism: classroom activity, 138; community in academic world, 137–38; Dewey, John, 136–37; impersonal and personal qualities, 136; ironic question, 138; as language for teaching morality in classroom, 217; participants, 138; storytelling, use in, 142–43; student's words as focus, 139; teaching in school, 185–86; teaching tool, 135–36; text, link to, 137; "to teach," 143–44

Adult education: education's meaning, 153–54; teaching attacked, 27–28; therapeutic languages, 105

Alexander the Great, 109

Ambivalence about teaching, 1–2

Animals: nonhuman animals as taught, 48; nonhuman entities as teachers, 47–48; physical skills, 50–51

Antireligious bias of education theory, 3

Apprenticeship, 164, 177–78

Aquinas, Thomas: books as teachers, 44; definition and use of term, 11; dialectical exchange, 133; double negative use, 108; language, uses of, 9; teaching and learning distinguished, 60, 61

Arendt, Hannah, 44, 118

Ariès, Philippe, 121

Aristophanes, 19

Aristotle: abstraction, definition of, 10–11; activity in teaching, 71; agent/patient relation, teaching as, 42; cause, teaching as, 41; human community as teacher of morality, 206–7; humility of teacher, 35; language, inquiry into, 9–10; leisure, 166; virtue, how to teach, 54

Arts as school performance areas, 189–91

Ashton-Warner, Sylvia, 65–66

Atlee, Clement, 97

Augustine, 185–86

Authority: of being called teacher, 203–4; moral authority of teacher, 205

Bailyn, Bernard, 155–56

Barkley, Charles, 52, 53

Barzun, Jacques, 6, 16–17, 19, 149

Beckett, Samuel, 131–32

Bible, interpretation, 128

Bickel, Alexander, 8

Blame, condemn as therapeutic language, 113

Books as teachers, 43, 44

Broudy, H. S., 39–40

Bruner, Jerome, 186–87

Buber, Martin, 129, 223

Buddhism, 17, 61–62, 107, 108

Camus, Albert, 110

Carter, Stephen, 213–14

Child abuse, teaching morality, 208

Child as teacher, 159–60

Child-centered classroom, 171–72

Clark, Manning, 90–91

Classroom: academic criticism, 162–63; as form of education, 161–63; morality teaching in, 212–18; teacher within, 162; teaching morality, see Teaching morality in classroom

Classroom teaching activities: academic criticism, 138, 185–86; dialectical discussion, 184–85; dramatic performance, 183–84; instruction, 29; instruction, education's meaning, 157; job performance as performance areas, 191–92; languages of teaching used, 181; lecturing, 95, 181–82, 185; physical accouterments, 180; preaching, 182; storytelling, 183; subject taught, styles of teaching, 187; teaching in school, see Teaching in school; therapeutic language, 183; verbal arts as school performance areas, 190–91

Coaching as metaphor for teaching in school, 178

Cohen, Brenda, 30

Comedy as play with language, 130

Comenius, Johann, 22, 68, 109

Comfort, therapeutic languages, 120–23

Commercials as preaching, 100

Communal activity, therapeutic languages, 112

Communal experience of school, 176

Community: academic, 137–38; example, 54–56; as teacher of morality, 206–7